FIGHT FOR THE
FINAL FRONTIER

FIGHT FOR THE
FINAL
FRONTIER
IRREGULAR WARFARE IN SPACE

JOHN J. KLEIN

Naval Institute Press
Annapolis, Maryland

Naval Institute Press
291 Wood Road
Annapolis, MD 21402

Library of Congress Cataloging-in-Publication Data
Names: Klein, John J., author.
Title: Fight for the final frontier : irregular warfare and competition in the space domain / John J. Klein.
Other titles: Irregular warfare and competition in the space domain
Description: Annapolis, Maryland : Naval Institute Press, [2023] | Includes bibliographical references and index.
Identifiers: LCCN 2023009276 (print) | LCCN 2023009277 (ebook) | ISBN 9781557507358 (hardcover) | ISBN 9781557507488 (ebook)
Subjects: LCSH: Space warfare. | Strategy. | BISAC: HISTORY / Military / Aviation & Space | HISTORY / United States / 21st Century
Classification: LCC UG1530 .K575 2023 (print) | LCC UG1530 (ebook) | DDC 358/.8–dc23/eng/20230627
LC record available at https://lccn.loc.gov/2023009276
LC ebook record available at https://lccn.loc.gov/2023009277

∞ Print editions meet the requirements of ANSI/NISO z39.48-1992 (Permanence of Paper).
Printed in the United States of America.

30 29 28 27 26 25 24 23   9 8 7 6 5 4 3 2 1
First printing

*For the space strategist—past, present,
and future*

⇒ CONTENTS ⇐

⇒ FIGURES ⇐

⇒ PREFACE ⇐

Irregular warfare at its root is still warfare.
—Colin Gray[1]

The genesis for this book was my attempt to wrestle with the prevalent thinking in the national security space community that many of the ongoing nefarious and malicious events in space—like jamming and lasing—were outside of our collective understanding of strategic history and war. I pondered how to reconcile this with a Clausewitzian sensibility for strategic competition in space and the daily events below the threshold of war. How could this be done? How did these events fit within an understanding of war's enduring nature and warfare's changing character?

I concluded that many of the malicious, nefarious, and irresponsible behaviors displayed to date in the space domain can be labeled as *irregular* in style or form. By considering present competition and malicious activities in space as irregular, policy makers and military strategists can better understand how these activities fit within millennia of human experience with conflict and strategic competition. The subject is indeed relevant, because rivals of the United States and their proxies are increasingly seeking to prevail through their own use of irregular forms of warfare and competition, deliberately pursuing political and strategic objectives in a competitive arena below any threshold that is likely to provoke a U.S. conventional military response.

After concluding that irregular warfare is a helpful strategic concept for considering today's competitive environment in space, I decided to write this book because of the dearth of literature on the subject. Certainly, there is an ever-growing list of books that address geopolitics in space, spacepower, and space warfare, and there are seminal works on irregular styles of warfare and competition, by Sun Tzu, Carl von Clausewitz,

Mao Tse-tung, T. E. Lawrence, David Galula, Roger Trinquier, and others. Yet foundational literature about irregular styles of warfare and competition in the space domain is difficult to find. This condition is troublesome because irregular approaches for achieving political ends are in daily use within the space domain and are not well understood in a strategic context. Because of the persistence of irregular actions in space, I daresay that these "irregular" activities are more regular in occurrence than supposedly "regular" ones.

This work considers irregular styles of warfare and competition in the space domain, to include the particular methods used and appropriate counterstrategies. The book's chapters explain ways of achieving political ends with respect to the space domain apart from solely conventional, large-scale military conflict. Importantly, this work addresses irregular approaches in the space domain using both military and nonmilitary means. So, while the use of force to achieve political aims and strategic goals will be addressed, so too will the use of diplomatic, informational, economic, and legal means.

Given the teachings of the Prussian strategist Carl von Clausewitz and his understanding of the general theory of war and warfare, it is understood that warfare in space—including that in an irregular style or form—will be a complex phenomenon and that its essential nature will not change.[2] With a strategist's Clausewitzian sense, it is understood that irregular warfare in the space domain must obey the fundamental lore of war, along with the universal principles of strategy and essential unity in all strategic experience. The space strategist can look to historical experience and knowledge of past conflicts for insight into the functional character of irregular space warfare, as the epigraph above suggests. The theory and strategy of irregular warfare in space constitute merely a subset of the overall theory and strategy of general space warfare, which is likewise merely a subset of the theory and overarching strategy of war and warfare. The characteristics of irregular warfare, consequently, should be expected to be relevant to all domains—including the space domain. Because of war's enduring nature, this work will frequently note historical experience, refer to past military strategists, and employ strategic analogies to explain irregular warfare and competitive approaches.

As they always have, the strategic and geopolitical environment are constantly changing. When I wrote my last book, *Understanding Space Strategy: The Art of War in Space* (2019), the phrase *return of great-power competition* was in vogue, highlighting the rivalry among China, Russia, and the United States. Today, the phrases *strategic competition* and *gray-zone operations* are similarly in style, connoting that while the three countries are indeed still rivals, much of the resulting competition and actions will occur below the threshold of actual armed conflict. Additionally, competition is better understood as being relevant to all countries—including middle and emerging powers—and not just to great powers. Today, the national security community generally understands that there is a wide range of potential competitors, with a large array of military and nonmilitary means available to achieve political aims. This book seeks to explain how space strategies and activities fit within this present-day thinking of rivalry as spanning the breadth of geopolitical competition. This book's chapter 3, "Small Space Wars," is a homage to British army officer and noted military theorist Charles Callwell and his book *Small Wars: Their Principles and Practice* (1898), which had a profound impact globally on military thinking.

Importantly, the United States cannot merely focus on the wars it wants to fight and ignore the rest. Irregular and messy small wars have a way of challenging the United States despite its conventional military strength and ability to plan for large contingency operations. The space strategist should have hope, however, because all strategies have suitable counterstrategies. As such, irregular styles of warfare and competition in space have inherent weaknesses, which can be exploited for strategic effect. This book will address these weaknesses of irregular space warfare and offer viable counterstrategies.

Chapters 1 and 2 lay the foundation for considering irregular styles of warfare and competition in the space domain. Chapter 1 addresses the enduring nature of war, noting that war and strategy have—indeed must have—constant natures throughout history and with respect to politically motivated violence in all modes.[3] Yet warfare's character is constantly changing, and irregular forms of warfare will likewise always be changing. Chapter 1 also defines relevant terminology and firmly places irregular warfare and competition within the overarching theory of war and warfare. Chapter 2 details the most important characteristics of irregular space warfare and how they can be employed, which will be critical for understanding how irregular space warfare functions and for developing suitable counterstrategies. Subjects covered include the indirect approach, cumulative strategy, asymmetric advantage, deception and surprise, dispersal and concentration, and hybrid warfare. Also, chapter 2 highlights the nonmilitary dimension of irregular forms of competition, especially in relation to the indirect approach and cumulative strategies.

Chapter 3 examines small space wars—that is, conflicts using force in space and against space architectures but occurring below the threshold of major, conventional conflict. This chapter describes how irregular space warfare seeks to achieve political aims and serve the purpose of space strategy—ensuring access to and use of space. The operational art associated with using force of an irregular style in the space domain is detailed, including the ways and means of doing so, like kinetic or nonkinetic, reversible or irreversible methods. Chapter 3 examines the concepts of command of space, Fabian strategy, maneuver warfare, proxies and proxy war, debris generation, and terrorism, along with the means and methods of generating nonkinetic effects, all to explain how space strategy fits within the framework of irregular warfare.

Next, chapter 4 builds upon the previous chapter by examining the ancillary effects associated with the threat and use of limited space forces, along with the manner in which they are applied. Included in this discussion are gray-zone operations and gunboat diplomacy as applied to the space domain. The movement, placement, and proximity of spacecraft are examined, especially when such proximity entails a potential threat or coercive action. This chapter details the indirect effects achieved through such irregular space activities as technological demonstrations, space exercises, and limited space warfare.

Chapter 5 details the concept of *lawfare*—the intentional distortion and misuse of legal regimes for competitive advantage—and its relationship to space activities and operations. This chapter describes past and current examples of lawfare by China and Russia, while noting how lawfare works as a part of an overarching strategy. Chapter 5 also provides space-centric examples of likely uses of lawfare and concludes with practical methods of countering lawfare's long-term, coercive influence within the space domain.

The roles of commercial and quasi-commercial entities during competition and conflict within the space domain are considered in chapter 6. Almost all space capabilities entail dual-use technologies, so it is critical to examine how states are using commercial capabilities or may employ commercial space companies as proxies and for security and peacekeeping roles. Commercial-related topics such as the differing definitions of commercial space, proxies, private military companies, privateers, space pirates, and space militias are discussed in this chapter. The implications of hybrid space architectures are detailed, including the integration of small and large satellite constellations, governmental and commercial capabilities, and exquisite and less costly satellites across various orbital regimes. Furthermore, the chapter discusses the legal questions arising from the intermingling of governmental and commercial capabilities and services, along with the long-term implications of misinterpreting space as a global commons.

In chapter 7 the motivations for using space technologies in warfare are highlighted. Discussions include how technology and technological innovation are used to achieve asymmetric advantage and shape future operational concepts for war fighting in space. This examination also addresses China's view of exploiting innovative space technologies and the implications of dual-use space technologies. Additionally, this chapter details the potential unintended consequences of innovative space technologies within the context of international relations theory, such as the creation of power imbalances among competitors and international instability.

Lastly, chapter 8 is a synthesis, explaining why the study of irregular styles of conflict and competition in space matters in today's security environment. To that end, the chapter answers the skeptic's key question, "So what?" The commonly debated shortcomings of an American style of war are examined in relation to how future competitors will exploit any perceived U.S. shortcomings in irregular space warfare. More importantly, this concluding chapter describes how countries like the United States and other liberal democracies can successfully counter a rival's strategy of irregular warfare and competition in space and provides specific solutions for doing so.

This work highlights the continuities of historical experience, along with analyzing how and when irregular warfare and competitive approaches can be used to achieve strategic and operational objectives in the space domain. It is my intent, by shedding light on the past and putting today's space activities in the proper perspective, to illuminate the future of space warfare and promote sound strategies during the decades to come. It is my sincerest hope that thinking now about irregular space warfare against a background of historical and strategic experience will help future policy makers and military leaders glean practical insights and be better equipped to protect national security interests, deterring conflict, and avoiding strategic miscalculation.

⑈ ⑈ ⑈ ⑈ ⑈

I am indebted to the many who educated me during my journey of strategic exploration. Thank you to my amazing and insightful students at the George Washington University, Georgetown University, and Institute of World Politics. You all make teaching fun. Also, I am grateful to the wonderful students at Air University—including those in the Schriever Scholars and West Space Seminar programs—who have elaborated on my writings over the years. Great appreciation is due for the enduring support of my compatriots at the Space Policy Institute: John Logsdon, Scott Pace, Henry Hertzfeld, Dana Johnson, Pete Hays, and Aaron Bateman.

Benjamin Armstrong's *Small Boats, Daring Men: Maritime Raiding, Irregular Warfare, and the Early American Navy* served as the intellectual seed for writing this book, and his encouragement is much appreciated. Victoria Samson and Brian Weeden at the Secure World Foundation continue to provide thoughtful written analysis that has helped shape my research. Robert Jarman's expert analysis and suggestions on space law have been indispensable. For their in-depth review of the manuscript and helpful suggestions, thank you to Mike Fowler, Shawn Hackett, and Matt Jenkins. I greatly appreciate the unflagging efforts of Raj Dhillon, Sofia Fagan, and Lexie Weikert in their research assistance. Carole Sargent and her Georgetown University publishing group helped immensely in finding the best press for publication. To that point, I am grateful to Glenn Griffith and the staff at the Naval Institute Press for their enthusiasm about publishing this work.

I am fortunate to have friends and colleagues who reviewed and provided comments on specific chapter topics, and thank you to Chris Beauregard, Adam Brown, Henry Heren, Scott Sadler, and Jo-Anne Sears for your feedback. Additionally, Stephanie Bednarek, Nick Boensch, Dean Cheng, Carissa Christensen, Sandra Erwin, Theresa Hitchens, Kaitlyn Johnson, Bhavya Lal, Doug Loverro, François Raffenne, and Charity Weeden continue to provide valuable perspectives on the international community and commercial space sector. To the good folks in Montgomery, Alabama—Everett Dolman, Peter Garretson, Namrata Goswami, Andrea Harrington, Greg Miller, Michael Smith, Brent Ziarnick, and the unmentioned U.S. Space Force guardians and national security space professionals who helped shape the ideas here—thank you. Moreover, I am thankful for the lasting literary contribution of the late Colin Gray. His writings continue to inspire me and many others to understand better strategic theory and spacepower.

Finally, I would like to thank my family and friends for their enduring support and patience, as writing this book has consumed much of my time over the last year. Notwithstanding the invaluable feedback of others, I am fully responsible for the work's contents and conclusions and for any remaining flaws. The views expressed here are mine alone and do not reflect the official policy or position of the U.S. Department of Defense, the Georgetown and George Washington Universities, or Falcon Research, Inc.

—*JJK*

⇒ ABBREVIATIONS ⇐
AND ACRONYMS

AKM	apogee kick motor
ASAT	antisatellite
CASC	China Aerospace Science and Technology Corporation
CASIC	China Aerospace Science and Industry Corporation
CCP	Chinese Communist Party
CLOC	celestial line of communication
COIN	counterinsurgency
CSIS	Center for Strategic and International Studies
GEO	geostationary (also geosynchronous) Earth orbit
GPS	Global Positioning System
IDA	Institute of Defense Analyses
PLA	People's Liberation Army
PPP	public-private partnership
PPWT	Prevention of the Placement of Weapons in Outer Space and of the Threat or Use of Force against Outer Space Objects
PRC	People's Republic of China
RPO	rendezvous and proximity operation
SDA	space domain awareness
SJ-17	Shijian-17
SJ-21	Shijian-21
SOE	state-owned enterprise
SO/LIC	special operations/low-intensity conflict
STARCOM	Space Training and Readiness Command
UN	United Nations
UNCLOS	United Nations Convention on the Law of the Sea
USSF	U.S. Space Force

CHAPTER I

The Enduring Nature of Irregular Warfare

All wars are things of the same *nature.*
—Clausewitz[1]

Irregular warfare is not an irregular occurrence. Throughout history, there have been many occasions when leaders have used irregular warfare—or warfare apart from conflicts fought by major, conventional fighting forces—to achieve political ends. Indeed, polities, militaries, and groups have pursued irregular styles of warfare and competition either by choice or out of necessity. Because irregular warfare can be a preferred style of conflict, both policy makers and strategists should consider these forms of competition and aggression as part of the enduring nature of war, particularly within the framework prescribed by the Prussian military officer and strategist Carl von Clausewitz.

Clausewitz notes that war has an enduring nature, even though war and warfare take on ever-changing characteristics. In his *On War*, written almost two centuries ago, he describes how "war is a remarkable trinity" composed of violence and hatred, chance and probability, and political considerations and asserts that all these elements play out through the interaction of people, military forces, and governments.[2] Putting Clausewitz's lasting insights into proper perspective, military historian Peter Mansoor notes, "These [Clausewitzian] factors have been a part of war since the dawn of recorded history."[3] Although war changes its characteristics under various circumstances and over time, war is still war. So, when considering irregular warfare in the space domain, the space strategist can still study and apply the lessons of strategic history and mankind's collective understanding of war and warfare. The enduring nature of war makes this true.

Irregular warfare and nontraditional approaches to strategic competition have been part of our collective experience since recorded history, but despite irregular warfare being an enduring phenomena, the terminology used to describe these activities has varied. Some of the terminology—it is certainly not an exhaustive list—used during the past few decades in reference to irregular or nontraditional approaches to warfare and competition are *asymmetric warfare, counterinsurgency, gray-zone operations, guerrilla warfare, gunboat diplomacy, hybrid warfare, low-intensity conflict, paramilitary operations, political insurrection, small wars*, and *terrorism*.

Unfortunately, the routine rebranding of irregular warfare's central idea and the changing terminology that results have led some strategists and military professionals to infer mistakenly that the nature of war has changed or that irregular methods of warfare and competition are new phenomena. An example of the rebranding of irregular warfare comes from the U.S. defense community's response to the 9/11 terrorist attacks. During the effort to defeat the Taliban in Afghanistan and the insurgents in Iraq following the collapse of the Baathist regime, the terms "counterinsurgency"—or COIN—"and special operations/low-intensity conflict"—or SO/LIC—became fashionable. In the early 2000s the defense community used the phrase to describe an operational style of warfare. Some defense analysts erroneously characterized these approaches to war and warfare as new, believing that the nature of war had changed.[4]

Irregular warfare does not have a distinctive nature. Warfare is warfare, and war is war—period. Yet irregular warfare often does have a sharply distinctive character, one that can take a variety of forms and be practiced in different operational styles, even in the same conflict. Irregular warfare has had an enduring place in strategic history. As a rebuttal to the occasional thinking that irregular or nontraditional forms of combat are matters for separate or unique consideration, Colin Gray reminds us that nontraditional kinds of military power must function according to the general "lore of war." Gray declares that the "objective nature of war described by Clausewitz is enduring and universal regardless of the geography of combat."[5] Indeed, Clausewitz highlights that war is not an ever-changing phenomenon: "War is more than a true chameleon that slightly adapts its characteristics to the given case."[6] So, when considering irregular styles of competition and conflict, strategists can be confident that strategic history can be used to inform current and future problems.

The U.S. Department of Defense's 2020 *Irregular Warfare Annex to the National Defense Strategy* hits the mark: "The character and form of war are constantly changing, yet its fundamental nature remains the same. Though Great Power Competition is now our primary national security challenge—a departure from conducting almost two decades of continuous irregular war against violent extremist organizations worldwide—the requirement for mastery of irregular warfare persists. Far from abandoning these critical competencies, we will sharpen these capabilities for application against peer competitor, nation-state adversaries."[7]

The operational styles used during conflict and over time vary according to a polity's changing predisposition in using technology, strategy, and forms of conflict in applying military force. Likewise, a nation's broader defense community's interest in irregular forms of warfare will wax and wane according to changing circumstances as well as to societal and cultural predispositions, yet irregular warfare will remain an enduring part of the time-honored "lore of war" (humanity's traditional knowledge or belief about conflict).

Ultimately, this work is about the use of irregular styles of warfare and competition in the space domain. Yet space strategy is just a subset of general military theory and strategy. So while this chapter can inform the potential use of irregular warfare in all domains, a foundational understanding is necessary before focusing on irregular warfare specific to space. Given the teachings of Clausewitz and his understanding of the general theory of war and warfare, it is understood not only that warfare in space—including that of an irregular style or form—will be a complex phenomenon but also that its essential nature will not change.

War, Strategy, and Irregular Warfare: What's in a Name?

War is thus an act of force to compel our enemy to do our will. —Clausewitz[8]

While there is a downside to parsing terminology and ideas, some rigor is needed to address irregular warfare in the space domain adequately, given the at times murky waters of strategy and war fighting. Certainly, these distinctions in terminology matter, because some words carry a heavy burden of implied wisdom and advice.[9] Nevertheless, Colin Gray warns would-be theorists against taking this approach to an extreme and of the risks in categorizing on the basis of specific definitions: "Theory is constructed by the making of distinctions. It is an activity at which we theorists are truly expert. Unfortunately, the Cartesian method of analysis, basically to dissect, is always likely to lose the plot, as analysts delve ever more deeply into this or that sharply defined category of military or strategic behaviour."[10] Therefore, policy makers and military planners should be cautious when employing or arguing for terms of reference and definitions at the expense of developing sound strategies.

War and Warfare

In his seminal *On War*, Clausewitz writes that war is an extension of policy by other means: "The political object—the motive for the war—will thus determine both the military objective to be reached and the amount of effort it requires."[11] Further, *war* and *warfare* can be differentiated, as Peter Browning explains: "Warfare is the act of making war. War is a relationship between two states or, in a civil war, two groups. Warfare is only a part of war, although the essential part."[12] Thus, war is the overall contest between competing states or groups, while warfare is the overall activity of using force and potential violence to achieve political objectives. Also, in this text *conflict* is meant in the context of *warfare*, and the two terms will be used here interchangeably.

War and its conduct, then, should serve the ends of politics, and this idea also holds for irregular warfare. Irregular warfare and nontraditional forms of strategic competition should serve the ends of policy and politics, but ensuring that they actually do and in a sound manner requires a properly aligned strategy. As irregular warfare in space is considered further in this work, strategists should keep the central premise at the forefront of their thinking: irregular styles of conflict and competition have inherently political dimensions.

Furthermore, when considering what is and is not war, it is worth underscoring that war and the act of making war have a deadly component, regardless of whether the war is vast or small, regular or irregular. Clausewitz refers to this deadly aspect as "primordial violence," linking it to an "act of force" in the above epigraph.[13] If hostilities fail to result in significant loss of life or large-scale destruction to property, arguably other labels besides *war* or *warfare* should be used instead, such as *military action* or *operations other than war.*[14] While war is not only about violence, that is its distinguishing feature.

War, warfare, and the use of force play a role in strategy. *Strategy* refers to the art and science of marshaling and directing resources to achieve some objective.[15] Or put simply, *strategy* refers to the balancing of one's ends with one's means.[16] The key element of this latter definition is *balancing.* If political ends cannot be achieved with available means, then those ends should be made less ambitious or additional means and capabilities should be developed, procured, and used. If political ends and available means are not balanced, then the strategy is misaligned and faulty. Pursuing a poorly developed strategy often results in failure and disaster—with the potential for great expenditure of both blood and treasure—as historical experience repeatedly underscores.

Irregular Warfare

For *irregular warfare*, the noun matters more than the adjective.[17] Fundamentally, once again, irregular warfare is still warfare. Michael Handel describes *irregular warfare* as "apart from major, conventional wars against an enemy who takes a similar approach."[18] It is perhaps less than satisfactory to define a term by what it is not, but Handel's definition is useful in distinguishing this form of conflict from more traditional forms of warfare. Indeed, defining strategic terminology by its opposite is fairly common, as is illustrated by the terms *irregular, indirect,* and *asymmetrical,* which are all inherently empty concepts except when defined with reference to their opposites.[19] Irregular warfare is warfare waged in a style, or several styles, that are typically nonstandard for the regular fighting forces. Because it is defined in terms of its opposite, and because regular warfare has a character that changes with circumstances and time, irregular warfare, likewise, can have no fixed character.

Other definitions for irregular warfare exist, many of which align with the previous discussions. For example, the doctrinal publication of the U.S. Army and Marine Corps, *Insurgencies and Countering Insurgencies*, states, "*Irregular warfare* is a violent struggle among state and non-state actors for legitimacy and influence over the relevant population(s). Irregular warfare favors indirect approaches, though it may employ the full range of military and other capacities in order to erode an adversary's power, influence, and will. Because of its irregular nature, U.S. involvement in a counterinsurgency demands a whole-of-government approach."[20]

Like Handel, counterinsurgency and counterterrorism scholar Seth Jones defines irregular warfare in terms of its opposite, arguing that irregular warfare is distinct from conventional warfare—sometimes referred to as *traditional* or *regular* warfare.[21] Jones writes that irregular warfare refers to "activities short of conventional and nuclear warfare that are designed to expand a country's influence and legitimacy, as well as to weaken its adversaries."[22] Additionally, the irregular-warfare annex to the 2020 U.S. National Defense Strategy observes that irregular warfare "favors indirect and asymmetric approaches, though it may employ the full range of military and other capabilities, in order to erode an adversary's power, influence, and will."[23] In total, irregular warfare includes numerous tools of statecraft that governments can use to shift the balance of power in their favor, tools that have utility across the peace-war continuum.

Writing in 1964 about irregular strategy for opposing insurgencies, the French military officer and theorist of counterinsurgency warfare David Galula noted that such a struggle is defined by opposites: the presumably more capable power versus the less capable insurgent; conventional versus unconventional methods; order versus disorder; and symmetry versus asymmetry. Galula wrote, "This phenomenon results from the very nature of the war, from the disproportion of strength between opponents at the outset, and from the difference in the essence between their assets and their liabilities."[24] Irregular (specifically, protracted guerrilla) warfare is "so cheap to carry out and so expensive to suppress."[25] For his part, "the insurgent has to grow in the course of the war from small to large, from weakness to strength."[26] The counterinsurgent, likewise, has a heavy liability, being responsible for maintaining order throughout the country, while the insurgency need only aim to convert its intangible assets into concrete ones. Because the counterinsurgent cannot escape responsibility for maintaining order, the expenditure ratio is high when compared to that of the insurgent.[27] Having few responsibilities, the insurgent will promote disorder in every way until able to assume power and in the meantime will use every trick available to succeed.[28]

The last point to be made here is that irregular styles of warfare should not be linked solely to the choice of nonstate actors; Stephen Biddle, a historian and international-affairs expert, argues the prevalent and intuitive picture of nonstate irregular warfare is a fallacy.[29] "In fact there is nothing intrinsic to nonstate status in the conduct of war. And nonstate status is both a less important signpost to meaningful differences of degree than often assumed, and one that matters less with every passing year."[30] Beginning in the 1900s, those adopting comprehensive war-fighting systems have had to, at times, combine both "conventional" and "irregular" approaches.[31]

To synthesize: *irregular warfare as used in this work refers to conflict apart from major, conventional wars.* Certainly, this definition is broad: it includes both state and nonstate actors, along with the use of force during armed conflict and actions below the threshold of armed conflict.

Irregular Warfare in Strategy

War is war and strategy is strategy. —Colin Gray[32]

Policy makers and military leaders may in particular cases prefer irregular styles of warfare and competition to achieve their political ends given the limitations of available means and the need to achieve a sound strategy's requisite balance. Some polities and their militaries may adopt irregular warfare and other competitive approaches as their long-term method for contesting an adversary's power or gaining time for achieving political goals. Rivals of the United States and their proxies are increasingly seeking to prevail through irregular styles of conflict and competition, deliberately pursuing political and strategic objectives in a competitive space below any threshold that is likely to provoke a conventional military response.

Less capable powers looking for asymmetric advantage and strategic effect may choose an irregular style, thereby employing small forces or expending relatively little blood and treasure. In contrast, great powers may turn to irregular warfare when their political objectives are limited or when the political environment will not support the deployment of large, conventional forces. Given the innumerable possible variations and relative competitive advantages between competitors, polities and state leaders frequently view irregular warfare as the way to achieve political ends with the means at hand.

As Colin Gray hints in the previous epigraph, strategically approached, there is only war and warfare.[33] It does not matter whether a conflict is of largely regular or irregular character; Clausewitz's general theory of war and strategy applies equally to both. The threat or use of force, regardless of the style used, is employed as the instrument for political purposes. Styles of warfare are of no relevance whatsoever to the authority of the general theory of strategy. In short, irregular warfare—waged by a range of irregular enemies—is governed by exactly the same strategic experience as regular warfare.[34]

Because of this constancy in war and warfare, irregular warfare may employ either an offensive or defensive strategy—or a combination of both—depending on the desired political ends and military objectives. In Clausewitz's framework of a general theory of war, offensive strategy is aimed at acquiring or wresting something from the adversary—a "positive" objective. He notes that the destruction of the enemy's forces always offers the highest probability of victory and that accordingly an offensive strategy is a preferred instrument for the stronger power.[35]

In contrast, the objective of a defensive strategy is to preserve one's forces, assets, or capabilities or to prevent the enemy from acquiring something or achieving a political objective.[36] Thus, defense has a "negative" objective. Clausewitz underscores the superior strength of defense, despite the considerable advantages an attacker might enjoy during the opening phases of hostilities: "So in order to state the relationship precisely, we must say that *the defensive form of warfare is intrinsically stronger than the offensive.*[37] He elaborates that a defensive strategy should be assumed when one is weaker than the adversary and should be abandoned once one is able to pursue an offensive strategy.

Irregular warfare and nontraditional competition have aims that are either offensive—seeking to acquire something from the adversary—or defensive—seeking to prevent the adversary from acquiring or achieving something. In many historical examples, irregular forms of warfare include simultaneously both offensive and defensive elements, the interrelationship changing in relation to time, location, and fluctuations in the competitors' relative strategic advantage.

In addition to the intermingling of offense and defense, irregular-warfare elements may be employed concurrently with traditional, conventional forms. In contemporary literature this mixing of conventional and irregular styles of conflict is called *hybrid warfare.*[38] Further blurring any existing discrete lines in terminology, Colin Gray observes that regular, conventional wars can convert into irregular ones: "A state or coalition may defeat a regular enemy in a regular style of warfare, only to discover that a new phase of hostilities begins, which is characterized by irregular warfare."[39] This was the experience for U.S. and coalition forces in Iraq in the mid-2000s and the reverse experience of that in Vietnam.

Other Nontraditional Approaches

Military space power can be combat power as well as military operations other than war through or from the space medium. —Brent Ziarnick[40]

Because warfare pertains to an act of force—per the writings of Clausewitz and a strict definition of warfare—it is best to use special terminology for activities apart from the direct military use of force.[41] Phrases such as *nonmilitary activities* and *nontraditional approaches* are helpful for efforts meant to achieve political ends without the direct military use of force. While not part of warfare, whether of a regular or irregular form, these nontraditional approaches are still quite relevant to the achievement of political ends and strategic effects; also, they are in themselves means to coerce an adversary. Moreover, these operations and approaches are relevant to space warfare, as the epigraph above underscores.

Militaries can coerce potential adversaries through the movement, placement, and proximity of forces and assets. In the context of Thomas Schelling's writings, *coercion* is a method of achieving an objective by affecting another party using threats to make them act in a certain way.[42] Coercion can include employing one or several nonoffensive measures to change another's strongly held view or line of action. Coercion occurs short of open military hostilities; it may result from the perceived threat caused by the proximity of military forces and assets. Most often, coercive actions are focused on causing an adversary's leadership to acquiesce to some demand, reverse a prior decision, or decide in favor of something that may not best support its own interests. Coercive activities can help achieve political ends, strategic effects, and operational objectives. Coercion—along with power projection and forward presence—will be explored further in chapter 4.

States, organizations, and groups can achieve political ends and strategic effects through nonmilitary instruments of national power, which include diplomatic, informational, and economic activities. Nonmilitary activities can seek either to coerce a rival into a decision contrary to its initial sentiments or to encourage allies and partners to maintain a current decision or action. Additionally, nonmilitary methods may include the intentional distortion and exploitation of legal regimes and rule-based orders for competitive advantage—that is, *lawfare*, described further in chapter 5. Furthermore, states, organizations, and groups may employ both military and nonmilitary means simultaneously in the same region, or in different regions, all depending on their political and military objectives.

Reasons for Choosing Irregular Warfare

Political and military leaders may determine that irregular warfare is to be preferred to major, conventional forms of warfare. This point is especially true for warfare in the space domain. The decision to employ irregular approaches should be informed by a sound and practical strategy, especially with regard to trade-offs between political ends and available means. Questions of whether to pursue irregular forms of conflict and competition will be influenced by the characteristics of irregular space warfare, which will be developed further in chapter 2. That said, there are two broad reasons for choosing irregular warfare and associated nontraditional approaches in space: irregular actions are viewed as occurring below the threshold of armed conflict, and sometimes they are the only currently available and viable options to achieve desired aims.

As with any dissection of an overarching strategic framework, there are disadvantages in devising a segmented rationale for choosing irregular warfare. Certainly, the strategy of irregular warfare and its implementation are complex phenomena, and there may be several logical reasons for pursuing such a strategy. Yet it is important to convey to the space strategist that irregular styles of conflict and competition in the space domain may be the best choice in certain strategic and political environments.

Actions below the Threshold of Armed Conflict

While war is war, irregular warfare often is considered something different in Western countries, including the United States. Frequently, irregular styles of conflict involve relatively small forces and few assets, for which reason many malicious actions are not perceived to be acts of armed conflict or warfare. It is important to convey to American policy makers and military leaders that competitors may turn to irregular warfare and competition because the United States has an established history of difficulty in deciding on suitable responses to such actions. Competitors may decide to use irregular styles of warfare to achieve political objectives as a matter of exploiting strategic and cultural weakness in Western views of peace and war—of a bifurcated peace-conflict continuum. The fact that a malicious activity is considered below the threshold of an armed attack may complicate the invocation of mutual defense agreements, collective action by an alliance or coalition, or application of the inherent right of self-defense under either the standing or supplemental rules of engagement. The resulting confusion and lack of consensus among international allies may delay—or even prevent—any collective military response.

Questions and complications regarding activities below the threshold of armed conflict are especially difficult in the space domain. Many space systems are autonomous and unmanned. There is the frequently mentioned adage that "satellites don't have mothers," which implies that actions in space are inherently less severe or significant than terrestrial ones.[43] Political and military leaders may question whether malicious actions against spacecraft warrant deliberate responses, let alone military ones. Consequently, the party whose satellite has been irreversibly damaged by a purposeful, state-sponsored irregular action may view a diplomatic, economic, or legal response as more appropriate than a military one. What is more, given the present-day proclivity for jamming and lasing of on-orbit systems, the prevalent and presumably acceptable use of reversible, nonkinetic methods of interference only reinforces the point that irregular activities in space are considered different from terrestrial actions and that accordingly malicious actions against space systems seldom result in military responses.[44] This is a critical point when considering space strategy, because if a rival's irregular actions are not countered satisfactorily, these seemingly minor malign actions can achieve strategic effect over time.

Another reason that irregular methods are often deemed attractive to potential perpetrators is the difficulty of attributing an irregular attack or malicious action to a single source or actor. This pertains to the need for *space attribution*, the ability to trace the origin of an action against space architectures.[45] The U.S. cyber community has noted an analogous and overlapping difficulty in identifying the origins of the cyberattacks with which it must perpetually deal, sponsored by state and nonstate entities. Jamming and lasing attacks against satellites may be difficult to trace to a source, and cyberattacks against space-enabled communications and architectures can be, as noted, difficult to attribute. In addition, it can sometimes be difficult to distinguish between intentional actions to disrupt or damage satellites and the effects of natural phenomena or space debris.

Creating Asymmetric Advantage

States often choose irregular approaches because these methods create asymmetric advantages. The chief of the General Staff of the Russian Armed Forces, Valery Gerasimov, whose "Gerasimov Doctrine" of hybrid warfare is often quoted in the West, underscores the point: "Asymmetric actions have come into widespread use, enabling the nullification of an enemy's advantages in armed conflict."[46] In the context of irregular warfare, creating an asymmetric advantage is simply achieving big results with little effort. We will consider asymmetric advantage in the broader context of space strategy in chapter 2, but the idea is helpful here, in regard to reasons for choosing irregular styles of conflict and competition. Moreover, a belligerent may undertake irregular actions in the space domain because of the perceived advantage that accrues from attacking vulnerable, national-level space systems and the ease of doing so. Jamming and lasing are relatively inexpensive measures compared to "exquisite" (i.e., highly sophisticated and very expensive) space systems; significant effects can be achieved with little effort using commonplace technology. Furthermore, cyberattacks against satellite communications and associated networks may also create asymmetric advantage.

Space powers may adopt asymmetric approaches to achieve political ends. In the case of great space powers, political and military leaders may find irregular warfare attractive as a way to achieve policy aims with minimal outlay. A large, conventional fighting force simply may not be a viable option, whether for political reasons or because of the overall competitive environment. Instead, leadership may decide that using the few military assets and space capabilities required for irregular operations is best suited for achieving limited political aims with minimal risk.

For midlevel or emerging space powers competing with more capable opponents, irregular modes may be the only practical method of achieving political aims, in effect a lower barrier of entry. In fact, there may be simply no other choice—for midlevel and emerging space powers recourse to irregular warfare for its asymmetric advantage may be a "nonchoice." This is not an original insight by any means: history offers many examples of belligerents seeking an asymmetric advantage against more capable adversaries. The space strategist must acknowledge the applicability of irregular warfare to developing both competitive strategies and counterstrategies.

Utility of History and Strategic Analogies

Knowledge of the past is prerequisite to an understanding of the present.

—Michael Howard[47]

Historical experience is essential for understanding irregular warfare and nontraditional approaches, both present and future. Failure to read about and reflect upon historical experience warps our capacity to act intelligently in the contemporary world and to contemplate usefully the future.[48] Furthermore, history provides insights into strategic competition that policy makers and strategists need to ask the correct questions as the epigraph above highlights. This especially holds true for irregular action in the space domain.

An understanding of historical experience helps equip humanity to consider a range of potential futures regarding irregular space warfare. Irregular warfare in space must fit within our collective understanding of the enduring nature of war, notwithstanding the changing character of space warfare. Colin Gray explains, "War, and warfare, has an enduring, unchanging nature, but a highly variable character. It follows that history is our best, albeit incomplete, guide to the future."[49] Historical experience can reveal the nature and function of strategies, including practical space strategies of both regular and irregular warfare.

Whether history teaches actual lessons, however, is a matter of debate. As the late acclaimed British military historian Michael Howard observed, since the earliest times history has been expected to teach lessons.[50] History "was defended, in the 1579 translation of Plutarch's *Lives*, as a 'certain rule of instruction which by examples past, teacheth us to judge of things present and to foresee things to come.'"[51] Howard cautions, "In short, historians may claim to teach lessons, and often they teach very wisely. But 'history' as such does not teach."[52] As for historical experience predicting the future, Howard is again skeptical: "The theories they (history and the social sciences) formulate are at best explanatory or heuristic. They can never be predictive. Even the most convincing of their theories should be regarded as tentative hypotheses to be critically re-examined as new data becomes available."[53] So, while an understanding of historical experience is essential for explaining the present and suggesting potential futures, there are indeed limits to its benefits.

Taking a somewhat more utilitarian view of history—along with its potential for teaching lessons—is the military historian Williamson Murray, who laments that

> unfortunately, history does repeat itself, but mankind seems largely unwilling to accept the comment that Thucydides made two and a half millennia ago that "it will be enough for me, however, if these words of mine are judged useful by those who want to understand clearly the events which happened in the past and which (human nature being what it is) will at some time or other and in much the same ways, be repeated in the future."[54]

For Murray, much of the present represents echoes of the past—making it all the more necessary to study, debate, and understand historical events.[55]

Maritime historian John Hattendorf bridges the gap between these two perspectives and offers the space strategist a beacon to follow: "Historical study provides the practical basis of, and its approaches develop the intellectual tools for, an understanding of the nature of strategy and the process it involves. In this connection, historical understanding and knowledge of past events is not the object but rather one of several means to improve the ability of professionals to solve problems more wisely than arbitrary choice, pure chance, or blind intuition would allow."[56] Through a study and better understanding of historical experience, strategists can glean greater insight than they would otherwise, offering a hope that their political and military leaders will need not relearn unnecessarily (and painfully) the lessons of the past. The study of history offers insight and helpful questions, but not answers.

Relatedly, but differently, insights into the functioning of strategy can be mined from analogies to history, especially given how few the decades of space experience are from which conclusions can be drawn. Space strategist Brad Townsend observes, "Developing a theory of space power is made doubly difficult because, unlike the sea, space is an untested domain. Humanity lacks any empirical evidence on the nature of conflict within it."[57] Consequently, such analogies can offer a way to mitigate the scantness of empirical evidence. Spacepower theorist Joshua Carlson highlights the benefits of using strategic analogies: "Reasoning by analogy is an accepted method of seeking truth about an unknown thing—comparing a known and an unknown to attempt to explain the unknown."[58] Like the study of history itself, the use of analogies can produce powerful insights into practical space strategies and help us ask important questions, but it cannot provide specific, definitive answers.

Colin Gray finds enduring value in analogies, especially from antiquity: "In point of fact, from the perspective of the strategic educator there is a major advantage in pointing students and others toward temporally distant episodes. The would-be strategist is less likely to bring unhelpful cultural baggage to the examination of medieval or ancient cases as strategic behavior, than he or she would to contemporary affairs."[59] Gray argues that one can learn about statecraft and strategy from any period, and that there is no real advantage in modernity as opposed to historically distant times.[60]

This work will frequently employ analogies to historical experience to understand irregular warfare and competitive approaches in the space domain. In particular, analogies to historical experience in the maritime domain will be utilized, because of the similarities in the national interests and strategic environments of the maritime and space domains. National interests common to maritime and space domains include the interrelationships of science, technology, industry, economics, trade, politics, international affairs, communications, international law, social affairs, and leadership.[61] Shared strategic considerations include expansive lines of communications (such as the routes traversed by ships or spacecraft going from one distant place to another), distant hubs of activity, movement of people and commerce, and strategic positions.[62] Moreover, maritime strategy is inclusive of the interaction between sea and land, just as a properly understood space strategy is inclusive of the interaction between the Earth and space.

Michael Howard offers an important caution to the would-be historian (for whom, generally, his advice was originally meant) or strategist seeking to search either historical experience or analogies for strategic insights. It concerns individual bias and prejudice: "Historians are as prone as anyone else unconsciously to formulate conclusions on the basis of temperament, prejudice and habit, and then collect the evidence to justify them. It would be dishonest to pretend otherwise."[63] So strategists must be ever vigilant to fight their own biases and avoid cherry-picking historical events to substantiate unconscious agendas or predetermined conclusions.

Space and Irregular Warfare

It is a central argument of this work that many of the competitive, nefarious, and irresponsible behaviors displayed to date on the world stage in space can be labeled as *irregular* in style or form. Some of these irregular behaviors involve military actions or militarized capabilities. The militarization of space, and relatedly the prevalence of "dual-use" (having applications for either military or nonmilitary purposes, or both) technologies, is part of humanity's collective experience, as space-power theorist Everett Dolman emphatically asserts: "The militarization and weaponization of space is not only an historical fact, it is an ongoing process."[64]

Among recent reports and analyses highlighting the ongoing competition in space is the Defense Intelligence Agency's 2022 *Challenges to Security in Space*. It notes that both the Chinese and Russian military doctrines identify space as important to modern warfare: "China and Russia, in particular, are developing various means to exploit the perceived U.S. reliance on space-based systems and challenge the U.S. position in the space domain. Beijing and Moscow seek to position themselves as leading space powers, intent on creating new global space norms. Through the use of space and counterspace capabilities, they aspire to undercut U.S. global leadership."[65] Similarly, Brian Weeden and Victoria Samson observe "from a security perspective" that "an increasing number of countries are looking to use space to enhance their military capabilities and national security. The growing use of, and reliance on, space for national security has also led more countries to look at developing their own counterspace capabilities that can be used to deceive, disrupt, deny, degrade, or destroy space systems."[66] A number of countries are developing capabilities in the categories of direct-ascent (specially launched from the ground), co-orbital (already in space, in the same orbit), electronic-warfare, directed-energy, and cyber attack, along with conducting significant research and development across a broad range of destructive and nondestructive counterspace capabilities.[67] In November 2021 Gen. David Thompson, U.S. Space Force's vice chief of space operations, commented that both China and Russia are regularly attacking U.S. satellites with non-kinetic means, including lasers, radio-frequency jammers, and cyber.[68] According to Thompson, the United States is dealing with reversible attacks on its government satellites every single day.[69] That is, countries are in fact conducting activities in the space domain below the threshold of major force-on-force engagements to achieve political effects, and these activities should be considered irregular in style and form.

Seth Jones notes that countries like China and Russia have histories of competing with the United States using irregular methods because conventional and nuclear warfare are far too costly. "Unfortunately," he writes, "the United States is woefully unprepared for this type of competition—both at home and abroad. U.S. government agencies and departments have erroneously focused too much on planning for conventional and nuclear war, including scenarios like nuclear exchanges and conventional wars in the Baltic states, Taiwan Strait, and South China Sea."[70] Furthermore, Jones observes, China has engaged in irregular activities to expand its global influence, such using fleets of fishing vessels to harass those of other nations and creating artificial islands to assert territorial and resource claims in the South China Sea.[71] Russia, under President Vladimir Putin, often employs a mix of offensive cyber operations, espionage, covert action, and information and disinformation campaigns to weaken the United States and expand Moscow's influence.[72] While Jones' examples are not space-specific, the prospect that China and Russia would use irregular action in the space domain is real.

Competitors may turn to irregular means in space for various reasons. First, coercive and aggressive actions in space may not be perceived as armed attacks or actual violence. In fact, competitors may employ reversible and nonkinetic effects to achieve political aims with relative impunity. Second, belligerents may see desirable asymmetry in going after highly valuable space-based assets with relatively inexpensive and unsophisticated capabilities. Chapter 2 will detail the characteristics that make irregular space warfare the arena of choice for many competitors.

It is worth underscoring here that the purpose of space strategy is to ensure access to and use of space.[73] As a result, if decided-on strategies fail to promote those ends, then those strategies should be reevaluated.

Furthermore, any counterstrategies to irregular warfare and competition should also embrace the purpose of space strategy. Importantly, if a rival's irregular actions lack significant consequence for one's access to and use of space, then no resources or efforts need be devoted to countering them—a great position to be in.

So What?

Skeptical war fighters could well ask why they should care. Perhaps conveniently categorizing routine, malicious, and nefarious activities as irregular warfare has no practical value in solving today's most pressing security challenges. Critics could argue that any explanations about warfare in the space domain are just general truisms—or worse, banal observations. Such potential criticisms must be acknowledged and addressed, because discussions of strategy must have practical value if they are not to be worthless and if books like this one are not to become authorial self-indulgences.

Through understanding historical experience and placing space domain actions in the proper perspective, policy makers and strategists can discern insights that could not be gained otherwise. The practical value is that senior political and military leaders need not relearn old lessons. Military historian Williamson Murray notes graphically the persistent problem of relearning past lessons and its disastrous effect. "Mankind marches ever forward into the future sure that everything is new and thus fills body bags with dead soldiers rather than reaching back into the past for the lessons others have learned at such great cost."[74] Throughout history, political and military leaders have embarked on wars with preconceived assumptions, many of them faulty. What matters is how quickly leaders align their assumptions with the reality of these conflicts. With respect to irregular warfare, policy makers and military leaders need to prepare more to fight irregulars effectively from the beginning, not just after a period of adjustment and adaptation.[75] A historical understanding of such conflicts—including those where irregular warfare played a significant part—would be a good place to start.[76] It is indeed best to think about these questions during peacetime, not after a threat has actually manifested itself.

Critically, this work's focus on irregular styles of warfare and competition is not meant to discount conventional warfare planning. As Seth Jones correctly advises, "The United States does not need to choose *between* conventional and irregular competition. Both are important."[77] The challenge is finding an equilibrium as part of a holistic national security strategy. It is important for political and military leaders to prepare for a range of potential futures and contingencies, spanning the range of conventional and irregular competition. This work's focus on irregular strategies and approaches, particularly in the space domain, is a response to the slightness of foundational literature on the subject and prevalence of misunderstandings of it within the national security communities.

Ultimately—and to answer the skeptical war fighter's "So what?"—the practical value of the discussion here is a better understanding of how irregular styles of warfare and competition in the space domain might promote peace and stability. More clarity facilitates the development of improved competitive strategies as well the formulation of sound counterstrategies to future adversaries. Through thoughtful deliberation, policy makers and military leaders can equip themselves to develop useful deterrence strategies, along with the requisite space systems and architectures. If conflict cannot be prevented, a better understanding can mean fewer lives lost and less expense. Lastly, the exploration of irregular warfare in this work should not be construed as a heedless embrace of war and warfare in the space domain. Far from that, the purpose of this work is to provide policy makers, strategists, and military leaders material for formulating sound space strategies, deterring aggression, and avoiding unnecessary losses—as best as humanity can.

⇒ CHAPTER 2 ⇐

Characteristics of Irregular Space Warfare

*Irregular warfare is an old, old story, and so are
the methods applied to wage it, on both sides.*
—Colin Gray[1]

T his book is about forms of irregular warfare and competition in space; this chapter focuses on those irregular warfare characteristics that most apply to conflicts beyond Earth's atmosphere. Given the Clausewitzian sense about the enduring nature of war (from the previous chapter), it is understood that irregular warfare in the space domain must obey the fundamental lore of war, along with the universal principles of strategy and the essential unity of all strategic experience.[2] The space strategist can look to historical experience and knowledge of conflict for insight into the functioning of irregular space warfare, as the above epigraph suggests. Once again, no matter how unfamiliar the military technologies or strange the geography or domain, warfare is still warfare.[3] Certainly, the theory and strategy of irregular warfare in space is merely a subset of the overall theory and strategy of space warfare, which is likewise merely a subset of the theory and overarching strategy of war and warfare. The general characteristics of irregular warfare, consequently, should be expected to be relevant to all domains, including the space domain.

Along with the enduring nature of war, Clausewitz explains the nuances of the ever-changing character of war and its conduct. He held that the "grammar" and character of strategy are in a constant state of change, even though strategy's fundamental nature and logic are eternal.[4] It should be no surprise to the space strategist, therefore, that war in space, including that waged in an irregular style, has its own distinctive characteristics.

According to Clausewitz, the character of war refers to the changing way that war as a phenomenon manifests itself in the real world. Because war is a political act that takes place in and among societies, war's specific character will be shaped by those politics and those societies, or what Clausewitz calls the *spirit of the age*. Clausewitz writes, "The aims a belligerent adopts, and the resources he employs, must be governed by the particular characteristics of his own [geopolitical] position; but they will also conform to the spirit of the age and to its general character."[5] The space strategist, therefore, should expect that the particular characteristics of irregular warfare in the space domain to vary with strategic circumstances and cultural predispositions.

Military theorist and strategist Antulio Echevarria interprets Clausewitz as saying that the elements that shape policy and strategy are both situational and cultural, objective and subjective.[6] The cultural aspect mentioned by Echevarria is critical for strategic preferences involving irregular space warfare. Polities are predisposed to certain styles of warfare, including irregular styles, based on societal, cultural, and historical experiences. Indeed, polities and their militaries often prepare for and fight wars according to their strategic cultures and distinctive characters, at least insofar as adversaries allow. The differences in strategic preferences between China, Russia, and the United States are widely acknowledged, and these differences should be expected to manifest themselves in the chosen operational styles of warfare. Examples would be a U.S. preference for regular styles of warfare over irregular styles compared to China's and Russia's preference for irregular and unconventional methods.[7] Because of the competitive nature of strategies and their implementation, policy makers and military leaders must be self-aware as to their own biases in styles of warfare, along with those of competitors. This ideal holds when considering U.S. preferences for competition and conflict in space (see chapter 8).

What comes next in this chapter are characteristics of irregular warfare in space. There is always some downside to distinct, neat categories, and the strategist must always be fully cognizant of this hazard. Many of these characteristics overlap with one another, but there is still value in considering these areas individually. Notable intersections and interdependencies can be helpful for developing strategies meant to protect national security interests, and counter those of adversaries, in space. Irregular warfare in space includes the use of military force; however, aspects of this chapter also pertain to the broader topic of strategic competition, which includes methods apart from using force. A more complete exploration of nonmilitary activities and nonforcible actions will be detailed further in chapters 4 and 5.

Political and Terrestrial Reference

War is simply a continuation of political intercourse, with the addition of other means. —Clausewitz[8]

Though space is a relatively new domain with regard to conflict, war in space, like war in all other domains, should serve the ends of policy in pursuit of political objectives. Irregular warfare and competition in the space domain have meaning only in terms of policy and political objectives. In the epigraph above, Clausewitz asserts that war is an extension of policy by other means. Similarly, Mao Tse-tung, who routinely paraphrased and echoed Clausewitz's thoughts, notes the linkage between war and politics: "'War is the continuation of politics.' In this sense war is politics and war itself is a political action; since ancient times there has never been a war that did not have a political character."[9] It is noteworthy that both renowned military theorists—Clausewitz describing the universal framework for war and strategy and Mao expounding protracted, irregular warfare deemed it critical to highlight the policy/political dimension of war and warfare.

Colin Gray, comparing irregular warfare to traditional forms of military conflict, finds that the irregular style too is undergirded by politics: "Of course, all warfare is about politics. It is only the political dimension that gives meaning to the bloody activity. But, in regular warfare, at least for the soldiers, politics typically takes a backseat until the military issue is settled. Not so in irregular warfare. In the latter case there will probably be no recognizable military decision. Military behavior must be conducted for its political effects because those effects, in the minds of the public, comprise the true field of decision."[10] Irregular warfare in space too will have a political context. Because of its protracted nature and often the absence of any definitive military resolution, irregular warfare in space will have more the character of a contest of political wills than do regular forms of military conflict in space. The converse of this relationship can also be true: when the desired ends are mostly political, irregular styles may be the best suited to them. The lesson for today's national security community is that using space for political gain will likely necessitate irregular forms of competition and conflict.

Furthermore, war and warfare in the space domain must have terrestrial dimensions, at least in the foreseeable future. For conflict to have the greatest impact and affect the strategic level of war, military operations must affect the preponderance of people where they live, which at present is on land. This is because strategic effect is decided by the target, not by the means of attack.[11] In most cases, when seeking strategic effect the chosen target should affect the adversary's polity. As a result, there will be practical limits to what space warfare can achieve strategically, no matter how significant the success or how well operations are executed. Although the use of force in space may indeed achieve strategic effects—even the potential employment of space-to-Earth weapons—actions there will be strategically decisive in determining a war's outcome only on the rarest occasions. The indispensability of a terrestrial reference holds true for both regular and irregular forms of space warfare and will do so at least until such time as polities' interests expand significantly outward from near-Earth matters.

Limited vs. Unlimited Objectives

Irregular styles of warfare and competition, including those in the space domain, may be limited or unlimited with respect to the desired political object. Leaderships should decide on what kind of war they are embarking, whether the aims are limited or unlimited; as Clausewitz explains, "The first, the supreme, the most far-reaching act of judgment that the statesman and commander have to make is to establish by that test [of fit with political aims] the kind of war on which they are embarking; neither mistaking it for, nor trying to turn it into, something that is alien to its nature. This is the first of all strategic questions and the most comprehensive."[12] Policy makers and military leaders should heed Clausewitz's advice when contemplating irregular warfare and ensure that this form of warfare is appropriate given the strategic environment and the availability of both time and means. Surely, irregular warfare may play a critical part if it meets the needs of strategy and balances political ends and available means. Yet in other circumstances, irregular warfare may be ineffectual, impractical, and inefficient, and consequently more-conventional methods may be a better choice (if they are even an option for the would-be belligerent). The strategist will earn his or her keep if only by determining the correct balance of regular and irregular approaches.

Like Clausewitz before him, the maritime strategist Julian Corbett helpfully differentiated between limited and unlimited aims. In limited war "we merely seek to take from the enemy some particular part of his possessions, or interests."[13] In contrast, a state fights an unlimited war to overthrow the adversary completely, forcing the adversary to submit to avoid destruction.[14]

A state, organization, or group less capable than its enemy may explore irregular forms of warfare to achieve either limited or unlimited political objectives. This point is commonly understood in the contexts of insurgency and guerrilla warfare. An insurgent's political objective may become unlimited—to overthrow the current regime and establish a new government—but at an earlier stage may be more modest, limited aims, such as harassing the government's forces while preserving one's own. Andrew Krepinevich notes how an insurgent's desired objectives change, from intermediate to final aims, throughout the struggle: "An insurgency is a *protracted struggle* conducted methodically, step by step, in order to obtain specific intermediate objectives leading finally to the overthrow of the existing order."[15] The objectives of irregular warfare, therefore, may have temporal dimensions, including short-term, limited aims but also long-term, unlimited ones.

By comparison, a larger, more capable power may use irregular warfare, for whatever aims. First, the more capable power may find it an appropriate and efficient method to counter an adversary's attempt to use irregular warfare for an asymmetric advantage. This would essentially be responding in kind—irregular force against irregular force—to nullify any perceived strategic advantage the adversary might otherwise have, while achieving the unlimited aim of causing an insurgent's force eventual demise. Second, for the stronger power, irregular warfare may be an economical method, one having a minimal "footprint," to achieve limited political aims—that is, strategic effect using limited means.

Julian Corbett writes extensively about using a small force against a larger one in the maritime domain, with relevance for irregular styles of warfare in space. In particular, he explains how small forces can achieve limited objectives and strategic advantage.[16] He highlights the British experience during their wars with Napoleon, during which they sent small amphibious forces to invade the continent or divert the Napoleonic forces to the coast. The small amphibious force "was always out of all proportion to the intrinsic strength employed or the positive results it could give. . . . Its value lay in its power of containing [a] force greater than its own."[17] In fact, Corbett goes on to say, "the limited form of war has this element of strength over and above the unlimited form. . . . The point is of the highest importance, for it is direct negation of the current doctrine that there can be but one legitimate object, the overthrow of the enemy's means of resistance and that the primary objective must always be his armed forces."[18] From Corbett's writings on limited war it emerges that a small, contingent force (modest in size and presumably with an ancillary role or mission) with limited aims can gain strategic advantage almost immediately, without exposing itself to unacceptable risk from counterattack.

Furthermore, Corbett writes, a country with overwhelming maritime superiority can fight with limited aims to prevent the opponent from escalating the conflict into an unlimited war. In the maritime realm, "a war may be limited not only because the objective is too limited to call for the whole national force, but also because the sea may be made to present an insuperable physical obstacle to the whole national force being brought to bear. That is to say, a war may be limited physically by the strategical isolation of the object, as well as morally by its comparative unimportance."[19] Therefore, according to Corbett, not only the political objective but the strategic environment may constrain a belligerent's aims in war. He calls the ability to prevent an adversary from escalating a limited conflict into an unlimited one the "power of isolation," whereby one is able to defend against an unlimited counterstroke.[20] In Corbett's view, this isolation is an effective barrier to action.[21]

While the foregoing discussion of limited and unlimited political objectives during irregular warfare is relevant for all domains, irregular warfare in space can be expected to have characteristics of its own. First, a less-capable force or insurgency may wage irregular warfare in the space domain or against space architectures for time-limited objectives—such as short-term tactical success but long-term overthrow or collapse of the adversary's government. Second, a more capable space power may be able with a small, contingent space force to achieve limited political aims more efficiently than with a larger force. Third, a more capable space power can, by exercising the "power of isolation," prevent the adversary from responding effectively in space. Such a "barrier to action," created by a space force to isolate the adversary and limit its options, can help control escalation in space or elsewhere.[22]

Time as a Weapon: Protracted Strategy

For there has never been a protracted war from which a country has benefited.

—Sun Tzu[23]

As mentioned, irregular warfare itself frequently has temporal dimensions, and so too will irregular space warfare. This temporal dimension often is understood in terms of the strategic advantage enabled by a protracted strategy. The protracted characteristic of irregular warfare has long been noted, as Sun Tzu's epigraph above illustrates, and historical experience illustrates that belligerents conducting irregular warfare have been willing and able to extend wars in time to achieve long-term goals. While insurgents and others choosing irregular warfare may fight from a point of initial weakness with respect to the forces they oppose, they can use the element of time by protracting the conflict. In a long conflict the stronger force may be worn down and weakened while the less-capable force becomes stronger and finds the strategic environment changing in its favor. Combatants in irregular space warfare often will use a protracted strategy, the element of time, to gain these benefits.

Mao's writings frequently note the temporal aspect of successful insurgencies: "Because the reactionary forces are very strong, revolutionary forces grow only gradually, and this fact determines the protracted nature of our war. Here impatience is harmful and advocacy of 'quick decision' is incorrect."[24] Similarly, in the Arab revolt of 1916–18 a protracted approach played an important part for irregular forces. A British participant, T. E. Lawrence ("Lawrence of Arabia") recalled, "Final victory seemed certain, if the war lasted long enough for us to work it out."[25] Through a protracted strategy, irregular forces can test the patience and resolve of their opponents.

Fundamentally, time is a determinant between victory and defeat in irregular warfare. Colin Gray makes the point powerfully:

> Of all the many dimensions of strategy, time is the most intractable. Compensation for deficiencies elsewhere and corrections of errors are usually possible. But time lost is irrecoverable. The Western theory of war and strategy pays too little attention to war's temporal dimension. In particular, there is too little recognition that time itself can be a weapon. It can be used purposefully to compensate for material or other weakness, and to expose and stress the vulnerability of the enemy. In irregular warfare, the materially disadvantaged combatant is obliged to try to win slowly, for no other reason than [that] he cannot win swiftly.[26]

Protracted, irregular warfare looks to buy time, delaying potential defeat until fortunes can improve—to that extent, in essence, it is a defensive strategy. In fact, Sun Tzu's epigraph above implies that a powerful, centralized state can be worn down in a protracted conflict. This style of warfare, then, is likely to be advantageous to a less-capable insurgency against a more powerful opponent.

Furthermore, in protracted irregular warfare, irregular forces do not necessarily need to "win"—just not to "lose." More important than winning a specific tactical engagement in a protracted strategy is being able to fight another day. An irregular opponent need not aspire to defeat a larger, more capable force in battle. It does not need to. A larger, traditional force seeking decisive victory against an irregular opponent is chasing a chimera; it will likely only exhaust itself, undermine its domestic political support, and dissipate its strength.[27] Moreover, a protracted conflict works against the stronger force by increasing the scope for chance, uncertainty, and the unforeseeable. As John Mearsheimer explains, "It is difficult [for the stronger force] to feel fully confident about the final outcome of a protracted conflict, simply because that outcome is likely to be influenced by unforeseen events."[28] Less capable, irregular forces hope for and count on these contingencies and the long-term problems they create.

Indirect Approach

There are two related but distinct aspects of protracted war specifically in the space domain—the indirect approach and cumulative strategy. It is noteworthy that Mao's idea of a protracted strategy embraces both, without using those terms. Historical experience should teach policy makers and strategists that a less-capable power's space strategy is likely to be indirect and cumulative. More capable powers may also employ these approaches to achieve strategic effect in the space domain using minimal means.

The British strategist B. H. Liddell Hart's writings frequently address the indirect approach, and his strategic conception is particularly helpful. While regular forms of warfare and traditional, large-scale forces may employ it as well, the indirect approach is quite likely to play a key role in protracted, irregular warfare.

In his *Strategy*, Liddell Hart argues that the indirect approach incorporates the idea that strategy should adjust as the situation develops. That is, he explains, "The longest way round is apt to be the shortest way home."[29] A direct approach to the object exhausts the attacker and hardens the resistance by compression, whereas an indirect approach loosens the defender's hold by upsetting his balance.[30] Liddell Hart contends that the indirect approach is a key counterview to Clausewitz's theory, in the mainstream interpretation, that strategy should seek solely to overcome the adversary's resistance. Liddell Hart writes that, rather, a sound wartime strategy should exploit the elements of movement and surprise to achieve operational advantage by throwing the enemy off balance before being struck.[31] By doing so, an indirect approach can lead to greater operational success with fewer casualties. Liddell Hart explains,

> The art of the indirect approach can only be mastered, and its full scope appreciated, by study of and reflection on the whole history of war. But we can at least crystallize the lessons into two simple maxims, one negative, the other positive. The first is that, in face of the overwhelming

evidence of history, no general is justified in launching his troops to a direct attack on an enemy firmly in position. The second, that instead of seeking to upset the enemy's equilibrium by one's attack, it must be upset before a real attack is, or can be successfully, launched.[32]

In Liddell Hart's view, a successful wartime strategy should seek not battle so much as strategic situations so advantageous that if the situation does not in itself produce a decision, the ensuing battle is sure to do so.[33]

Mao contends that flexibility is "a concrete expression of the initiative in guerrilla warfare, whereas rigidness and inertia inevitably lead to passivity and cause unnecessary losses."[34] Because wartime conditions are constantly changing, military leaders must adjust their strategy as well, as Mao highlighted: "War is a contest of strength, but the original pattern of strength changes in the course of war."[35] Part of this requisite adaptability includes avoiding the opponent's strength and attacking his weaknesses, which agrees with the indirect approach. By creating strategic advantage through the adjustment of strategy to exploit the opponent's weakness, an irregular force can be able to achieve its political aims and military objectives.

Cumulative Strategy

We should recognize the existence and power of these cumulative strategies and integrate them more carefully into our basic strategic thinking.

—J. C. Wylie[36]

The naval officer and strategist J. C. Wylie offers in his *Military Strategy: A General Theory of Power Control* remarks on cumulative strategy that are helpful in understanding a protracted style of irregular warfare. According to Wylie, a cumulative strategy uses the "minute accumulation of little items piling on top of the other" until their aggregate mass becomes critical.[37] A sequential strategy, in contrast, refers to a series of discrete actions where the success of any one depends on the success of the one that precedes it.[38] In Wylie's words, "There is a type of warfare in which the entire pattern is made up of a collection of lesser actions, but these lesser or individual actions are not sequentially interdependent. Each individual one is no more than a single statistic, an isolated plus or minus, in arriving at the final result."[39] A cumulative strategy produces results not by any single action or sequence of actions but by the cumulative effect of numerous actions over time. According to Wylie, commerce raiding in maritime strategy is a classic example: the loss of a single ship is not especially significant, and there is no need to sink ships in any particular order. Specific types of ships (like tankers) might be more valuable than others, but the sinking of any ship contributes directly to the raider's victory. The effectiveness of the strategy comes from cumulative losses over time.[40]

Wylie views psychological warfare, economic warfare, naval blockade, and guerrilla warfare as operations and activities commonly employing a cumulative strategy.[41] For example, a small contingent of insurgents might be discovered and militarily defeated, but the overall insurgency remains intact as long as other guerrilla forces remain, believe in the cause, and continue the fight. Wylie is forthright and transparent about the limitations of a cumulative strategy: it is rarely sufficient to defeat the enemy, achieve the requisite level of control, and decisively conclude a conflict. However, he finds, when sequential and cumulative strategies are integrated, maximum pressure on the enemy is achieved.[42]

Furthermore, Wylie views Mao's strategy of guerrilla warfare as sound.[43] Wylie acknowledges the well-established and historical understanding of guerrilla warfare, that there is, in fact, no novelty about it.[44] Wylie views Mao's theory of conflict as exemplifying many of his own ideas on cumulative strategy: "It is important to note here that while the normal strategy of the continental or Clausewitz theory is a sequential strategy, a main weight of the Mao theory is based on a cumulative, not a sequential, concept."[45]

For his part, Mao writes, "If each month we could win one sizable victory . . . it would greatly demoralize the enemy, stimulate the morale of our own forces, and evoke international support. Thus, our strategically protracted war is translated in the field into battles of quick decision. The enemy's war of strategic quick decision is bound to change into protracted war after he is defeated in many campaigns and battles."[46] Mao saw the accumulation of victories over time as vital for successful protracted guerrilla warfare.

As the space strategist should know well, there is a danger in seeking neat, tidy definitions and discrete terminology. War and warfare are a messy business. So too will be war and warfare in the space domain. Therefore, it may be ultimately unhelpful to argue whether an action or method is protracted, indirect, or cumulative. In the end, what the space strategist needs to understand is that irregular styles of conflict and competition will likely include protracted, indirect, and cumulative strategies, all of which seek to achieve long-term, strategic advantage. Holistic and strategic consideration of these ideas will be the soundest way to achieve success.

Additionally, policy makers and military leaders should consider how these elements can be appropriately blended and balanced in each domain. For example, a future wartime strategy may need to consider how and why the maritime, space, and cyberspace domains use indirect and cumulative methods, while the land and air domains employ more traditional, direct, and sequential ones. There is no "one size fits all" approach to strategy, and each domain may have its own approach for achieving political aims, depending on time and place.

Asymmetric Advantage

In its very nature irregular warfare is structurally asymmetrical. —Colin Gray[47]

While having some overlap with the concept of the indirect approach, asymmetric advantage as part of irregular warfare is a distinct enough concept to warrant separate discussion. The indirect approach, broadly considered, seeks strategic effect by means apart from direct, large force-on-force engagements. In contrast, asymmetric advantage seeks to take advantage of one's strengths against an opponent's weakness, either of them military or nonmilitary, to achieve strategic or tactical effects. Sun Tzu's writings touch on asymmetric advantage, in regard to attacking the enemy's emptiness and avoiding its strength.[48] Therefore, one of the key distinctions between the indirect approach and asymmetric advantage is that the latter *may or may not* involve major military engagements, while the indirect approach, as evoked by Liddell Hart, is best understood as apart from them. Ultimately, both asymmetric advantage and the indirect approach may seek strategic effect by exploiting imbalances. As part of a competitive strategy, seeking asymmetric advantage entails understanding fully one's own strengths and weaknesses and those of the adversary.

It is worth underscoring that asymmetry can have a nonmilitary dimension. Nonmilitary instruments of national power—whether diplomatic, informational, economic, or legal—are vital elements of asymmetric strategies. The writings of two People's Liberation Army (PLA) officers, Qiao Liang and Wang Xiangsui, though not representing the official views of China's military establishment, relate the concept of *unrestricted warfare* to asymmetry. In 1999 they asserted, "No matter whether it serves as a line of thought or as a principle guiding combat operations, asymmetry manifests itself to some extent in every aspect of warfare. Understanding and employing the principle of asymmetry correctly allows us always to find and exploit an enemy's soft spots. The main fighting elements of some poor countries, weak countries, and nonstate entities have all used 'mouse toying with the cat'–type asymmetrical combat methods against much more powerful adversaries."[49] In short, to these two PLA officers, asymmetry means refusing to confront head-on the armed forces of a stronger country, and unrestricted warfare transcends all boundaries and limits.[50] Anything goes, anything that might work. Warfare can be military, quasi-military, or even nonmilitary. It can be violence, or it can be nonviolent, waged on the battlefields of politics, economics, culture, and the psyche.[51]

In irregular warfare, asymmetric advantage is often a matter of using a small force to achieve big results. The space strategist should presume that competitors, whether peer competitors or less-capable powers, will do just that, which frequently means going after presumably vulnerable, high-value assets. In 2017 Gen. John Hyten, then commander of U.S. Strategic Command, referred to certain American satellites as "large, big, fat, juicy targets."[52] An adversary may well go after "juicy targets" with inexpensive ground-based systems, like lasers. Alternatively, high-value assets may be rendered ineffective with even less of a physical footprint or presence, if any, by cyberattacks against telemetry, tracking, and control communications; space-enabled computer networks; or a space architecture's ground segment.

Furthermore, asymmetric advantage in space, as part of an overarching irregular warfare and competition strategy, may be achieved in good measure by nonmilitary means. Nonmilitary methods may achieve political aims and military objectives. Such means and methods—under the rubric of trying anything that might work—might include exploiting a competitor's domestic and political weaknesses, creating new (or aggravating old) divisions between allied countries, using disinformation and propaganda to cause confusion, misconstruing international law or creating ambiguity in accepted norms, and undermining existing economic frameworks or "most-favored" trading agreements.

Deception and Surprise

Take advantage of the enemy's unpreparedness; attack him when he does not expect it; avoid his strength and strike his emptiness, and like water, none can oppose you. —Sun Tzu[53]

Deception and surprise are interrelated and mutually reinforcing aspects of irregular warfare. Deception can create opportunities for surprise. The strategic or tactical advantage generated may create an asymmetry that did not exist beforehand. Sun Tzu frequently writes on deception and surprise, declaring, for example, that "all warfare is based on deception" and that it is best to take your adversary unaware, by surprise attacks where he is unprepared.[54] Sun Tzu elaborates, "If I am able to determine the enemy's dispositions while at the same time I conceal my own then I can concentrate my forces and he must divide. And if I concentrate while he divides, I can use my entire strength to attack a fraction of his. There, I will be numerically superior. Then, if I am able to use many to strike few at the selected point, those I deal with will fall into hopeless straits."[55] This passage encapsulates the idea of using deception and surprise to generate asymmetric advantage (in this case numerical) that in turn creates strategic effect.

In the space domain, it is not merely possible, or even probable, that competitive deception and surprise will be employed, but certain. A 2015 U.S. Department of Defense white paper addressed the synergistic effect of deception and surprise with respect to space.[56] It noted that deception is a long-standing practice by which adversaries hide their strengths, weaknesses, and intent so as to achieve operational and strategic surprise.[57] Commanders of space national security assets must consider deception in their planning for space operations to ensure the survival and resilience of their space mission.

We define deception as measures taken to confuse or mislead an adversary with respect to the location, capability, operational status, mission type, and/or robustness of a national security system or payload. While many deception measures could be taken at the system level, such as constructing different payloads or components in a manner that would make them difficult to distinguish from others that perform different functions, there are deception measures one could take at an architectural, operational, or organizational level as well. To the degree that deception measures are successful, an adversary either: (a) will not attack a given space system or capability that he would attack if he realized what and where it was or the actual function it performed; or (b) may be induced to attack systems that do not provide the capabilities that he is attempting to degrade. Given the physics of space defense and attack, deception is likely a critical element of any space system resilience effort.[58]

War is a duel between thinking adversaries. Therefore, the space strategist should remember that while deception and surprise are helpful, one's adversary will use them too. Furthermore, deception and surprise in military actions are discovered soon after the actions occur, so planning should acknowledge the eventual counterattack.

Remaining Elusive: Dispersal and Concentration

Move when it is advantageous and create changes in the situation by dispersal and concentration of forces. —Sun Tzu[59]

Constant alternation of dispersal and concentration is a key dimension of irregular warfare, particularly of a protracted strategy that avoids decisive battle. Sun Tzu knew that dispersal and concentration are not separate concepts but constitute a singular idea, each constantly flowing into the other based on the strategic or tactical environment. Mao Tse-tung, who routinely quotes and paraphrases Sun Tzu, develops the idea in the context of guerrilla warfare:

Flexibility in dispersal, concentration and shifts of position is a concrete expression of the initiative in guerrilla warfare, whereas rigidness and inertia inevitably lead to passivity and cause unnecessary losses. But a commander proves himself wise not just by recognition of the importance of employing his forces flexibly but by skill in dispersing, concentrating, or shifting them in good time according to the specific circumstances. This wisdom in sensing changes and choosing the right moment to act is not easily acquired; it can be gained only by those who study with a receptive mind and investigate and ponder diligently. Prudent consideration of the circumstances is essential to prevent flexibility from turning into impulsive action.[60]

Military leaders should, with due consideration of timing and specific circumstances, employ dispersal and concentration to achieve desired aims and minimize potential losses.

The interconnection of dispersal and concentration is also well established in maritime strategy. Naval officer and strategist Alfred Thayer Mahan explains in detail the idea relative to naval vessels and how they should work in a coordinated fashion:

> It is not the keeping of the several vessels side by side that constitutes the virtue of this disposition; it is the placing them under a single head, thereby insuring co-operation, however widely dispersed by their common chief under the emergency of successive moments. Like a fan that opens and shuts, vessels thus organically bound together possess the power of wide sweep, which insures exertion over a great field of ocean, and at the same time that of mutual support, because dependent on and controlled from a common centre. Such is concentration, reasonably understood; not huddled together like a drove of cattle, but distributed with a regard to a common purpose, and linked together by the effectual energy of a single will.[61]

Julian Corbett agrees, adding that the concept involves being able to assemble "the utmost force at the right time and place" and yet also to stop the concentration and rapidly shift direction.[62] Holding back on the massing of ships, as circumstances and environment allow, gives an opponent less indication of where and against what the expected concentration will be directed. This flexibility and near-real-time decision-making denies the opponent critical intelligence of the fleet's actual distribution and intention.[63] The "oneness" of dispersal and concentration corresponds with Mahan's image of the "effectual energy of a single will."

One of the key advantages of dispersal and concentration is its compatibility with elusiveness. Being elusive and avoiding a decisive battle is paramount in guerrilla styles of warfare, to prevent an irreversible defeat. Critically, dispersal and concentration offer small forces the flexibility and adaptability they need. Mao argues that a long-term guerrilla strategy is best accomplished by fluidity in dispersing and concentrating forces and effects.[64] The British amphibious-warfare proponent and strategist Col. Charles Callwell, collecting over a century ago the lessons for imperial powers of their colonial "small war" experiences, underscores how dismaying to a stronger force the elusiveness and indecisiveness of irregular warfare can be. It is quite difficult, Callwell observes, to persuade or coerce an irregular enemy to come out and fight so that he can be duly slaughtered in satisfactorily large numbers.[65]

The concept of dispersal and concentration is one of space warfare's defining characteristics.[66] Its strategic environment—including expansive celestial lines of communication (CLOCs) and distant hubs of activity—demands flexibility in dispersal and concentration. The interests of polities, organizations, and groups need to be advanced and protected, thereby demanding dispersal to wherever those interests lie. Yet, available forces and resources will be insufficient to protect all interests, activities, and CLOCs at all times. It is the space domain's vastness that makes irregular warfare viable there.

A strategy of irregular space warfare will likely seek to attack and harass an opponent far from the preponderance of the opponent's forces, infrastructure, or space architectures, perhaps his rearward, terrestrially based logistical lines of communication and supply (see chapter 3). Like guerrillas, combatants in irregular space warfare avoid single, deciding battles so as to survive to fight another day. They should disperse systems, architectures, and effects to wherever their vital space interests are located. By dispersing spacecraft and architectures in various celestial regions or along distant CLOCs, irregular space forces can keep an adversary uncertain; as in other domains, as noted, a viable irregular space warfare strategy provides for agile alternation between dispersal and concentration. That is, irregular space forces, systems, and architectures should be dispersed to cover the widest possible region and yet retain the ability to concentrate force or effects rapidly, wherever and whenever needed.

Hybrid Space Warfare

But of all the grisly forms that war takes, hybrid conflicts would appear to be the nastiest. —Williamson Murray[67]

It is important to discern the implications of hybrid warfare for irregular warfare in space. In *hybrid warfare* both conventional and irregular forces, perhaps state and nonstate actors, work in tandem.[68] Hybrid forms of warfare are nothing new or particularly exceptional, except that historically hybrid approaches are often most challenging.[69] Historian Williamson Murray explains, "The historical record suggests that hybrid warfare in one form or another may well be the norm for human conflict rather than the exception. Moreover, history also suggests that such conflicts may well be the most difficult conflicts to win."[70] Moreover, as Peter Mansoor notes, hybrid warfare's "pedigree goes back at least as far as the Peloponnesian War in the fifth century BC."[71] In the twentieth century, Mao Tse-tung and his subordinate commanders became experts on integrating regular and irregular forces and symmetric and asymmetric attacks.[72] Both opponents might choose hybrid styles, as occurred during the French and Indian War (the North American theater of the Seven Years' War, 1755–63), where each side used a combination of regular military forces, colonial militias, and native irregulars.[73]

During the last decade or so, however, "hybrid warfare" has become something of a buzzword, fashionable jargon in the U.S. defense community. In 2009, Secretary of Defense Robert Gates first employed the phrase publicly, predicting a future security environment defined by "more complex forms of warfare."[74] Gates' comments followed years of analysis and debate by academia and thinktank communities. In a 2007 policy paper titled, "Conflict in the 21st Century: The Rise of the Hybrid War," Frank Hoffman warned that instead of future adversaries "with fundamentally different approaches (conventional, irregular, or terrorist) we can expect to face competitors who employ all forms of war and tactics, perhaps simultaneously."[75] Of note, the 2010 U.S. Quadrennial Defense Review acknowledged a need for increased capacity for COIN as well as for stability operations and counterterrorism, because "today's hybrid approaches demand that U.S. forces prepare for a range of conflicts."[76]

Buzzword or not, history shows that hybrid forms of warfare are frequently employed. Because of its convoluted character and the difficulty in formulating even a simple strategy—let alone counterstrategy—hybrid warfare is quite tough to wage successfully. Stephen Biddle places hybrid warfare on the spectrum between conventional and irregular warfare; in view of its complexity, this "midspectrum war fighting requires unusually resource-intensive training and poses serious dilemmas of conflicting interests and collective action."[77] But then, it can be equally complex for both belligerents and consequently remains an attractive option to create a balanced strategic environment.

Hybrid space warfare includes traditional military forces in coordination with nontraditional efforts—irregular forces, militia, or state-sponsored commercial entities. It will be a hybrid of both symmetric and asymmetric combat, of traditional space constellations and architectures and irregular space capabilities and services.[78] An example might mix traditional, exquisite satellites, conventional war fighting, and nontraditional, nonstate spacecraft for on-orbit servicing and active debris removal. Inferring the actual purpose of nonstate spacecraft or state-sponsored commercial satellites with dual-use technologies will be difficult, and in any case they may change over time or as the strategic environment dictates.

Additionally, hybrid warfare may involve different styles of combat in various war-fighting domains, as predicated on the relative strengths and weaknesses of the belligerents. Consequently, a hybrid strategy may pair the lethality of conventional land forces with the elusiveness of an irregular space force effort. Alternatively, the hybrid strategy may see terrestrial irregulars—whether guerrillas, insurgents, or terrorists—in coordination with traditional space forces and systems, such as satellite communications and Earth observation satellites. (The role of commercial capabilities as part of a hybrid space architecture is explored in chapter 6.) Because of its complexity of potential styles of warfare and domains of conflict, a hybrid approach must be fully synchronized and coordinated in an overarching strategy.

A Russian cyberattack ahead of Russia's 2022 invasion of Ukraine was a real-world example of hybrid space warfare, combining attacks against commercial space systems with the movement of military land forces. An hour before Russian troops crossed the border, Russian government hackers conducted cyberattacks against the American satellite company Viasat.[79] The attack resulted in an immediate and significant loss of communication in the early days of the war for the Ukrainian military, which relied on Viasat's satellite services for command and control. This cyberattack against a commercial satellite provider is considered typical of Russia's playbook and its propensity toward hybrid warfare.[80] Morten Bødskov, the Danish defense minister, noted, "Russia's coordinated and destructive cyberattack before the invasion of Ukraine shows that cyberattacks are used actively and strategically in modern-day warfare, even if the threat and consequences of a cyberattack are not always visible for the public."[81] Furthermore, acts of hybrid space warfare such as cyberattacks against spacecraft and space architectures can do great damage to countries' critical infrastructure. In this instance, the damage to Viasat spilled over from Ukraine to affect thousands of internet users and internet-connected wind farms in Central Europe.[82]

Conclusion

Irregular warfare in the space domain should not be seen through the lens of discrete, tactical actions. As with all forms of warfare, irregular space warfare should support an overall strategy that aims to achieve political aims. Mao asks, "Why is it necessary for the commander of a campaign or a tactical operation to understand the laws of strategy to some degree? Because an understanding of the whole facilitates the handling of the part, and because the part is subordinate to the whole. The view that strategic victory is determined by tactical successes alone is wrong because it overlooks the fact that victory or defeat in a war is first and foremost a question of whether the situation as a whole and its various stages are properly taken into account."[83] Irregular forms of warfare and competition should be integrated into the overall war plan, with provision for synchronization of regular and irregular elements supporting an all-encompassing strategy. Resorting to irregular warfare is not a shortcut for thinking hard about strategy.

The space strategist should expect some states, organizations, and groups to protect their respective interests and achieve political objectives by means of irregular styles of warfare. If strategy involves the balancing of political ends with available means, certain powers will prefer irregular styles of conflict and competition. The choice will be shaped by a variety of factors, including technology, law, ethics, politics, and military culture. This will hold true for the space domain as well. Also, what characteristics of irregular space warfare are incorporated into a wartime strategy will also depend on time, place, and competitive environment. The characteristics of irregular space warfare described in this chapter, if properly integrated and synchronized, can help maximize the inherent strengths of an irregular space force, reduce the adversary's strengths, and mitigate risks.

CHAPTER 3

Small Space Wars
Irregular Warfare in Space

We must therefore be prepared to cope—even better, to **thrive—**
in an environment of chaos, uncertainty,
constant change, and friction.
—U.S. Marine Corps, Warfighting, MCDP 1[1]

T his chapter focuses on conflict in the space domain apart from major, conventional forms of warfare. In particular, this chapter explores the ways, methods, and operational styles of irregular space warfare, whether kinetic or nonkinetic, reversible or irreversible. While the previous chapter discussed the characteristics of irregular space warfare, this chapter details the operational art of using force in the space domain in an irregular style or form. Irregular space warfare will be chaotic and uncertain, an environment in which war fighters must be able to thrive.

Policy makers and strategists should remember that the employment of force, or military action, is not in and of itself the ultimate goal—the goal is to support the achievement of desired policy ends and strategic aims. The use of the military instrument of national power is meaningless, in a strategic sense, if divorced from the context of political aims. Similarly, the concepts of irregular space warfare are hollow if they are not directly supportive of an overarching strategy and associated policy objectives.

Space powers across the spectrum, whether great, middle, or emerging, will find this chapter relevant. Stephen Biddle advises that irregular warfare is waged by both state and nonstate actors.[2] Consequently, the concepts here are relevant for both, the highly capable and the less so. Because actors have a variety of motives, goals, and resources, in practice irregular warfare in space will entail a wide range of military means and operational styles, depending on the correlation of strengths and weaknesses between given belligerents.

Defining Small Space Wars

This chapter's main title is "Small Space Wars"—in other words, force and violence in the space domain below the threshold of major, conventional forms of warfare. The definition aligns with Clausewitz's overall premise that war is an act of force to compel an enemy to do one's will.[3] Additionally, the phrase harks back over a hundred years to the strategic concept of small wars. One of the best-known works addressing small wars is Colonel Callwell's *Small Wars*, published in 1896 as a guide for the conduct of colonial wars and imperial policing. In seeking to establish the lexicon for his argument, Callwell writes, "*Small war* is a term which has come largely into use of late years, and which is admittedly somewhat difficult to define. Practically it may be said to include all campaigns other than those where both the opposing sides consist of regular troops."[4]

For Callwell *small* has no connection with scale but simply "denote[s], in default of a better, operations of regular armies against irregular, or comparatively speaking irregular, forces."[5] Callwell later suggests that "small wars may broadly be divided into three classes—campaigns of conquest or annexation, campaigns for the suppression of insurrections or lawlessness or for the settlement of conquered or annexed territory, and campaigns undertaken to wipe out an insult, to avenge a wrong, or to overthrow a dangerous enemy. Each class of campaign will generally be found to have certain characteristics affecting the whole course of the military operations which it involves."[6] Callwell offers a comprehensive listing of the wide array of reasons for why small wars may be the most suitable choice for achieving strategic goals and political objectives, and he demonstrates how operational styles will differ according to desired aims.

Callwell's wisdom is illuminating for irregular warfare in space as well.

> The conditions of small wars are so diversified, the enemy's mode of fighting is often so peculiar, and the theatres of operations present such singular features, that irregular warfare must generally be carried out

on a method totally different from the stereotyped system [of regular war]. The art of war, as generally understood, must be modified to suit the circumstances of each particular case. The conduct of small wars is in certain respects an art by itself, diverging widely from what is adapted to the conditions of regular warfare, but not so widely that there are not in all its branches points which permit comparisons to be established.[7]

Irregular warfare in space, or small space wars, likewise will be conducted using methods and styles differing from those of major, conventional wars. Individual small space wars will take on specific operational forms and military styles that reflect the peculiarities and circumstances of the situation at hand.

Humanity's collective experience makes clear that the topic of small space wars is worthy of exploration. Many military publications and national-security scholars note that small wars outnumber major, conventional wars in our historical record. One is U.S. Marine Corps doctrine: "Military operations other than war and small wars are more probable than a major regional conflict or general war."[8] David Kilcullen, an analyst of counterinsurgency, points out that since 1816 about 83 percent of all conflicts have fallen under the heading of "civil wars or insurgencies," or small wars.[9] Similarly, Max Boot, of the Council on Foreign Relations, finds that U.S. involvements in small wars—such as the Boxer Rebellion in 1900, the Philippine Insurrection in 1899, Bosnia in 1992, and Kosovo in 1999—actually outnumber the major conflicts in which the nation has participated.[10] Boot argues that these small wars were fought not to attain decisive victory but to inflict punishment, ensure protection, achieve pacification, or even to benefit from profiteering.

In fact, American participation in small wars was so commonplace that the Marine Corps felt obliged to publish the *Small Wars Manual* in 1940. The manual, which addresses counterinsurgency and peacekeeping, defines *small wars* as "operations undertaken under executive authority, wherein military force is combined with diplomatic pressure in the internal or external affairs of another state whose government is unstable, inadequate, or unsatisfactory for the preservation of life and of such interests as are determined by the foreign policy of our Nation."[11] These small wars vary from simple demonstrative operations to military interventions. They need not be "small" in size, theater of operations, or cost in property, money, or lives.[12] The manual noted the United States had historically viewed intervention through small wars as legitimate under international law, because a state may protect, or demand protection for, its citizens and their property regardless of location.[13] Because of that propensity, displayed by many countries, and not only by the United States, such forms of warfare can be expected to be relevant for competition and the advancement of political objectives in the space domain.

The Inevitability of Space Warfare

Our own generation knows from experience that no society has a dispensation from catastrophe, and that history provides no sure formula for avoiding one.
—Michael Howard[14]

To better understand space warfare's place in humanity's history and future, it is worth acknowledging the inevitability, however regrettable, of armed conflict in space. Although commentary on space as a war-fighting domain has become prevalent in recent years, the fact that irregular warfare and competitive actions in space are already everyday occurrences is not widely recognized at present.[15] For these two reasons, it is worth underscoring that thinking about the use of force in space, in a strategic and historical sense, is really nothing new.

Countries and their polities have national interests that they advance and protect. Such advancement and protection are at times exercised through the military instrument of national power. Throughout the ages, country-specific agendas and nationalistic feelings have powerfully driven nations to action to achieve political aims. "Nationalism remains, even after two hundred years, by far the most effective instrument of social mobilisation—and so a most effective tool of war," as Michael Howard observes.[16] Policy makers and strategists should fully consider that nationalism and the advancement of polities' goals will remain at the center of international relations and competitive strategy.

Colin Gray asserts the inevitability of acts of force and space warfare, whether of a regular or irregular style, in a poignant way: "It is a rule in strategy, one derived empirically from the evidence of two and a half millennia, that anything of great strategic importance to one belligerent, for that reason has to be worth attacking by others. And the greater the importance, the greater has to be the incentive to damage, disable, capture, or destroy it. In the bluntest of statements: space warfare is a certainty in the future because the use of space in war has become vital."[17] Space capabilities and services are critical national interests; therefore, the many spacefaring nations will want to protect them. Likewise, an adversary may seek to deny them freedom of action in space, not in a totally preclusive manner but in a way that makes access to and use of space unreliable and space a nonpermissive operational environment.

Space warfare, in both irregular and regular forms, is thus a certainty. Interests there will need to be protected and defended through military means, and future adversaries will find that attacking these interests serves their own.

Establishing and Disputing Command of Space

A polity's leadership will at times deem irregular styles of military action suitable to its political aims and strategic objectives. To be effective, irregular space warfare must work in concert with the purpose of space strategy —ensuring access to and use of space.[18] Irregular actions not directly supporting the purpose of space strategy are likely to be ineffectual or, worse, counterproductive.

Irregular space warfare in support of space strategy raises the concept of *command of space*: the ability to ensure access to and use of space when needed to achieve political aims and strategic objectives.[19] The concept embraces occasional efforts to prevent or deny access to and use of space to adversaries—who are, reciprocally, seeking to establish their own command of space for their own aims and objectives. Consistent with the time-honored maritime strategies of Alfred Thayer Mahan and Julian Corbett, command of space—also referred to as *space control* or *space supremacy*—cannot be achieved in an absolute sense. Command of the sea is normally in dispute; in fact, as Corbett explains, "the normal position is not a commanded sea, but an uncommanded sea."[20] The space domain is vast, with expansive CLOCs and distant hubs of logistical activity (such as dispersed spaceports and satellite communication nodes); therefore, it will be impracticable to protect all interests in space against the inevitable competitor who disputes one's command of space.[21] Moreover, by extension from maritime history, the "default" condition for command of space is to be in dispute between rivals.

General and Local

For the above reasons, though it will be necessary to work toward command of space, it will be possible to establish it only to some degree, and this degree has both spatial and temporal elements. At its most basic level, *command of space entails efforts to conquer the tyranny of distance, as to both place and time.* With regard to spatial elements, command of space may be general or local.[22] General command of space is achieved when an adversary is no longer able to act dangerously against one's access to and use of CLOCs and cannot adequately defend its own. With only minor exceptions, *general* command means unfettered access to and use of space for diplomacy, trade, commerce, informational services, or military operations.

In contrast, *local* command is less than total in a region wherein a state's, organization's, or group's interests lie. Local command is less than ideal but is often acceptable recourse for those whose space-related military "footprints" are relatively small for its space forces, systems, and architectures. Local command protects one's most vital CLOCs and potentially denies the adversary access to and use of its own in that same limited region.

Persistent and Temporary

Under the rubric of the temporal element, command of space may be persistent or temporary.[23] *Persistent* command means that the element of time is no longer significant in the execution of a space strategy, despite the adversary's best efforts. When command of space is both general and persistent, one's adversary can still act, but only in ineffectual ways unlikely to affect the war's outcome at the strategic level. When command is both local and persistent, the most vital CLOCs are protected in a specified region for the foreseeable future, but the adversary can act effectively outside the disputed region, and a conflict's outcome is not assured.

Temporary command, either general or local, is established for a specific period. This mode of command has a strong temporal characteristic: the military situation can change rapidly, with operational and tactical advantage repeatedly alternating between belligerents. An irregular space force may achieve command that is both local and temporary by concentrating forces, assets, and nonkinetic effects (such as spacecraft repositioning, laser dazzling, or communications jamming) where its opponent is not.[24]

Certainly, the establishment and dispute of command of space in its various modes—general and local, persistent and temporary—will be important during the conduct of irregular space warfare. Command of space is a helpful theoretical framework because it includes both the potential tradeoffs between desired ends and available means and the actions of a thinking, competent rival. The concept of command of space illuminates the prospect that smaller, irregular forces may seek to exercise local and temporary command of space at points along expansive CLOCs and at distant hubs of activity. Furthermore, the concept equips policy makers and military leaders to understand more fully that command of space will normally be in dispute. As a result, there will be an ongoing push and pull between rivals, as each seeks to ensure its own access to and use of space and degrade its competitor's.

Fabian Strategy and Maneuver Warfare

Fabian strategy and maneuver warfare, albeit different concepts, have commonalities that are helpful in connection with small space wars. Additionally, while Fabian strategy and maneuver warfare share certain characteristics with several of the elements discussed in chapter 2—the indirect approach, cumulative strategy, and elusiveness through dispersal and concentration—they warrant separate discussion here. Both these concepts have been applied by large, conventional forces in the past; they are particularly relevant to the ways and methods of irregular warfare, whether for great, middle, or emerging powers, including in space.

Fabian Strategy

Quintus Fabius Maximus Verrucosus (280–203 BC) was a Roman general during the Second Punic War, one of a series of conflicts in which Rome and the North African city-state of Carthage contested primacy of, effectively, the Mediterranean world. He advocated avoiding open and direct battle, convinced that the Romans would lose any such engagement against the Carthaginian general Hannibal Barca, having already been crushingly defeated several times by him.[25] In a Fabian strategy, therefore, one side intentionally avoids large-scale, decisive battles for fear of the outcome and can succeed only by wearing down, through attrition, its opponent over time, usually by an unrelenting campaign of small skirmishes.[26]

Stephen Biddle explains that Fabian strategy entails several elements: an absolute unwillingness to accept exposure or to defend ground by a decisive engagement, dispersed military operations with no local concentrations in excess of the normal combatant density, exclusive reliance on coercion, and insistence on concealment.[27] During a Fabian land campaign, Biddle observes, "Dispersed operations with only light weapons and no local concentrations in excess of the [normal and existing] theaterwide combatant density mean that pure Fabian raids will be small, unlikely to destroy heavily defended positions, and limited largely to soft targets such as unescorted convoys, isolated posts, economic infrastructure, or civilian gatherings."[28] In addition to seeking to attrite the adversary's forces, Fabian strategy will often disrupt logistical supply lines, attack isolated and dispersed outposts, and negatively influence the adversary's morale. The side employing a Fabian strategy typically believes that the element of time is in its favor; consequently, Fabian strategy is commonly associated with delaying and protracting conflict, without a decisive battle.[29] Moreover, a Fabian strategy employing hit-and-run methods of attrition may be adopted when no feasible alternative can be devised.

Irregular warfare in space will share many of the attributes of Fabian strategy. Small numbers of space forces and systems may seek to contest the space command of an adversary by harassing dispersed and remote hubs and lines of communications used for commerce and trade. Small-scale, hit-and-run operations using Fabian methods will seek to degrade an adversary's space forces, systems, and architectures, thereby reducing the rival's overall competitive advantage. Regardless of the primary domain of military operations, space-related attrition can prolong the conflict until one's fortunes improve, meanwhile avoiding a major, potentially disastrous battle.

Maneuver Warfare

Earth orbit is a cosmic coastline suited for strategic manoeuvres.
—Bleddyn Bowen[30]

Maneuver, sometimes coupled with *movement*, is frequently acknowledged as an enduring principle of war, and U.S. joint doctrine lists it as one of the principles of joint operations.[31] In language that perhaps causes unintended confusion for strategists and military professionals, U.S. joint doctrine describes the purposes of movement and maneuver together: "[Movement or maneuver] encompasses the disposition of joint forces to conduct operations by securing positional advantages before or during combat operations and by exploiting tactical success to achieve operational and strategic objectives. Maneuver is the employment of forces in the [operational area] through movement in combination with fires to achieve a position of advantage in respect to the enemy."[32] The difficulty is that many professionals in the U.S. Marine Corps and Army view maneuver and movement as separate concepts, each with its own distinct definition and characteristics. Nevertheless, the two ideas have common themes, which are helpful when examining irregular warfare in space.[33]

Foundational literature exists regarding the importance of maneuver and movement during warfare. Over two thousand years ago Sun Tzu wrote, "Move when it is advantageous and create changes in the situation by dispersal and concentration of forces."[34] Likewise, Mao Tse-tung, paraphrasing Sun Tzu, addressed fluidity of maneuver during guerrilla warfare: "The enemy advances, we retreat; the enemy camps, we harass; the enemy tires, we attack; the enemy retreats, we pursue."[35]

Beyond Sun Tzu and Mao Tse-tung, the writings of the French naval officer and strategist Raoul Castex are helpful. His *Strategic Theories*, published from 1931 to 1939, addressed among other subjects how maneuver can create strategic advantage during war. With respect to maritime strategy, Castex observed that ships need to move purposefully to achieve strategic advantage, a concept he called *manoeuvre*.[36] Castex used *manoeuvre* to mean, "to move intelligently in order to create a favorable situation."[37] Also, he viewed *manoeuvre* as an art, as essentially a creative activity.[38] If performed successfully, *manoeuvre* creates security and freedom of action for one's forces.[39]

A second foundational work is David Galula's *Counterinsurgency Warfare.* Galula was concerned with movement during warfare between insurgent and counterinsurgent forces and argued that an insurgency "requires an overwhelming and sudden concentration of insurgent forces against an isolated counterinsurgent unit caught in the open—not entrenched; hence a *movement warfare* in which the insurgent can exploit his fluidity, his better intelligence, and the simple but effective cross-country logistical facilities afforded by the organized population."[40] During warfare between insurgencies and counterinsurgencies, Galula singled out as of special importance movement warfare and its relation to the fluidity of attacks, shock effect, and negative impact on logistical and supply facilities.[41]

Moving to space operations, U.S. joint doctrine highlights the role of movement and maneuver for operational advantage: "Space operations movement and maneuver include the deployment, repositioning, or re-orientation of on-orbit assets and joint space forces. These movements may support service optimization, protection from environmental hazards, passive defense from threats, or the positioning of assets to enable active defensive or offensive measures. Changing the position or operating frequency of spacecraft can make them more difficult to target. Joint space force movement and maneuver occurs in each of the three space-system segments: space, link, and ground."[42] Examples of operational maneuver and movement in space include moving satellites into different near-Earth orbits; changing a spacecraft's location between lunar and geostationary orbits; maneuvering in cislunar space (the volume of space lying between the Earth and the Moon or the Moon's orbit); concentrating various nonkinetic effects, whether jamming, lasing, or cyberattacks; changing operating frequencies; shifting users to other satellites (commercial or military); frequency hopping; dispersing space capabilities and services across a space architecture and other domains, while remaining able to focus military effects when needed.[43]

The strategic environment of the space domain—with expansive CLOCs, dispersed logistical hubs, and activities spanning prestige, national security, information, commerce, and trade—will necessitate making the combined concept of maneuver and movement a fundamental part of space warfare, regular or irregular. Maneuver and movement will facilitate elusiveness through dispersal and concentration, protract conflicts, move between defensive and offensive operations, and create an asymmetric advantage—to name just a few areas (see chapters 1 and 2). Bleddyn Bowen, a British lecturer and author on space policy, notes that even ancillary and mundane space operations can trigger adversary actions in other domains, including terrestrial.[44] This is an important point: to maneuver a spacecraft can trigger adversary actions in nonspace domains. During small space wars, maneuver and movement will be defining features.

Proxies and Proxy War

Some participants in irregular space warfare may be external third parties, whether state or nonstate actors. Indeed, land and naval warfare have historically seen repeated use of third-party organizations, groups, and participants. In land warfare, soldiers of fortune and mercenaries—people who hire themselves out to fight, those who do so voluntarily for their own reasons, or auxiliaries hired out to another party by their own government (like the "Hessians" of the American Revolutionary War, soldiers of the German state of Hesse "rented" to the British army)—frequently have played vital roles during military operations.[45] In naval warfare, privateers have done the same, notably during the early days of the United States. Soldiers of fortune, mercenaries, and privateers are all examples of proxies used during wars. These third parties may be national or extranational, which is consistent with Stephen Biddle's general observation that, historically, both states and nonstates have fought and will fight using irregular styles of warfare.[46]

In the context of irregular warfare, *proxies* are organizations, groups, or participants fighting on behalf of another. Andrew Mumford has written extensively on *proxy wars*, which he defines "as conflicts in which a third party intervenes indirectly in order to influence the strategic outcome in favour of its preferred faction."[47] Mumford links proxy war to Liddell Hart's strategic concept of the indirect approach: "All proxy wars can be considered contemporary acts of the indirect approach."[48] Mumford reinterprets Liddell Hart's concept, however, arguing that the indirect component of modern warfare is not necessarily about repositioning forces to avoid the adversary's strength and its large conventional forces but instead about fundamentally shifting lethal activity to and through a third party, or proxy.[49]

> This can involve the provision of weapons, money and other forms of assistance, but crucially absolves the intervening party (often described as a benefactor or sponsor) from having to undertake its own direct military intervention in a pre-existing conflict by outsourcing the lethal activity to a proxy, such as a militia group or other national military (often labelled a surrogate). Proxy wars are fought at arms-length by those who want to simultaneously protect or expand their interests whilst avoiding the exposure and costs of a direct military intervention.[50]

The indirect approach can manifest itself in a variety of ways during modern proxy wars, such as third parties conducting information operations, psychological operations, cyberattacks, or sponsoring terrorist attacks by the indirect provision of money, weapons, or logistical or communications equipment.[51] Some contemporary scholars stress involvement by nonstate actors in proxy wars but in so doing fail to capture the full range of state, extranational, transnational, and commercial entities that have historically been drawn in by great powers. Mumford views proxy war as a mode of modern warfare that is likely to be used even more frequently in the future.[52]

Irregular space warfare too will involve proxies. Space proxies are valuable during irregular warfare generally as by alternative, indirect means of force and coercion. Space proxies may have state, nonstate, transnational, or commercial affiliations (see chapter 6 on commercial and quasi-commercial entities). Their sponsors, by purchasing the services and aid of space proxies, in effect convert fiscal resources and economic power into military power. Examples in irregular space warfare include acquiring the auxiliary services of another country's on-orbit, dual-use space capabilities to coerce a rival, hiring hackers to launch cyberattacks against critical space-related networks, and employing private military companies.

Cyberattacks against Space Architectures and Networks

Cyberattacks against space architectures and associated networks involve an indirect approach and utilize asymmetric methods to create strategic effects. While cyberattacks may not have the same temporal dimension as some other irregular warfare methods—such as those associated with a protracted approach where the effects potentially accumulate or increase over time—in some situations and depending on how computer networks and associated software are affected, there may be a protracted character to cyberattacks against space capabilities and services. Lt. Gen. Stephen Whiting, commander of U.S. Space Operations Command, notes the potential threat of cyberattacks to space architectures: "Cyberspace is the soft underbelly of our global space networks."[53] As a result, space professionals should focus more than they do now on defending against cyberattacks.

In a real-world example, Maj. Gen. Michel Friedling, the head of France's Space Command, says that Russian cyberattacks just before the invasion of Ukraine sent a critical message, telegraphing Russia's intentions to invade its neighbor.[54] The February 24, 2022, Russian cyberattack against Viasat—a California-based provider of high-speed satellite broadband services and secure networking systems covering military and commercial markets worldwide—was meant to cripple Ukrainian command and control, as Russian forces advanced as part of the invasion (see chapter 2).[55] Of the Russian cyberattack against Viasat, Friedling explains: "What Ukraine has shown us well is that things will begin in cyber and space domain[s] before beginning on the ground. The cyberattack against Viasat was done the day before the beginning of the ground invasions. This is very significant. And this is very interesting. This is a big lesson. I would say it's something we were thinking [about] but now it's real."[56]

Defense policy analyst Andrew Krepinevich defines *cyberspace* as the world's "computer networks, both open and closed, to include the computers themselves, the transactional networks that send data regarding financial transactions, and the networks comprising control systems that enable machines to interact with one another."[57] The cyberspace domain utilizes expansive lines of communication involving a global network, along with hubs of activity at server farms or network hardware locations.[58] Cyberspace also involves near-simultaneous communications, the prevalence of nonkinetic effects and actions, rapidly advancing technology, a greater opportunity for anonymous actions, interdependence with the other domains, and an evolving understanding of its relative importance.[59] Cyber activities involve international commerce and finance, social media, information sharing, and military-related activities. Cyberspace as a whole is not the sovereign territory of any one state, but it incorporates both shared infrastructure that may be uncontrolled and widely distributed hardware located in sovereign territory.[60] For many countries, including the United States, malicious and hostile cyberattacks present difficulties with attribution and accountability.[61] Additionally, policy makers and military leaders may be challenged when determining suitable responses to cyberattacks, because malicious cyber activity frequently falls below the threshold of what is considered the use of force and armed conflict.[62]

Remarkably, many of the cyberspace-domain characteristics and considerations noted above are identical to those of the space domain. Indeed, cyber warfare and space warfare share to a considerable extent the same environment and strategic considerations. Because space capabilities and services routinely utilize computers, networks, ground stations, and software, the space and cyberspace domains are intertwined and inseparable. The result is that cyber warfare and cybersecurity are important for space warfare, particularly of an irregular style.

American space policy recognizes the critical importance of cybersecurity for providing vital space capabilities and services. Released in December 2020, the White House's National Space Policy states the need to integrate cybersecurity into space operations and capabilities to "retain positive control of space systems and verify the integrity of critical functions, missions, and services they provide."[63] The policy directs that cybersecurity principles be integrated across all phases of space systems design, development, acquisition, and deployment. Additionally, the policy emphasizes the critical intersection between cyberspace and the

U.S. Global Positioning System (GPS), by noting the need to "improve the cybersecurity of GPS, its augmentations, and federally owned GPS-enabled devices, and foster commercial space sector adoption of cyber-secure GPS enabled systems consistent with cybersecurity principles for space systems."[64] Governmental and commercial space architectures are interdependent; consequently, the U.S. government should collaborate with industry to mitigate unauthorized access to critical space system functions, reduce vulnerabilities, protect ground systems, promote cyber-security "hygiene" practices, and manage supply-chain risks.[65]

Further, cyberattacks against space architectures and networks may frequently involve third-party proxies. Cyberattacks and cyber warfare offer a relatively high degree of anonymity, a point that enhances the appeal of an indirect, proxy-war strategy.[66] Combined with the fact that computer technology is easier and less conspicuous to turn over to proxies than large caches of weapons, cyberattacks add a further layer of "plausible deniability" during proxy warfare.[67] These proxies may entail cyber units acting on behalf of a sovereign sponsor. Alternatively, the cyber proxies may be organizations and groups unaffiliated with a state actor, seeking perhaps to hack space-related networks as a personal challenge or to cause purposeful harm. This latter category also includes *hacktivism*, a portmanteau of *hack* and *activism*, which involves such computer-based techniques as hacking as a form of civil disobedience and protest to promote a political agenda or social change.[68]

Jamming, Lasing, and Electromagnetic Attack

Those employing irregular warfare in the space domain will want to achieve big results with little effort. Jamming, lasing, and electromagnetic attack generally can provide significant results while requiring little materiel or fiscal resources. *Electromagnetic attack* is the use of electromagnetic or directed-energy weapons against capabilities and infrastructure to degrade, deny, or destroy them.[69] Radio-frequency jamming, electromagnetic deception (spoofing), lasers, and high-powered microwave weapons all fall under the heading of electromagnetic attack.[70] Particle-beam weapons are also included in this category, even though they do not rely on the electromagnetic spectrum for the movement of their destructive effects through space. Electromagnetic warfare is the overall activity of which electromagnetic attack is one category.[71]

Air Vice Marshal Harvey Smyth, director of space at the Ministry of Defence space directorate in the United Kingdom, summarizes the overall problem with electromagnetic attack: "Space is increasingly contested by adversaries who are engaging in gray-zone warfare, acts that are below the threshold that would instigate an armed conflict."[72] Smyth notes that radio-frequency interference, laser dazzling, and signal jamming are routine in today's increasingly competitive space environment but that governments are finding it challenging to formulate deliberate responses.[73]

Indeed, electromagnetic attack will be attractive to those engaged in irregular space warfare because of its flexibility and versatility in delivering effects. First, electromagnetic attack can advance both defensive and offensive aims. For instance, jamming, lasing, and other methods of electromagnetic attack can help ensure one's own ability to access and use space against an adversary's action, thereby supporting a defensive aim. Or these same methods can take away the adversary's ability to access and use space, an offensive aim.

Second, electromagnetic attack provides a wide range of effects. Radio-frequency jamming and spoofing of GPS signals can inflict nondestructive, temporary effects against the adversary's spacecraft and architectures. In contrast, laser dazzling of highly sensitive electro-optical sensors and employment of high-power microwave weapons against vulnerable satellites can deliver destructive, permanent effects.[74] Consequently, the various methods of electromagnetic attack constitute a range of both reversible and irreversible effects, depending on how they are employed.

Third, as Air Vice Marshal Smyth points out, policy makers and military leaders may have difficulty in determining what, if any, response is warranted following an electromagnetic attack: whether, as noted previously, electromagnetic interference rises to the threshold of armed conflict as well as whether a response is warranted at all, especially a military one. This ambiguity arises particularly during temporary and nondestructive electromagnetic attacks. As technology historian Aaron Bateman explains, this issue was raised as early as the Gerald R. Ford presidential administration.[75] Additionally, like cyberattacks, some forms of electro-magnetic attack against space systems and architectures are difficult to attribute with high confidence. Attributing responsibility in space can be especially difficult when it is third parties or proxies that conduct electro-magnetic attacks.

Real-world experience, however, provides some hope that effective solutions can be found. In May 2022 Russia jammed broadband internet communications signals from SpaceX's Starlink constellation serving Ukraine. SpaceX founder and chief executive officer Elon Musk states emphatically that Starlink continued to provide internet services in Ukraine despite Russian attempts to disrupt it. According to Musk, the Starlink network "has resisted Russian cyberwar jamming and hacking attempts so far, but they're ramping up their efforts."[76] Of the episode Gen. David Thompson, vice chief of space operations of the U.S. Space Force, says, "You may be able to deny a piece of it, but you can't eliminate the capability writ large."[77] Thompson asserts that the resiliency demonstrated by Starlink's constellation supporting Ukraine against Russian jamming validates the U.S. Space Force's strategy to use distributed and proliferated architectures for space communications.[78]

Purposeful Debris Generation

Like sea lines of communication, CLOCs are frequently shared among belligerents—meaning that while one can deny or degrade a rival's unfettered access to and use of space, doing so negatively impacts one's own. Moreover, detrimental actions can affect humans working and living in space. This ability to harm others, often in an indiscriminate manner, is painfully apparent when it comes to purposeful debris generation in space.

The purposeful generation of space debris falls soundly in the realm of irregular space warfare for primarily two reasons. First, especially in low-Earth orbit, it represents a protracted strategy, by virtue of the subsequent cascading collisions between existing debris or orbital systems, which can extend for years, decades, or longer. This is simply debris creating more debris. This temporal dimension and inherently protracted nature can help those employing such a simple operational concept achieve a strategic effect over time. Second, purposeful debris generation can serve as an asymmetric advantage. Creating space debris is relatively simple to do: a small action results in a big effect. A single deliberate act, like an anti-satellite weapon test or demonstration, has the potential of impacting large orbital regions and vital CLOCs.

Moreover, purposeful debris generation along shared orbital regions and CLOCs may serve either defensive or offensive strategies. On one hand, debris generation and the consequent fouling of orbital regions can impede an adversary's ability to access and use space, which is defensive to the extent that it may prevent the adversary from achieving or gaining something.[79] On the other hand, the orbital debris can take away an adversary's current ability, destroy its spacecraft, the essence of an offensive strategy.[80]

The November 2021 Russian direct-ascent, antisatellite missile demonstration against one of its own satellites illustrates how widespread and harmful the impacts of purposefully generated debris are. While debris generation may be unintentional—residual rocket bodies of upper-stage launch vehicles, gloves lost by humans during space walks, or the residue of accidental satellite "conjunctions"—Russia's weapon demonstration appears to have been deliberate, given the knowledgeable and experienced Russian space workforce and the event's wide-reaching harmful effects. The purpose or reason behind it, however, remains unclear.[81]

The U.S. State Department was quick to condemn the action, charging that the Russian Federation had acted recklessly.[82] The debris increased the number of close approaches to active satellites in low-Earth orbit, in some cases tens of thousands of close approaches in a week.[83] Secretary of State Anthony Blinken publicly rebuked Russia's irresponsible behavior:

> This test has so far generated over fifteen hundred pieces of trackable orbital debris and will likely generate hundreds of thousands of pieces of smaller orbital debris. The long-lived debris created by this dangerous and irresponsible test will now threaten satellites and other space objects that are vital to all nations' security, economic, and scientific interests for decades to come. In addition, it will significantly increase the risk to astronauts and cosmonauts on the International Space Station and other human spaceflight activities. The safety and security

of all actors seeking to explore and use outer space for peaceful purposes has been carelessly endangered by this test.[84]

Also, immediately following the Russian demonstration, the astronauts and cosmonauts aboard the International Space Station were required to take shelter for two hours in their docked spaceship capsules, for fear that the resulting debris would cause catastrophic harm to the space station and the personnel on board.[85]

Following the characterization and tracking of the Russian debris fields, it was reported that the demonstration had created "surges of close approaches" with active satellites in low-Earth orbit—"conjunction squalls."[86] Moreover, the squalls are, at this writing, still affecting a great number of remote-sensing satellites operating in sun-synchronous orbits. In many cases, the Russian-caused debris overlaps with the orbits of remote-sensing satellites but moves in the opposite direction. Space situational-awareness expert Dan Oltrogge advises, "When they [debris squalls and satellites] sync up, you have the perfect storm: they're in the same orbit plane but counter rotating, crossing each other twice an orbit, again and again."[87] The number of conjunction squalls is expected to increase over time, affecting Earth-observation and remote-sensing satellites of commercial companies like Planet, Spire, and Swarm. Furthermore, satellites operating outside of sun-synchronous orbits will also be affected, among them SpaceX's Starlink constellation, whose satellites must maneuver to dodge the growing regions of orbital debris.[88]

Russia's irresponsible actions make clear the long-term, negative impact to human and robotic systems caused by debris generation. What makes purposeful debris generation, whether for defensive or offensive purposes, so problematic is that it is indiscriminate—affecting target, perpetrator, and neutrals alike. Debris generation has, along with its ability to take away or to minimize the adversary's capabilities and military advantage in an indirect and asymmetric way, a kinetic and irreversible component.

Ultimately, purposeful debris generation can be seen as the great equalizer, denying everyone's ability to use certain orbital and celestial regions reliably. That is, the belligerents suffer together. Though indiscriminate, purposeful debris generation will most affect states, organizations, and companies most reliant on space. Those less reliant on space may feel relatively free to resort to it. For these various reasons, irregular space warfare will create long-lived debris to deny or impede a competitor's access to and use of space.

Space Strikes and Raiding

Wartime strikes and raids have been historically frequent, and it should be expected that the space domain will be no different. Both are military operations to support political aims and strategic objectives. *Strikes* are conducted to inflict damage on or destroy an objective.[89] Strikes may be delivered to punish offending nations or groups, uphold international law, or prevent states, organizations, or prevent groups from launching their own offensive actions.[90] In contrast, *raids* are usually small in scale and temporary, involving swift penetration of a hostile area—to secure information; confuse the enemy; capture personnel; confiscate equipment, property, and resources; or destroy installations and capabilities—followed by a planned withdrawal.[91]

Space strikes and raids are relevant for space powers across the spectrum—great, middle, and emerging, both state and nonstate. Strikes and raids may be important elements during irregular space warfare and can contribute to either unilateral or multinational efforts. Space strike and raiding operations can demonstrate political resolve, display military capabilities, complement the nonmilitary instruments of national power, or terminate a contentious situation on favorable terms. Their focus, however, should be the achievement of political and policy aims, not the exercise of military force for its own sake.

Space Strikes

The space and maritime domains share many strategic interests and characteristics, including dispersed hubs of activity and expansive lines of communication used for commerce, commercial, diplomatic, and informational activity. Consequently, maritime experience can be a source of insight transferrable to the strategic context of the space domain.

In fact, naval irregular warfare was a vital, albeit now mostly ignored, sidebar of the U.S. Navy's operational history.[92] Naval historian and war studies professor Benjamin Armstrong explains, "From the American Revolution to the dawn of the Steam Age, maritime raiding and naval irregular warfare were common and important operations conducted by the United States naval forces."[93] In peacetime, irregular maritime operations filled the gray area between war and peace, limited combat operations required to advance national objectives and protect interests.[94] In fact, the legendary John Paul Jones extensively used "war by raiding" and is considered to be the American "father of naval irregular warfare."[95]

James Cable, whose seminal book *Gunboat Diplomacy* has been considered authoritative for decades, addresses irregular approaches to maritime conflict and competition. Cable pertinently notes, "A resort to force is more likely to meet with acquiescence [i.e., on the part of the target power] if it is immediate in its application, instantaneous in its effect and appropriate in its nature."[96] Because, when successful, space strikes and raids can achieve political aims and strategic objectives, they will be viewed as viable options.

By extension from the general definition offered above, *space strikes* are military operations in, through, or from space conducted to inflict damage or destroy an objective. Space strikes may be used for punishing an offending state, organization, or commercial company; upholding international law or rules-based order; or preventing other actors from launching their own offensive actions. These strikes may be against space-centric targets—like spacecraft, satellite communications and networks, high-value units, logistical hubs, radio-frequency spectrum, or other space architectures—or they may be against objectives in the other domains. In general, they will be irreversible in their effects (whether kinetic or nonkinetic). Especially in the context of irregular space warfare, space strikes likely will entail asymmetric attacks against vulnerable systems and assets. Examples of space strikes causing irreversible damage would be using antisatellite weapons (whether direct-ascent or co-orbital) against high-value space capabilities; lasing exquisite electro-optical satellites; and causing the permanent failure of a space-based radio-frequency transmitter.

Space Raiding

Historically, raiding has had success; logically, therefore, it is relevant in the space domain as an operational concept. Military historian James Bradford speaks of *guerre de razzia*, "war by raiding," and of its long history in land warfare. Examples include the American colonialists' conflicts with Native Americans and French colonial counterinsurgency operations during the mid-twentieth century in North Africa.[97] As for naval operations, in 1776 John Paul Jones was first in American service to advocate *guerre de razzia* as, especially in irregular naval warfare, an alternative, third school of maritime strategy: "a style of [maritime] warfare in which the main goal of operations is not the capture or destruction of the enemy's commerce as in *guerre de course*, or the defeat of his fleet as in *guerre d'escadre* [squadron warfare], but the raiding of his coasts and colonies."[98] According to Armstrong, *guerre de razzia* is "best labeled as naval irregular warfare" and can be understood best through the study of naval irregular operations, beginning with the Age of Sail.[99]

Admittedly, the concept of raiding in space is challenging to visualize in a practical way, and attempting to evoke it is to risk criticism for overexuberance, fancifulness, or departure from the realm of space strategy to that of science fiction. Analogies to naval boarding or landing parties and the taking of "prizes" may seem somewhat unrealistic in the space domain at present. Therefore, in what follows it is important to avoid overstatement and embellishment and to think at the highest conceptual level.

Given those important disclaimers, *space raiding* comprises small-scale, temporary, and swift action against an adversary's space capabilities and services to secure information; deny space services; confuse the enemy; apprehend personnel from space stations or lunar bases; confiscate property, resources, and equipment; capture valuable regions, positions, or radio-frequency spectrum; or destroy systems, installations, and capabilities. Space raids are typically brief, ending on completion. During irregular space warfare, raiding will often occur in areas considered remote and vulnerable—like distant terrestrial or celestial bases, posts, and communication stations. Space raiding around the periphery of an adversary's area of strength is consistent with Clausewitz's advice that it is best for an insurgency to operate on exterior lines of communication and "nibble at the shell and around the edges" of the adversary's operating area.[100]

In addition to physical targets, space raiding pertains to actions against such nonphysical assets as the electromagnetic frequency spectrum and cyberspace-reliant networks. Given that, examples of space raiding include confiscating lunar landers and scientific equipment; acquiring a rival's usable frequency spectrum and lines of communication; securing information and intercepting vital communications; destroying or ravaging an adversary's most vital space capabilities and services through cyberattacks; and denying capabilities through the covert installation of malicious software. Because space raiding has a strong temporal characteristic— typically involving swift, temporary operations—some raiding tactics may be reversible, such as disruption of critical communications and jamming of vital radio frequencies.

Space Prizes

Tied closely to the concept of raiding is the idea of space prizes, which raiding operations may produce. Considered generally, *space prizes* are captured or confiscated space-related personnel; important equipment, property, and resources; critical capabilities and services; and valuable orbital regions, positions, and spectra. More specific examples are seizure of critical satellites, facilities, logistical bases, networks, and space architectures; confiscation of valuable cislunar and lunar resources, such as water ice (often formed in permanently shadowed features near the poles); commandeering preferred geostationary orbital slots and Lagrange points (where objects tend to hold their positions relative to others); and the appropriation of the adversary's most vital frequency spectrum. Often, the taking of space prizes is considered special and extraordinary, and public knowledge of them can result in morale boosts for the raiding side.

Drawing on the experience of land and naval warfare, space prizes are most likely to be taken along expansive CLOCs, from distant logistical hubs of activity, and around the periphery of the adversary's strength. Raiding itself is more likely along exterior lines of communication or in remote regions, so to avoid direct engagement with the adversary, and raiding operations may be staged for the purpose of taking prizes.

Terrorism as Irregular Space Warfare

Like irregular warfare itself, terrorism is not a new strategic concept. Acts of terror are to be expected—terrorism is merely a mode of irregular warfare.[101] Terrorism seeks to influence the actions and thinking of others; in the words of the canonical Cold War scholar and author Thomas Schelling, terrorism is "violence intended to coerce the enemy rather than to weaken him militarily."[102] Its goals and methods can differ from those typical of other irregular warfare approaches. Moreover, terrorism can be a strategy or even a goal in itself. Some terrorists are not interested in overthrowing a government or seizing conventional political power. Many ideological terrorists, such as certain ecological activists, have no desire or intent to progress beyond terrorism employing military-like means; they just want their championed policies, ideologies, or political agendas publicized and adopted. Others who have traditionally employed terror simply want to destroy the government as such without replacing it: anarchists have no positive aim whatsoever.[103] Strategically, Boone Bartholomees (a retired Army colonel now at the Army War College) writes, "The theory behind terrorism is fairly straightforward. A weak, usually nongovernmental, actor uses violence, either random or carefully targeted and often directed against civilian targets, to produce terror. The aim is to make life so uncertain and miserable that the state against which the terror is directed concedes whatever political, social, economic, environmental, or theological point the terrorist pursues."[104]

History demonstrates, however, that it is difficult for terrorists to effect lasting change. Their long-term effectiveness is questionable, because an organization that expresses its frustration, anger, and ambition solely by committing isolated outrages is going nowhere and can pose no fundamental danger to a basically stable society.[105] Regardless, terrorism is comparatively cheap, easy to conceptualize and execute, and effective for gaining publicity.[106] Moreover, like many irregular warfare approaches, terrorism can be difficult to counter successfully. Michael Howard deduces from British historical experience that "even in societies as stable as Britain [terrorism] can compel an allocation of resources to combat it on a scale quite out of proportion to its significance."[107] Despite the low prospect of having lasting impact, terrorists and their heinous acts can still negatively affect a government and, of course, their targets.

Inevitably, terrorism is a mode of irregular space warfare. Terrorists may attack space systems, capabilities, architectures, and networks. The considerations raised above associated with Fabian strategy, proxy war, and cyberattacks are equally applicable to terrorist groups. Again, some may have political objectives and consider attacks on vulnerable and expensive space capabilities and services a convenient way to draw publicity to their causes. Yet others, as above, seek only anarchy, chaos, or the disestablishment of a state.

Terrorism against space capabilities and services will seek to cause fear in the most dramatic and public way possible. Terrorists will want to avoid detection ahead of an attack and may not be in a position to counter defenses; therefore, again, terrorists likely will attack exposed, remote, and vulnerable locations, assets, and regions. Their aims may entail inflicting a large number of casualties; damaging major space infrastructure, high-value assets, or high-profile assets of commercial space companies; and attacking launch sites, stations, and bases, particularly those with historical, cultural, religious, political, or symbolic significance.[108]

Conclusion

The concepts of command of space, Fabian strategy, maneuver warfare, proxies, debris generation, and terrorism—all inferred from history—and that of nonkinetic effects all point to how space strategy fits, in a strategic sense, in the framework of irregular warfare. Even as "small wars," though not new, are still differently defined and interpreted, small *space* wars can be defined as Charles Callwell defines irregular warfare, by its opposite. Small space wars, then, are the opposite of major, conventional wars in space.

A word of caution, however, against taking these concepts to an extreme. Irregular styles of space warfare should acknowledge the importance of regular, traditional forms of conflict. Policy makers and military leaders need to consider and plan for both. Additionally, the space strategist should understand that the true subject of this chapter is not solely irregular space warfare, but *irregular space warfare and . . .* Indeed, space strategists cannot study and explore just one element of warfare and ignore the rest, that is focus on space warfare in isolation from the greater strategic context. Instead, they must discern how to make all the pieces of strategy fit together to solve the puzzle of achieving political aims with available means. Later chapters raise considerations of which the space strategist should remain cognizant: how irregular space warfare acts as an adjunct, supportive force during war; how it integrates with regular, conventional fighting forces as part of hybrid warfare; how it supports either limited or unlimited aims; and how it synchronizes with operations in the other domains.

To the point of understanding the broader strategic context, Clausewitz on the first page of his masterwork states emphatically, *"War is thus an act of force to compel our enemy to do our will."*[109] That is the essence. One does not set out to wage a regular or irregular war, a land or space war, as such. Rather, the mode of warfare—or more likely a mix of modes—is dictated by strategic circumstances.[110] The operational styles of all war-fighting domains and the various modes of irregular space warfare may be mixed and matched to achieve the aims of policy.

CHAPTER 4

Gray-Zone Operations and Gunboat Diplomacy
Using Presence and Coercion in Space

When thinking about the range of threats, it is common to divide the "high end" from the "low end," the conventional from the irregular, armored divisions on one side, guerrillas toting AK-47s on the other. In reality . . . the categories of warfare are blurring and do not fit into neat, tidy boxes.
—Robert Gates, 22nd U.S. Secretary of Defense[1]

T his chapter focuses on the ancillary effects—albeit still significant—associated with the threat and use of limited space forces, along with the manner in which they are applied. It emphasizes the "knock-on," indirect effects of irregular space activity and, consequently, the nuances of location, proximity, and threat. It also examines technological demonstrations, space exercises, and limited space warfare. Ancillary effects can profoundly affect a rival's decision calculus, possibly coercing a rival into taking actions that it would not have otherwise.

Irregular activities tend to occur in times of neither peace nor war, thereby posing problems for tidy minds seeking to bin military activity into either "peacetime" or "wartime." Therefore, the idea of coercive operations in the gray zone (see chapter 3) can be difficult to dissect and explore, especially using existing American and Western frameworks.[2] Furthermore, historically, gray-zone activity in the messy middle of the peace/conflict continuum is more commonplace than large-scale armed combat.[3] Development of effective responses to gray-zone operations in advance is problematic because of the wide range of possible actions and coercive effects. The effectiveness of gray-zone coercive actions and the difficulties of response make them especially relevant to irregular space warfare.

Indeed, the phrase "gray zone" is a bit of a catchall, embracing many diverse subjects related to competition and conflict, and it tends to blur the line between military and nonmilitary action. A U.S. Department of Defense report offers an all-encompassing (and somewhat long-winded) definition: the gray zone is "a conceptual space between peace and war, occurring when actors purposefully use multiple elements of power to achieve political security objectives with activities that are ambiguous or cloud attribution and exceed the threshold of ordinary competition, yet fall below the level of large-scale direct military conflict, and threaten US and allied interests by challenging, undermining, or violating international customs, norms, or laws."[4] The central idea here, especially in the contexts of irregular conflict and competition in space, is that the gray zone pertains to both military and nonmilitary actions occurring below the threshold of large-scale military conflict to achieve political aims or strategic objectives.

At times gray-zone operations complicate *attribution*, the determination of the source or pathway of an attack. The space domain can be ideal for cloaking malicious actions. According to a RAND report, gray-zone operations typically unfold gradually and in some cases in ways meant to disguise the aggressor.[5] States employing gray-zone tactics against other powers often are hoping to use the ambiguity they create to achieve gradual gains over time.[6]

As for the U.S. Space Force's role, Gen. John Raymond, chief of space operations, issued planning guidance for nontraditional conflict: "Adversaries actively create and exploit 'gray zones' in which they achieve political objectives through actions that avoid traditional triggers for conflict where the United States enjoys clear military advantage. The Space Force will provide unique space-enabled options, tailored to support operational commanders, to shrink gray zones. *Space domain awareness* (SDA), for instance, enables attribution that reveals illegal or hostile action and sets conditions for a better informed and legitimized response."[7]

According to the current deputy secretary of defense, Kathleen Hicks, space operations in the gray zone typically comprise disrupting normal space activity and space-enabled services by interfering with equipment, communications, and data.[8] Many gray-zone methods are reversible and nonkinetic, such as radio-frequency jamming, spoofing that creates believable but false signals, lasing that dazzles and temporarily blinds or disables satellites, and cyberattacks that harm space infrastructure.[9] Moreover, differentiating between purely passive on-orbit intelligence-collection and surveillance activities and more provocative proximity operations is becoming increasingly difficult, which makes space-based activity compatible with gray-zone operations.

Recent literature and debate about gray-zone operations may leave space strategists feeling ungrounded. Indeed, the subject could be construed as part of the "strategic netherworld," where the torch of strategic experience fails to light the way. Because irregular space warfare and the range of options are not as well understood as conflict in the other domains, it is valid to turn for insight to past military, including maritime, activity. When we do, we find decades', even centuries', worth of instructive historical lessons for the "messy middle."

Gunboat Diplomacy

Peace and war, however, have become regrettably hard to distinguish.

—James Cable[10]

We have seen that military activity below the threshold of large-scale armed conflict, to achieve political aims or military objectives, is not new as a strategic concept, despite the national security community's recent focus on gray-zone operations. For instance, in maritime history such activity is fairly commonplace, as are examples of ancillary effects. *Gunboat diplomacy* exemplifies this idea. In his book of that title, James Cable characterizes it as pertaining to "limited naval force as one of the instruments of foreign policy," and he points out that warships (whether or not actually rated as "gunboats") have been around and frequently used this way as long as has the naval gun.[11] Gunboat diplomacy is not an act of war but may secure an advantage, avert a loss, or further one's side of a dispute with a foreign nation or nationals.[12] Importantly, gunboat diplomacy includes not only the actual use of force but also the threat of force, implicit or explicit. Gunboat diplomacy may be exercised far from the country employing it. While the concept requires that the presence of naval forces be known—with none of the ambiguity sometimes associated with gray-zone operations—gunboat diplomacy is often associated with coercion between peace and war.

Naval historian Geoffrey Till, too, explains that gunboat diplomacy is the use of limited naval force to back up diplomatic efforts to support, persuade, deter, or coerce others.[13] Success often relies on fine graduation of naval force (in size, type, capabilities, etc.), taking advantage of the normally unstated, albeit self-evident, threat inherent in a warship's presence.[14] According to Till, gunboat diplomacy involves persuading others to do things they do not want to do (compellence) or not to do things they do want to do (deterrence).[15] As for the benefits of gunboat diplomacy, or naval diplomacy more generally, Australian naval doctrine observes that limited naval forces "possess the versatility and the range of response to be very useful tools in times of uncertainty and crisis, allowing governments the maximum freedom of decision."[16]

Through synthesis of Cable and Till's ideas, it can be inferred that gunboat diplomacy and the limited use of naval forces are helpful concepts with respect to irregular space warfare. Space forces and systems will likewise facilitate political goals, support of diplomacy, application of pressure, support of a government or group, and the persuasion, deterrence, or coercion of a rival. The limited use of space forces may be combined with diplomatic pressure to affect the internal or external affairs of a competitor.[17] This was, in fact, demonstrated during the 1970s when the James E. (Jimmy) Carter administration declassified information about U.S. photo-reconnaissance satellites to influence its arms-control discussions with the Soviet Union.[18] Limited operations of space forces may range from simple and friendly activity to military intervention short of actual war.

Maritime experience and gunboat diplomacy have further analogues to the threat and limited use of space forces and systems to serve the ends of policy: forward presence and demonstration of resolve, power projection and assurance of access, coercion, intimidation, and proximity operations, and technology demonstrations and space exercises.

Forward Presence and Demonstrating Resolve

The ideas of forward presence and demonstrating resolve are enduring concepts, routinely reflected in military strategy and service doctrine, and both have implications for space forces. First, *forward presence* demonstrates national commitment, lends credibility to alliances, enhances regional stability, and provides a potential crisis-response capability.[19] That is, sustained forward presence can promote a country's influence and regional access. Forward presence also embraces periodic and rotational deployments, multinational exercises, port visits, military-to-military contacts, and the like.[20] James Cable sees forward presence as a central element of gunboat diplomacy: "The last and least of the uses of limited naval force in furtherance of the objectives of foreign policy is the expressive, in which warships are employed to emphasize attitudes, to lend verisimilitude to otherwise unconvincing statements or to provide an outlet for emotion."[21] Forward presence is sometimes included in the concept of "showing the flag," through the positioning of naval forces near areas of potential discord as a symbolic expression of support and concern.[22]

Second, military forces are also used to demonstrate resolve. When nonmilitary instruments of national power, such as diplomacy and economic measures, are unable to influence a deteriorating situation, military forces and the threat of their use may be required to demonstrate a government's resolve and capability, support the other instruments of national power, or resolve the situation on favorable terms.[23] Military operations can also assert support for international rights and the rules-based order.[24] In general, demonstrations of resolve in times of heightened international tension include supporting national objectives, deterring war, and returning to a sustainable peacetime situation.[25] Demonstrating resolve should directly support political aims and diplomatic actions, or else they may be counterproductive.[26]

The missions of space forces and associated capabilities are aligned with the "vaguer purposes" of gunboat diplomacy, as Cable puts it: "Something, it is felt, is going to happen, which might somehow be prevented if force were available at the critical point."[27] The "vaguer purposes" below the threshold of major armed conflict can advance diplomatic, political, and strategic objectives. The sustained presence of space forces in-orbit or within cislunar regions can improve the chances for successful peacemaking by lending credibility and demonstrating resolve. Forward-postured space forces and architectures (including Earth observation capabilities, satellite communications, ground terminals, and robotic spacecraft on-orbit) will be enormously useful for demonstrating a government's commitment to its international partners and agreements and its ability to respond rapidly to tense situations, crises, and conflicts. The physical presence of space forces can serve in itself as an effective deterrent to potential aggressors, because it is widely understood that should deterrence fail, military action to compel compliance may follow—for example, strikes, raids, or other contingency operations (see chapter 3).

Some examples of forward presence and demonstrations of resolve are operating spacecraft in a country's most vital celestial regions, publicly launching spacecraft following a diplomatic statement and in response to heightened international tensions, moving lunar rovers to positions where they might compete with rivals and so support political objectives, building a new ground station near other countries' ground stations to emphasize one's view regarding a point of contention, and utilizing new frequencies in a highly sought-after radio-frequency spectrum.

Certainly, forward presence and demonstrations of resolve using space forces will play a vital role in the future when conducted concurrently with vigorous diplomacy. Space forces can assist in reaching a mutually agreeable, lasting, and peaceful solution to a crisis or tense international situation. Yet caution is warranted, because events often go awry. Speaking in 1974 on the importance of naval forward presence, Stansfield Turner, then president of the U.S. Naval War College, made a point relevant to space forces: "A well orchestrated Naval Presence can be enormously useful in complementing diplomatic actions to achieve political objectives. Applied deftly but firmly, in precisely the proper force, Naval Presence can be a persuasive deterrent to war. If used ineptly, it can be disastrous. Thus, in determining presence objectives, scaling forces, and appraising perceptions, there will never be a weapons system as important as the human intellect."[28] Likewise, space forces are useful tools for complementing diplomatic efforts and achieving political aims. Yet the employment of space forces in forward presence and demonstration of resolve must be circumspect and not haphazard, to avoid disaster.

Projecting Power and Ensuring Access

Power projection and access are as applicable in the space domain as in others. Power projection and the guaranteeing of access are interlinked and interdependent. The fact that one enables the other facilitates diplomatic and political objectives. Both involve the utilization of credible military force to underscore policy interests or commitment to an alliance or coalition. Most often, diplomatic and political aspects predominate, though the actions are inherently military.[29] Military forces conduct these operations within legal and political constraints and may also work with multinational forces.[30]

Power Projection

In maritime strategy, *power projection* is generally understood to be "the use of seaborne military forces directly to influence events on land," in Geoffrey Till's words.[31] It is an exercise of a navy's ability to launch sea-based air and ground attacks against an enemy ashore.[32] Commonly, power projection begins with the *ability to act* militarily, demonstration of one's means and will, but does not necessarily proceed to the actual use of force or violence. Maritime advocates often view power projection as the ultimate justification for having a navy.[33] A generalized definition spanning all the U.S. sea services, especially helpful here, is "the ability of a nation to apply all or some of its elements of national power—political, economic, informational, or military—to rapidly and effectively deploy and sustain forces in and from multiple dispersed locations to respond to crises, to contribute to deterrence, and to enhance regional stability."[34] Specifically, power projection rests on the ability to inflict costs on an adversary from the maritime domain to the degree of one's choosing, at the time and place of one's choosing, by means of strike, amphibious, or naval special warfare.[35] Maritime power projection "across the beach" obviates many diplomatic, military, and geographic complications and the reliance on nearby ports and airfields.[36]

A widely acknowledged ability to project power enhances a government's influence on the strategic environment. Many political and military leaders, including in the United States, expect to have the option to take the fight to the enemy. Power projection varies considerably in purpose, effort, and strategic impact, depending on the desired diplomatic and political aims.

Power projection will be vital in the limited use of space forces and systems. Space forces may be employed purposefully to change the policies and affect the decisions of a foreign government or its proxies. In the present context, power projection of space forces lies short of actual force but demonstrates the credible means and will to use it. Power projection in the space domain will involve discrete application of *spacepower*, or the totality of a nation's ability to exploit the space domain in pursuit of prosperity and security, for specific political aims in distant regions, terrestrial or celestial.[37] A nation's space forces and space-based assets project power by virtue of their publicly known ability to locate targets and support the navigation of precision weapons as well as to employ difficult-to-intercept space-to-ground weapons.

Ensuring Access and Freedom of Navigation

Ensuring access works in concert with projecting power. Military forces capable of overcoming many global geographic challenges may nonetheless be impeded by a competitor's anti-access and area-denial capabilities.[38] To support diplomatic and political aims, military forces require the access necessary to go wherever they want, to convey that they can do whatever they want. Gaining and maintaining access in an operationally contested environment or domain will often call for the full spectrum of a country's military and nonmilitary strength.

A special case of assured access is freedom of navigation. *Freedom of navigation* commonly refers to activities whose primary purpose is to assert a state's right under international law to be in or transit through certain sea or air zones or routes.[39] Exercises of freedom of navigation by aircraft flying through international airspace and the presence of ships in certain international waters or established shipping routes are well established, and freedom of navigation itself is a sovereign right granted by international law.[40]

In the maritime realm it is essential for global commerce. Inevitably, it is frequently threatened by state and nonstate actors who seek to disrupt legal activity and to commit piracy.[41]

Space forces will be instrumental in ensuring access to space and conducting freedom-of-navigation operations. Ensuring access to CLOCs, shared orbits, and cislunar regions will help safeguard states' ability to go wherever they want, in accordance with international law and the existing rules-based order. This assured access in space will, in turn, assist in projecting spacepower and conveying to rivals one's unfettered ability to act militarily. Military activity in support of access and freedom of navigation in space, in concert with diplomatic initiatives and congruent with the aims of policy, will undergird space-reliant trade. Access to space is assured through freedom of navigation and is exercised through the establishment of command of space.

An example of the means of ensuring access and freedom of navigation is a robust and responsive space-lift capability, including launch vehicles that can get spacecraft to a variety of orbital regimes and do so frequently. "Access" also applies to the radio-frequency spectrum, so as to use space-related networks and architectures. To be as effective and efficient as possible, these efforts will likely necessitate integrating the services of allies and commercial partners. They will have to contend with the attempts of adversaries to frustrate them, such as through jamming, lasing, counterspace weapons, and cyberattacks against computer networks.

Coercion, Intimidation, and Proximity Operations

Space forces can also be used in limited and bounded ways for coercion and intimidation, often by vigorous activities including proximity operations (examined below). Coercion and intimidation are imposed by threats, implicit or explicit, backed up by known capabilities and political will. Coercion is readily visualized in the land, maritime, and air domains as deployment of menacing forces in proximity to a competitor's territory, forces, or interests: armies moving toward the border, navies taking station off another's coast, and air forces flying near an adversary's national airspace. Yet coercion is also applicable in the space domain.[42]

In its most basic form, to *coerce* is to convince an adversary to act a certain way. In practice, coercion is the threat of force, backed up by actual force, to induce an adversary to behave differently than it otherwise would. Thomas Schelling developed the accepted theoretical framework for coercion, one in which coercion gradually raises the costs of resistance sufficiently to induce an adversary who is eager to avoid future costs to concede some disputed point.[43] Coercion is typically broken down into two subcategories (with names later adopted by Geoffrey Till, above, in a difference context): compellence and deterrence. *Compellence* involves attempts to reverse an action that has already occurred or otherwise overturn the status quo, such as evicting an aggressor from territory it has just conquered.[44] Schelling describes it as direct action to persuade an opponent to give up something they desire.[45] In contrast, deterrence involves preventing an action that has not yet occurred, such as by dissuading an aggressor from conquering a neighboring state.[46] As Schelling puts it, deterrence is persuading an adversary that it is in its interests to avoid certain courses of action.[47]

James Cable notes in connection with naval diplomacy how limited overt use of naval force can coerce others and achieve clearly defined objectives, all without drawing retaliation or interference.[48] Cable describes such a coercive effect as a "fait accompli," an accomplished fact, whereby a competitor's potential responses are rendered ineffectual or inconsequential: "A government embarking on an act of genuinely limited force should thus have a reasonable expectation that the force initially employed will be sufficient to achieve the specific purpose originally envisaged without regard to the reactions of the victim, whose options are thus confined to acquiescence or a retaliation which can only follow, and not prevent, the achievement of the desired result. In such cases the use of force is not merely limited, but also definitive: it creates a *fait accompli*."[49] The purposeful application of limited naval force "does not itself do anything: it induces someone else to take a decision which would not otherwise have been taken: to do something or to stop doing it or to refrain from a contemplated course of action."[50] Given the creation of a fait accompli, "all these factors combine to support the argument that, however infuriating, outrageous and immoral the original act of limited force, mere retaliation would be fruitless, dangerous and even wicked."[51]

Here we must deviate in an important aspect from James Cable's view of gunboat diplomacy and coercion. For Cable, coercion through the application of gunboat diplomacy is an option for the more capable against the less capable: "Gunboat diplomacy is traditionally a weapon employed by the strong against the weak and this somewhat exceptional instance thus demands careful analysis to establish whether it resulted from a chance combination of circumstances unlikely to be repeated or whether it can be fitted into a theoretical framework of more general application."[52] Yet, properly understood, coercion and intimidation are actually viable options for *less*-capable powers against a more capable one. By establishing command of the sea or of space, less capable forces can achieve a level of control, local or temporary, that in turn can coerce others (see chapter 3). Therefore, coercion and intimidation are available to great and small powers alike in the space domain.

To take an example, a midlevel space power might coerce a great space power by gaining control of an orbital regime or celestial region critical to both powers, such as an important section of the geostationary Earth orbit or valuable region on the Moon. If the middle power has significant space capabilities of a military nature, the great space power may be coerced in a specific region for a certain duration. Of course, the situation could change rapidly if the great space power brings additional assets to bear.

Proximity Operations in Space

Because coercion includes the implicit or explicit threat of some detrimental action, including military force, in the space domain *proximity* will play an important role. Proximity operations can enable coercion by bringing a significant military capability close enough to cause a competitor to take serious account of it. Proximity operations for the purposes of coercion will be conspicuous and attributable events but not hostile under most circumstances.

Proximity operations in space involve a series of orbital maneuvers executed to place and maintain a spacecraft in the vicinity of another space object on a planned path for a specific duration for particular reasons.[53]

A precursor to proximity is a *rendezvous*, which is a process whereby two space objects, whether artificial or natural bodies, are intentionally brought close together through matching planes, altitudes, and phasing.[54]

The concept and fact of rendezvous and proximity operations (RPOs) have been around for several decades, and on-orbit servicing by commercial industry has recently brought them increased attention.[55] Taken together, RPO technologies make possible a wide array of services that support civil and commercial space activity, including on-orbit inspections, repairs, refueling, assembly, and life extension. According to security experts at the Secure World Foundation, RPOs also can be applied to such military-related purposes as intelligence collection, surveillance, and the deployment of offensive weapons like co-orbital antisatellite systems.[56]

China has displayed sophisticated RPO and inspection capabilities in recent years. Both of China's Shijian-series satellites, Shijian-17 (SJ-17) and Shijian-21 (SJ-21), have performed on-orbit activities with cooperative Chinese spacecraft in geostationary Earth orbit (GEO). A Center for Strategic and International Studies (CSIS) space threat assessment summarizes, "China is no novice in performing RPOs in GEO."[57] In a statement to the Senate Armed Services Committee, the commander of U.S. Space Command, Gen. James Dickinson, stated that SJ-17 had a robotic arm on board, which had not previously been disclosed.[58] The mission of SJ-21, according to the Chinese state media, is mainly to "test and verify space debris mitigation technologies."[59] The CSIS report details, "Within its first couple of months on orbit, SJ-21 has performed several advanced tests and maneuvers, including the release of a subsatellite or apogee kick motor (AKM), close approaches with other satellites in GEO, and removal of a non-functioning satellite to a disposal orbit."[60] In the last-mentioned task, SJ-21 operated as a "space tug," moving one of China's defunct Beidou positioning, navigation, and timing satellites into a graveyard orbit.[61] These RPO and tug capabilities are akin to those of other on-orbit servicing, assembly, and manufacturing satellites, and the test was not run explicitly for counterspace purposes. However, the technical capabilities to perform such maneuvers—such as grappling inactive satellites—are necessary for co-orbital counterspace weapons.[62]

The effects of proximity are important during the maneuver and employment of space forces and systems. The transparent and publicly known movement of spacecraft in proximity to a rival's space assets can convey an implicit or explicit threat. Proximity to a competitor's critical and highly vulnerable space capabilities should be a deliberate "message" to the competitor's political and military leadership to decide in favor of something not in its best interest.

Space Force in Being

The essence of defence is mobility and an untiring aggressive spirit.

—Julian Corbett[63]

Proximity is not the only method by which military means may affect the decision calculus of a competitor. Other categories of coercion are not well addressed in the strategies of land or air warfare, but maritime strategy does illuminate the idea. In maritime history and strategy, active and capable naval forces may coerce a competitor without necessarily being close to its navy. This form of coercion falls under the concept known as a *fleet in being*.

It is important for a small navy to avoid decisive battle with a superior fleet; it should rather be kept "in being" until the situation develops in its favor.[64] A weaker but still capable "fleet in being" can tie up a stronger fleet, impeding its ability to project power elsewhere without actually engaging it. Julian Corbett viewed the concept of fleet in being as an element of the strength of the defense.[65] A fleet in being must be ready, and known to be, to do something injurious unless the rival takes, desists from, or refrains from some course of action.[66] A fleet in being can conduct minor attacks against maritime communications or coastal possessions, thereby thwarting the rival's attempt to gain command of the sea.[67]

Cdr. Kevin Rowlands, Royal Navy, argues that the fleet in being can be applied "at different points on the spectrum of conflict and thus be effectively used as tools of coercive naval diplomacy."[68] British maritime doctrine defines the concept in such terms: "Fleet-in-being. A state deprived of maritime superiority might choose, or be forced, to adopt a strategy of fleet-in-being. By avoiding confrontation with a superior enemy a state can hold back its own maritime forces but continue to threaten those of the enemy or their ability to carry out their mission. The submarine provides an excellent contemporary example of a fleet-in-being, as it could be held covertly in reserve but could also be operating undetected in an area vital to the superior force."[69] This document goes on to warn, however, that whatever potential a fleet in being has for coercing a competitor, it risks becoming overly passive.[70] Consequently, a fleet in being is best understood as *actively* in being, not merely in existence.[71]

Analogy to the space domain suggests a concept that has merit: the space force in being. Even a less-capable space force may be capable of compelling or deterring a competitor without moving into proximity to it. For example, a direct-ascent antisatellite capability that can destroy satellites in Earth orbit might represent a space force in being. Space-based lasers and radio-frequency jammers that operate from a distance might do so also. Additionally, and by analogy with the submarine, any spacecraft that can operate undetected and be held in reserve would also constitute a force in being in the space domain.

Technological Demonstrations and Space Exercises

Space-related technological displays and exercises are other related modes of coercing others. China's military literature and doctrine illuminate them. Even technology displays and space exercises not intended to coerce others may definitely do so as an ancillary effect, depending on what technology is demonstrated and how the exercises are conducted.

Dean Cheng, a senior fellow at the Potomac Institute for Policy Studies who has written extensively about PLA literature on space, perceives in it a hierarchy of actions pertaining to space deterrence. For times of crisis or conflict, PLA teaching materials and textbooks speak of a "deterrence ladder."[72] The rungs of this ladder are displays of space forces and weapons, military space exercises, space force deployments, and employment of space weapons.[73] Of these, displays and space exercises have significant intersections with gray-zone operations and gunboat diplomacy.

Technological Displays and Demonstrations

Displays and demonstrations have a context that warrants separate treatment. In the PLA literature, "displays of space forces and weapons' [*kongjian liliang xianshi*] occur in peacetime or at the outset of a crisis. The goal is to warn an opponent in the hopes of dissuading him from escalating a crisis or pursuing courses of action that will lead to conflict. Such displays involve the use of various forms of media to highlight one's space forces and are ideally complemented by political and diplomatic gestures and actions, such as inviting foreign military attachés to attend weapons tests and demonstrations."[74]

Cheng explains that for the PLA these displays and demonstrations, which are meant to coerce others, do not include solely military space capabilities but civilian systems as well.[75] This inclusion is a product of the well established and growing dual-use character of many space technologies. The implication is that civilian capabilities can morph rapidly into military ones, which can give a rival pause during times of heightened tensions. Consequently, civilian, commercial displays and demonstrations of space technology may be part of China's broader deterrence strategy.[76]

The PLA concept of displays and demonstrations of space technology has parallels in U.S. military literature. For example, U.S. joint doctrine comments, "Deterrence prevents adversary action *through the presentation of a credible threat* of unacceptable counteraction and belief that the cost of the action outweighs the perceived benefits."[77] So, the U.S. perceived value in the presentation of credible military capabilities as part of deterrence is similar to that in PLA literature. Indeed, American views, and Western views generally, frequently assert that maximum effectiveness of deterrence involves capability, credibility, and communication and that the presentation of capability will help establish the latter two.[78]

U.S. Space Force doctrine highlights the importance of displays and demonstrations for deterring aggression. General Raymond's *Planning Guidance* declares, "We are forging a warfighting Service that is always above. Our purpose is to promote security, assure allies and partners, and deter aggressors by *demonstrating the capability* to deny their objectives and impose costs upon them."[79] U.S. joint doctrine on space operations is congruent: "Displaying the resources and resolve to implement responses to an attack using all appropriate instruments of national power could cause an adversary to believe the cost of the attack is not worth the benefit."[80]

Space Exercises

Space-related military exercises can influence a competitor's calculations. U.S. joint doctrine defines *exercise*: "A military maneuver or simulated wartime operation involving planning, preparation, and execution that is carried out for the purpose of training and evaluation."[81] In general, a military exercise involves resources used in training (such as simulations) or preparing for military operations either to explore warfare effects or test strategies, in both cases without the actual use of force. Military exercises help ensure the combat readiness of deployable or forward-stationed fighting forces.

In the U.S. Space Force's Space Flag exercise series, space force personnel assess threats, plan and execute responses, and throughout, think critically about fighting in space.[82] Because its objectives include deterring real-world would-be aggressors, Space Flag activities are made public knowledge.

As Dean Cheng notes, space exercise represents a rung in the PLA deterrence ladder.

> "Military space exercises" [*kongjian junshi yanxi*] are undertaken as a crisis escalates if displays of space forces and weapons are insufficient to compel an opponent to alter course. They can involve actual forces or computer simulations and are intended to demonstrate one's capabilities but also military preparations and readiness. At the same time, such exercises will also improve one's military space force readiness. Examples include ballistic missile defense tests, antisatellite unit tests, "exercises demonstrating space strike" [*kongjian tuji*] capabilities and displays of real-time and near-real-time information support from space systems.[83]

The PLA, then, is clearly aware that space-related exercises, kinetic or non-kinetic, can coerce a rival into changing its plans. Space exercises are powerful tools in achieving political objectives. Of note, PLA writings mention antisatellite and space-strike exercises, activities that may be viewed as escalatory by political and military leaders outside of China. If publicized clearly and convincingly to a global audience, national and multinational space exercises can help deter potential adversaries, thereby promoting peace and stability. However, if communicated poorly and unconvincingly, these same military exercises can have the opposite effect.

Supporting Operations in Other Domains

Military space ventures have been inherently adjunct, supportive, and ancillary to the main terrestrial action of modern strategy. —Colin Gray[84]

As mentioned in connection with hybrid warfare (chapter 2), military space actions routinely support operations and irregular warfare in the other domains. Ancillary space actions are important and should not be discounted as inconsequential for achieving strategic effect. Colin Gray explains: "As the leading edge of overall U.S. combat potency, space power will decide the course and outcome of some conflicts, even though space forces may not themselves be combat forces with offensive capabilities."[85] Therefore, in a conflict, support that does not deliver combat power may nevertheless be decisive. Secondary and indirect space activities can make the achievement of desired effects more effective and efficient than it could have been without their support. The benefit of limited space action is especially relevant to irregular competition and conflict.

Military space capabilities perform a variety of tasks and missions that often support military operations. U.S. joint doctrine lists some of these: space situational awareness; positioning, navigation, and timing; intelligence, surveillance, and reconnaissance; satellite communications; environmental monitoring; missile warning; and space lift.[86] Many support military operations in other domains. In particular, communication satellites—along with intelligence, surveillance, and reconnaissance through Earth-observation constellations—routinely enable and directly support military activities on land, at sea, and in the air.

Space operations, along with cyberspace, are interconnected and interdependent with the military activities of the various geographical environments. At least presently, the strategic interest in space operations lies in the consequences of its application for deterrence and the conduct of war as a whole, especially in a terrestrial context.[87] Today—this may change in the future—there are practical limits as to what space operations can achieve strategically, however well executed and however significant a level of command of space they achieve. Each combat arm and potential coalition partner has distinctive strengths and limitations, and the integration of space forces with them must take those strengths and limitations fully into account. Space forces and their applications will be helpful in achieving political aims during future conflicts, but their precise roles and actual strategic utility will be unique to each class and case of conflict.[88] They must integrate and synchronize their actions in a joint and all-domain framework. Lastly, space professionals should embrace their supporting role, when they are indeed assigned to support land, maritime, air, or cyber capabilities and forces.

Limited Space Warfare and Asymmetric Advantage

In addition to supporting operations in the other domains, space forces can be employed in their own right in a limited manner to achieve great effect, using little effort. This aligns with Clausewitz and Corbett, regarding "war limited by contingent," which seeks low-cost victories through the creation of asymmetric advantage.[89] Ultimately, limited space warfare can help win, maximizing gains while minimizing risks and costs.

In *On War*, Clausewitz notes the idea of war using contingent or auxiliary forces, or what he defined a "fixed and usually modest force."[90] A polity with limited ambitions or inherent weaknesses can use a modest contingent force to achieve political aims during a defensive, limited war. A scholar of Clausewitz, Vanya Eftimova Bellinger, explains, "The concept of war limited by contingent also grew out of Clausewitz's realization about the complex relationship between political objectives and military means and the conditions that required their separation."[91] As she notes, however, the idea is not widely promulgated or anchored in Western strategic thought and war planning.[92]

Yet Corbett develops from Clausewitz's contingent-force concept a theory for a new form of limited war, especially maritime.[93] Corbett, as Michael Handel argues, "demonstrates how limited strength, coupled with a suitable strategy and a particular set of circumstances, can be used to expand the power of the state."[94] For Clausewitz, the decision to wage a limited war is first and foremost a political one and depends on available means; Corbett, however, moves away from solely political considerations and concentrates on the most effective use of limited means. Handel elucidates:

> The result is an integrated theory of combined naval and land operations, one that allows a small but effective naval power . . . to maximize the effectiveness of the limited means at its disposal. The success of such a "war by limited contingency" hinges upon "the intimacy with which naval and military action can be combined to give the contingent a weight and mobility that are beyond its intrinsic power." This is a case where the result achieved is truly more than the sum of its parts.[95]

According to Corbett, the idea is to win at the least possible cost, to take minimum risks for maximum gains. Corbett argues from Britain's maritime history that an intelligent, if limited, application of seapower to a tender diplomatic situation could produce results out of all proportion to its real physical potential.[96] He points out that a British threat of amphibious invasion by a small contingent force intended to divert enemy forces to the coast would have an effect that "was always out of all proportion to the intrinsic strength employed or the positive results it could give. . . . Its value lay in its power of containing [a] force greater than its own."[97]

Moreover, and departing from Clausewitz's theory, Corbett proposes that limited force can be applied as a force multiplier to obtain unlimited results, effectively creating an asymmetric advantage. For Corbett the use of limited contingent forces "is not a *form* of war, but a *method* which may be employed either for limited or unlimited war."[98] Corbett describes how during the Peninsular War, Britain applied naval warfare in a limited form to an unlimited war: "Our object was unlimited. It was nothing less than the overthrow of Napoleon. Complete success at sea had failed to do it, but that success had given us the power of applying the limited form, which was the most decisive form of offence within our means."[99] Clausewitz's continental version of war by limited contingent may escalate easily into an unlimited form of warfare, but according to Corbett, the British maritime version can remain limited.[100]

This synthesis of Corbett's analysis suggests that limited use of space forces may be less risky or costly than other military means. If the space forces are lost or destroyed during a conflict, that represents a minimal cost. This idea corresponds to what Corbett calls a "disposal force," the loss of which would be outweighed by what it might have achieved.[101] By logical extension, a "disposal" space force may be exposed to risk somewhat more freely in the knowledge that its loss would be acceptable.

Corbett's ideas regarding the strategic benefits of using modest contingent forces have relevance for space strategy, particularly during irregular space warfare. Limited space forces can help achieve aims that are either unlimited or limited in scope. For example, a war with unlimited political aims may involve unlimited means in terms of terrestrial forces but also limited space forces, which can achieve results out of proportion to their size or "footprint," thereby creating an asymmetric advantage. Alternatively, contingent space forces can be used to achieve limited political aims during limited war, as is already commonly understood.

Tactical-level examples can be offered of limited space warfare achieving asymmetric advantage. First, space forces can achieve kinetic effects through long-range, standoff military means to support a terrestrial fight, actions that would fall under the heading of space strikes (see chapter 3). Space forces would be somewhat protected by distance from terrestrial attack. Contingent space forces have the potential for achieving significant gains with low cost, even if destroyed. Second, modest space-based capabilities can achieve significant effects through reversible and nonkinetic jamming of space-reliant radio-frequency communications, thereby achieving a widespread effect using a small "space footprint" and relatively inexpensive systems. Regardless of how they are employed at the tactical level, over time limited space forces can achieve asymmetric advantage during war, whether for unlimited or limited political aims.

Conclusion

Historical experience demonstrates that competition frequently occurs in the middle region of the peace/conflict continuum, where space forces should be expected to contribute importantly through gray-zone operations and gunboat diplomacy. By the threat of or limited use of force, space forces can help achieve political aims and strategic ends during times of heightened tension. Even in situations where their effects are ancillary, space forces can, by such vigorous activity as moving into proximity to a competitor's assets, still help achieve a strategy's goals. The policy maker and strategist must remember that political ends and available military means should drive the style or mode of irregular space warfare, whether the aims are unlimited or limited in scope. Improperly balancing ends with available means will likely bring loss and disappointment.

The range of available options for using space forces and on-orbit systems in a limited manner is vast. Sometimes, just presence and demonstration of resolve are sufficient to affect the decision calculus of a rival, and in other situations proximity may coerce and intimidate others so as to achieve desired political aims. Overt displays of space-related technology and military prowess can also achieve notable results, but communicating intent is critical so as not to cause unintended escalation. Additionally, space forces may directly or indirectly—but not inconsequentially— support the terrestrial fight. The limited use of space forces in support of military operations in the nonspace domains can help achieve asymmetric advantage at minimal risks, which benefits the entire war effort.

Finally, it is worth underscoring that great, middle, and emerging space powers may decide on the limited use of space forces, whether ultimately for unlimited or limited political aims. More capable space powers may see a strategy of limited means as a way to reduce risk and minimize cost. For less capable space powers, there may simply be no better option.

≡ CHAPTER 5 ≡

Lawfare and Space

> *The military weapon is but one of the means that serve the purposes of war: one out of the assortment which grand strategy can employ.*
> —B. H. Liddell Hart[1]

There are a multitude of means to achieve political objectives and strategic aims. One such method is the intentional distortion and misuse of legal regimes for competitive advantage, or *lawfare*. The term is a portmanteau of the words *law* and *warfare*, which can be misleading, because acts of lawfare fall mostly outside the use of military force and violence. For many states seeking to employ unconventional, protracted methods of competition, lawfare can be a powerful method of achieving political aims. As suggested by historical experience, lawfare and its application should be expected to have relevance for irregular forms of warfare and competition, including in the space domain.

In a 2001 paper, Charles Dunlap (retired major general, former deputy head of the Air Force Judge Advocate General Corps) popularized the concept of lawfare as used predominantly today—that being "the use of law as a weapon of war."[2] In speeches and writings in the late 1990s, Dunlap explained that he wanted to create a "bumper sticker" phrase easily understood by a variety of audiences to describe how the law was altering warfare and perhaps forming a new relationship between itself and war.[3] In the next decade he elaborated on the idea: "At the time, I was trying to focus on the exploitation of real, perceived, or even orchestrated incidents of law-of-war violations being employed as an unconventional means of confronting American military power."[4] In 2008, he further refined the definition of lawfare to mean "the strategy of using—or misusing—law as a substitute for traditional military means to achieve an operational objective."[5] According to Dunlap, lawfare can make it appear that the United States is fighting in an illegal or immoral way, and its effects are as real as any caused by a traditional military campaign.[6]

Other definitions of lawfare exist. For instance, the founders of *Lawfare Blog* offer a double meaning of *lawfare*, which can include a negative context for American: "The name *Lawfare* refers both to the use of law as a weapon of conflict and, perhaps more importantly, to the depressing reality that America remains at war with itself over the law governing its warfare with others. This latter sense of the word, which is admittedly not its normal usage, binds together a great deal of our work over the years. It is our hope to provide an ongoing commentary on America's lawfare, even as we participate in many of its skirmishes."[7] The latter part of this definition does agree with the idea presented in this chapter of distorting and misusing legal regimes.

Along with Dunlap, other scholars have commented on lawfare's relationship to traditional military methods of conflict. Joel Trachtman observes how lawfare can achieve objectives and outcomes typical of military means: "Lawfare can substitute for warfare where it provides a means to compel specified behavior with fewer costs than kinetic warfare, or even in cases where kinetic warfare would be ineffective. As a result, lawfare can be strategically integrated into military command structures to bring about desired outcomes."[8]

Also noting the important role of lawfare throughout history is legal scholar Orde Kittrie, who writes on the increasing effectiveness of lawfare in achieving objectives typically associated with the use of military force.[9] He traces the first attempts at lawfare back to 1609, when legal arguments were used to bolster Dutch maritime power.[10] Kittrie attributes today's growing frequency of lawfare to several factors: the increased number and reach of international laws and tribunals; the rise of nongovernmental organizations focused on the law of armed conflict; and the advance of globalization and economic interdependence between states.[11] For many relatively weak states, lawfare is a means to compete in the courtroom or public discourse against a stronger power.

A wide range of meanings for the term *lawfare* has appeared in the scholarly literature during the last two decades, comprising positive and strict senses as well as negative and distorted contexts. To set some boundaries for this discussion, we posit first that lawfare is not generally warfare, or an act of force and violence. Second, the concept should not be appealed to for every minor connection of the law to armed conflict. Consequently, as used hereafter, *lawfare* connotes the intentional distortion and misuse of legal regimes to challenge another power in an unconventional manner, thereby achieving political or military objectives. It is worth emphasizing the unconventional, or nontraditional, aspect of lawfare's meaning. Therefore, in reference to linkages of the law with traditional competition and warfare, other commonly used phrases—such as *rule of law, international humanitarian law,* and the *law of armed conflict*—would be more accurate. (It is acknowledged, however, that savvy practitioners of lawfare will seek to co-opt the concepts, ideas, and language of traditional legal discourse to pursue objectives in a seemingly legitimate way.)

China's and Russia's Use of Lawfare

Security analysts and legal scholars in Western countries often use "lawfare" in the context of China and Russia's intentional misuse of legal regimes and associated distortions of the law. Their political leaders have sought by intentional omission and obfuscation to limit the superiority and military options of the United States and its allies, all while touting themselves as responsible stakeholders.[12] U.S. rivals and their proxies increasingly seek to prevail through their own uses of lawfare, deliberately pursuing political and strategic objectives in a competitive space below any threshold that is likely to provoke a conventional military response. China and Russia often practice lawfare as part of broader campaigns of disinformation, deception, sabotage, and economic coercion.

According to many security analysts, U.S. competitors view lawfare as an offensive weapon that is capable of hamstringing the United States while seizing the political initiative.[13] The concern is that U.S. rivals are preparing "legal-war plans" aimed at controlling or constraining the United States and its allies through the distortion or misuse of the law. American policy makers and military planners must be aware of lawfare and take steps now to prepare for its use by incorporating counterstrategies and countermeasures into campaign and contingency plans.[14]

Of the number that could be chosen, three broad examples of distorting and misusing legal regimes and their effects for competitive advantage will be examined here. They involve a draft treaty proposal by China and Russia regarding space weapons, the place of legal warfare in China's overarching strategy, and China's coercive actions in the South China Sea.

China and Russia's Space Weapons Treaty Proposal

Diplomatic leaders from China and Russia have proposed a draft "Prevention of the Placement of Weapons in Outer Space and of the Threat or Use of Force against Outer Space Objects," or PPWT. To many in the American foreign-policy and national-security communities, the PPWT is a classic example of lawfare.[15] China and Russia jointly submitted it at the United Nations (UN) in 2008, stating that one of the goals was "to keep outer space as a sphere where no weapon of any kind is placed."[16] The proposed language, however, defined "space weapons" to mean "any device placed in outer space, based on any physical principle, specially produced or converted to eliminate, damage or disrupt normal function of objects in outer space, on the Earth or in its air, as well as to eliminate population, components of biosphere critical to human existence or inflict damage to them."[17] The draft proposal further specified that "placing a weapon in space" meant inserting the object into an orbital trajectory or stationing it permanently somewhere else in space, such as the Moon. Therefore, the PPWT defined space weapons somewhat narrowly as space-to-space and space-to-Earth weapons, both kinetic and nonkinetic. The PPWT would not prohibit Earth-to-space kinetic weapons, such as the Chinese antisatellite (ASAT) missile tested in 2007.[18]

China and Russia's delegations to the United Nations jointly issued in 2014 an updated draft of the PPWT that modified the proposed definition of a space weapon to apply to any outer-space object and expanded a state's right of self-defense to include collective self-defense.[19] Importantly, the revised PPWT language continued to be limited to space-to-space and space-to-Earth forms of kinetic and nonkinetic weapons and to exclude Earth-to-space weapons such as ASATs.

American diplomats had, and continue to have, several objections to the PPWT. First, the most pressing threat to outer-space systems comprises terrestrially based ASAT weapons, to include direct-ascent, hit-to-kill capabilities, which the PPWT did not address and in which both China and Russia have proven capabilities.[20] Second, there were problems with how to verify and monitor compliance and regarding the definition of a space weapon. To many in the U.S. government, China and Russia's treaty proposal was a blatantly disingenuous attempt to preserve their terrestrial ASAT capabilities while constraining American on-orbit superiority. Ambassador Robert A. Wood explains, "It is clear from these examples that Russia and China believe it is currently acceptable to attack satellites in orbit from the ground, whether through directed energy or missile strikes. At the same time, they hypocritically profess their concern about attacks on satellites and serve as the main proponents of the draft PPWT."[21] From the perspective of many American diplomats, the PPWT episode draws attention to the fact that there is not at present an arms-control solution to the issue of weapons in space and makes clear that the PPWT is fundamentally flawed and has not been, is not, and never will be the solution to the threats facing the space domain.[22]

China and Legal Warfare

Members of the Chinese Communist Party (CCP) and the PLA are, according to Dean Cheng, approaching lawfare as an offensive weapon capable of hamstringing opponents and seizing the political initiative in wartime.[23] "Chinese writings often refer to the 'three warfares' (*san zhan*): public opinion warfare, psychological warfare, and legal warfare. Chinese analyses almost always link the three together, as they are seen as interrelated and mutually reinforcing."[24] "Legal warfare," in particular, is meant to raise doubts among the adversary, neutral military and civilian authorities, and the broader global population about the legality of the adversary's actions and thereby diminish its political will and domestic support. "Legal warfare" seeks to exploit international and domestic law to assert the legitimacy of China's claims, and the desired effect may be to weaken the adversary's military effectiveness.

Legal warfare should not be considered in isolation; it can undergird a successful public-opinion warfare strategy. Cheng cites a People's Republic of China (PRC) publication: "Legal warfare, at its most basic, involves 'arguing that one's own side is obeying the law, criticizing the other side for violating the law [*weifa*], and making arguments for one's own side in cases where there are also violations of the law.' The instruments of legal warfare include national laws as well as the full range of legal instruments: legislation, judicial law, legal pronouncements, law enforcement, and legal education."[25] Equally as important, however, PLA analysis suggests that international law, including treaties, must be considered through the prism of legal warfare as a source of opportunities to exploit competitors' weaknesses.

It is apparent that the PRC view about the utility of the rule of law differs from that of the West. The PRC's view is informed by important historical and cultural experiences, and the historical and cultural experiences of China's polity are very different from those of the West. The concept of the rule of law—the law existing as a distinct and autonomous entity, applying to both the ruler and the ruled—is one of the foundations of the West's legal traditions.[26] Cheng observes, "Despite its importance to the West, however, the rule-of-law maxim remained weak throughout imperial China and was ultimately devastated by Maoist rule."[27] During the early years of the PRC, its legal development was influenced by the Marxist perspective that the "law should serve as an ideological instrument of politics."[28] Consequently, during its formative years the CCP considered the law to be essentially an instrument of governance and not a constraint on the party.

Ultimately, there is little evidence that CCP decision makers see legal warfare as a misuse of the law. The CCP maxim is more "rule *by* law" than the Western "rule *of* law."[29] Seth Jones refers to the 2001 edition of the PRC's authoritative *Science of Military Strategy* as evidence that in China's view "international law is a powerful weapon to expose the enemy, to win over sympathy and support of the international community [for China], and to strive to gain the position of strategic initiative."[30] Given the instrumentalist role of the law in China's history, its employment for national and military goals is consistent with Chinese culture, but for the West the idea is problematic and often antithetical to its own.[31]

It is worth mentioning that in PLA analyses of recent conflicts, including the two Gulf wars, the United States appears as one of the leading practitioners of legal warfare. China perceives others, including the United States, as sharing its own instrumentalist perspective as well, at least in international relations and warfare.[32]

China in the South China Sea

China routinely uses lawfare to address competing interests in the South China Sea to its sweeping territorial claims. Of note, there are competing claims in the South China Sea by various regional countries, but China frequently pursues its own more coercively and antagonistically than other claimants do. Jill Goldenziel (a professor at the National Defense University's College of Information and Cyberspace) explains that China uses lawfare to "strengthen its legitimacy and undermine U.S. power."[33] International security analysts Nguyen Thanh Trung and Le Ngoc Khanh Ngan reinforce the point: "China has turned its naval fleets and disguised militia vessels into behemoths to outclass regional navies and law enforcement agencies. In this context, forcing vessels from smaller nations to comply with the law does not seem a very hard task for Beijing."[34] Two areas in particular are worth highlighting in the context of lawfare: China's construction of military and industrial outposts in disputed waters, and its use of its vessels to harass others, particularly excluding Filipino fishermen from the Scarborough Shoal.

In recent years, the PRC has launched an accelerated land-reclamation campaign across the South China Sea. A RAND report from 2019 concludes, "China's unprecedented expansion of artificial islands in the South China Sea and subsequent construction of logistics, maintenance, and storage facilities, along with airstrips, harbors, ports, and armament platforms, are in the process of further tilting the regional military balance in favor of China."[35] PRC actions include physically increasing the size of islands—in at least seven locations, its vessels have poured tons of sand to expand features occupied by China—and creating new features altogether. The PRC has also begun construction of additional infrastructure on much of this reclaimed land, including an airstrip capable of receiving military aircraft. Although other claimants have reclaimed land in the past, "China has reclaimed over 2,000 acres, more than all other claimants combined, and more than in the entire history of the region," according to the late Ashton Carter, then secretary of defense.[36]

The tension between China and Filipino fishermen in the Scarborough Shoal is seen as the most significant erosion of stability in the South China Sea in recent times.[37] There is a dispute over the shoal itself, and the two countries have quarreled over allegations of illegal poaching by Chinese fishermen for some time. In April 2012, the Philippine navy attempted to apprehend eight mainland Chinese fishing vessels nearby. The PRC responded by physically and coercively seizing the shoal. After a two-month standoff and continued allegations of illegal poaching by Chinese fishermen, the two parties agreed to withdraw from the shoal. Manila did, Beijing did not. Since then, China has excluded Filipino fishing boats from its waters. It routinely does so by means of a "maritime militia," commercial fishermen who work for the PLA in their off time.[38] When performing militia duties, these vessels do not fish but instead perform surveillance and other intelligence-gathering missions.[39]

In response to this escalatory move, the Philippines government filed an arbitration case against the PRC on January 22, 2013, under the auspices of the UN Convention on the Law of the Sea (UNCLOS). The Philippines' claim centers on maritime law, which China asserts cannot be resolved without first resolving territorial issues. Beijing has largely refused to participate in the proceedings, although it has drafted and publicly released a position paper opposing the tribunal's jurisdiction in the matter. In July 2016 an UNCLOS tribunal in The Hague issued a landmark ruling striking down many of the PRC's maritime claims in the South China Sea and actions in defense of those claims.[40] The tribunal found that China had violated the Philippines' sovereign rights and freedoms.[41]

The tribunal handed down decisions in four areas. First, it ruled that no land feature that was in dispute in the northern or southern sector of the South China Sea was capable of sustaining human habitation or economic life in its own right. Accordingly, none of them met the definition of an "island," or as the tribunal called it, "a fully entitled feature." The finding also underscored the illegal nature of the PRC's occupation of, much less the buildup on, another feature in contention, Mischief Reef (about three hundred miles north), given that the reef has a low-tide elevation (i.e., is above water only at low tide) on what is the now-undisputed Philippine continental shelf.[42] Second, the tribunal judged that China's "nine-dash line" claim to "historic rights" in the South China Sea was in fact an exclusive claim of sovereign rights and jurisdiction in the Philippines' economic exclusion zone. This, the tribunal ruled, was without lawful effect since, absent any Chinese-administered insular land feature capable of generating an exclusive entitlement beyond twelve nautical miles (as an "island" would), the PRC's claim exceeded the geographic and substantive limits of its entitlements under UNCLOS.[43] Third, the tribunal ruled that Beijing had violated its convention obligations by denying Filipino fishermen their right to traditional fishing in the territorial sea of the China-administered Scarborough Shoal, tradition-based rights being guaranteed by "other rules of international law."[44] Fourth, the tribunal found that China's law-enforcement vessels in the vicinity of Scarborough Shoal had repeatedly violated many international navigation-related regulations, notably the Convention on the International Regulations for Preventing Collisions at Sea.[45]

To the tribunal's stern findings have been added repeated diplomatic admonitions by world leaders, even Vice President Kamala Harris. In August 2021 she sharply rebuked Beijing for its incursions in the South China Sea, warning that they amount to "coercion" and "intimidation" and affirmed that the United States will support its allies in the region.[46] Harris commented, "Beijing's actions continue to undermine the rules-based order and threaten the sovereignty of nations."[47] That comment alone is telling as to the payoffs of lawfare for political objectives and strategic aims. Despite the best efforts of international courts, the rules-based legal regime, and diplomatic admonishment, the PRC's aggressive and coercive behavior under the cover of legal warfare remains unmitigated.

Lawfare as Strategy

Lawfare can be understood as part of holistic competitive strategies. Strategy involves balancing desired ends with available means, and

Strategy – Balancing Ends and Means

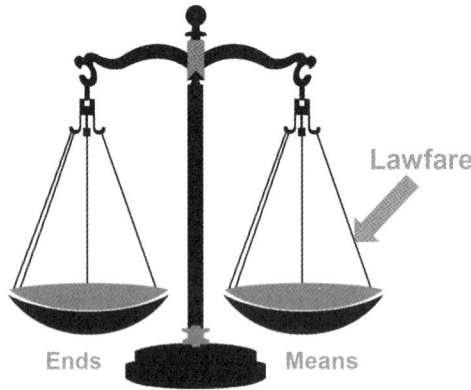

Figure 5.1. Lawfare and Strategy (*author*)

lawfare is one of the means available (see figure 5.1). Like other strategic approaches, lawfare works best when used as part of a comprehensive plan with other means—thus China's "three warfares" (public-opinion, psychological, and legal warfare).[48] History offers examples of states, organizations, and groups incorporating intentional distortion of international legal regimes into overarching strategies.

Indeed, lawfare is unlikely to be the sole determinant of strategic victory. Joel Trachtman explains, "Lawfare can be used to bring to bear the power of law in order to win victories or in order to hamper enemies. It would be ignorant to assume that law is irrelevant, but it is also ignorant to assume that law is always effective."[49] Fundamentally, lawfare works in an incremental, indirect manner. Lawfare seeks to change the context and the consensus among a group: lawfare aims to influence but can never control.

David Galula, writing of the irregular strategies of insurgencies, observes, "The insurgent, having no responsibility, is free to use every trick; if necessary, he can lie, cheat, exaggerate. He is not obliged to prove; he is judged by what he promises, not by what he does. Consequently, propaganda is a powerful weapon for him. With no positive policy but with good propaganda, the insurgent may still win."[50] The counterinsurgent, however, as Galula notes, is judged by his *actions*. A counterinsurgency is tied to its responsibilities and the facts of its past; lies and so on may bring temporary successes, but at the price of being discredited in the end.[51] This lesson holds for liberal democracies, including the United States. While U.S. rivals may be able to employ lawfare for strategic effect, the intentional distortion and misuse of legal regimes by Western countries can give only short-term gains and likely cause long-term problems.

Furthermore, all strategic approaches have inherent strengths and weaknesses, which tells the space strategist that lawfare can be defeated, or at least its most damaging effects mitigated. That assurance has particular relevance for the future misuse and distortion of law in the space domain, because the space domain does have an overarching legal regime, based on customary international law, international treaty law, and over six decades of historical precedent.

Indirect Approach

Lawfare is, by definition, an indirect approach. Liddell Hart, the indirect approach's most stalwart proponent, saw it as a way to avoid the carnage of war but still achieve political aims. It could contribute to victory not by overcoming the adversary's resistance but by exploiting movement and surprise to throw the enemy off balance before a strike.[52]

Liddell Hart argued that the responsibility of a strategist charged with winning a victory "is to seek it under the most advantageous circumstance in order to produce the most profitable result. *Hence his true aim is not so much to seek battle as to seek a strategic situation so advantageous that if it does not of itself produce the decision, its continuation by a battle is sure to achieve this.* In other words, dislocation is the aim of strategy; its sequel may be either the enemy's dissolution or his easier disruption in battle."[53] Lawfare fits well with Liddell Hart's thinking. While there is no evidence that he was thinking about using the distortion of the rule of law as an indirect approach, it is safe to say that lawfare aligns with his concept as a means of creating an "advantageous strategic situation."

Trachtman is specific about lawfare and overall strategy: "Lawfare can substitute for warfare where it provides a means to compel specified behavior with fewer costs than kinetic warfare, or even in cases where kinetic warfare would be ineffective. As a result, lawfare can be strategically integrated into military command structures to bring about desired out-comes."[54] In particular circumstances and geopolitical contexts, the distortion and misuse of international legal regimes can coerce others to behave in certain ways, often without the costs of kinetic warfare and the use of force. Also, lawfare can sometimes achieve results otherwise impossible for traditional, kinetic warfare alone.[55]

Cumulative Strategy

In addition, lawfare is potentially part of a cumulative strategy. J. C. Wylie (see chapter 2) believed that the strategist's role is to establish control not in an absolute sense but to some degree.[56] Wylie divided strategy into two kinds, "sequential" and "cumulative." A sequential strategy consists of a series of discrete actions, each of which depends on the one that preceded it, building all the way to a final decision.[57] He viewed the island-hopping campaign in the Pacific during World War II as an example. In contrast, the final success of a cumulative strategy does not rely on the success of each successive action but rather on the sum total of the individual actions. A cumulative strategy is "the less perceptible minute accumulation of little items piling on top of the other until at some unknown point the mass of accumulated actions may be large enough to be critical."[58] Wylie uses a naval blockade as an example: a few of the enemy's ships might make it through a naval blockade without compromising its overall effectiveness. A sequential strategy can be undermined by a single failure, but not a cumulative strategy. What counts is the aggregate effect.

Lawfare is of the latter kind of strategy: its effectiveness arises from the "piling up" of successes, whether to one's own benefit or the rival's detriment. Consequently, a strategy incorporating lawfare has a strong temporal dimension, as does the protracted strategy of guerrilla warfare as described by Mao Tse-tung.[59] If an adversary or rival fails to counter lawfare over an extended period of time, say several decades, lawfare's chance of success increases, even becomes guaranteed.

Obfuscate and Delay

Lawfare's potential success also comes from its ability to obfuscate and delay, for primarily two purposes. First, lawfare practitioners can, through confusing and ambiguous language and actions, cause competitors to waste time, energy, and resources. Second, obfuscation can delay the actions of others and lengthen the duration of a competitive episode, valuable where time is an enabler of strategic effect.

In the first case, rivals will distort or misuse the law to cause ambiguity as to the actual situation and cast doubt as to strategic intentions. Obfuscation through the intentional distortion of the rule of law is closely related to the time-honored practice of *deception*. The 2012 U.S. joint doctrine on military deception asserts that the purpose of deception is to cause an adversary to take, or not to take, specific actions, not just to believe certain things. It lists the functions of military deception as causing ambiguity, confusion, or misunderstanding in an adversary's perceptions of oneself, in critical ways; causing the adversary to misallocate personnel, fiscal, and material resources in ways advantageous to oneself; causing the adversary to reveal his own strengths, dispositions, and future intentions; conditioning the adversary to particular patterns of friendly behavior to induce expectations that can be exploited; and causing the adversary to waste combat power on actions either inappropriate or too late.[60] Yet again, much of this doctrine is valid for lawfare as well, especially at the strategic level of warfare.

For the purpose of obfuscation, lawfare can delay the actions of others. Lawfare may seek that effect by filing frivolous legal actions to swamp the court system and misdirect its time and energy. Lawfare can put a rival on the defensive, consumed by responding to all of one's legal arguments and judicial challenges. While lawfare is unlikely to be decisive in itself, it can be part of an indirect and cumulative strategy that ties up uselessly an adversary's time, energy, and resources and thereby enhances the effectiveness of other elements of an overarching competitive strategy.

Divide Allies

When he is united, divide him. —Sun Tzu[61]

Sun Tzu frequently highlights the importance of weakening the enemy's internal unity and alliances. Actions seeking to counter and negate an enemy's coalition and alliances follow from his general guidance, "Look into the matter of his alliances and cause them to be severed and dissolved.

If an enemy has alliances, the problem is grave and the enemy's position strong; if he has no alliances, the problem is minor and the enemy's position weak."[62] Lawfare can be a powerful tool in dividing an opponent's alliances, so weakening his overall position during a protracted campaign.

The law—particularly regarding a "use of force" and an "armed attack"—is interpreted differently within various judicial systems and the international community generally. There are frequent disagreements on whether a given action rises to force in a form grave enough to trigger the inherent right of self-defense and a military response, or whether it is on the lower end of the scale of force and coercion. This could lead, particularly in the space domain, to some allies and partners not believing that a threat exists or that force was used and other states determining that it does or has been. A rival can use lawfare to exploit these divisions, perhaps especially in the space domain, given the relative lack of precedent and state practice, and thereby attempt to weaken an alliance's collective resolve.

Lawfare and Space

Lawfare can also be used in other ways to achieve competitive advantage in space. Three primary examples have to do with the fact that satellites and autonomous spacecraft are inanimate, with distortion of the law of neutrality, and with due regard and safety zones on the Moon or other celestial bodies.

Satellites Don't Have Mothers

Divergence of views as to whether a coercive or aggressive action in space warrants a forceful response often comes down to the saying, "Satellites don't have mothers."[63] Satellites and autonomous spacecraft are objects and not as important as human beings, a point that affects the perceived gravity of any coercive act against one. If no human life is directly threatened by a malicious action, then it is arguable, in theory, that the question of inherent right of self-defense does not arise, let alone a response using military force.

International treaty law may add to the confusion by not specifically defining the key terminology. For example, the Charter of the United Nations provides in Article 2(4), "All Members shall refrain in their international relations from the *threat or use of force* against the territorial integrity or political independence of any State, or in any other manner inconsistent with the Purposes of the United Nations."[64] Article 51 adds, "Nothing in the present Charter shall impair the inherent right of individual or collective self-defence if an *armed attack* occurs against a Member of the United Nations, until the Security Council has taken measures necessary to maintain international peace and security."[65] Questions remain, however, as to how the Charter's language should be interpreted for operations in the space domain. For instance, national-security and legal professionals debate whether jamming and lasing satellites and other space systems, whether causing irreversible damage or not, rise to a use of force or armed attack.

The existence of such disparate views means that individual countries probably will join coalitions to respond to aggression in space on some occasions and not others. A country's determination will depend on its view of the gravity of the situation and its constitutional and legal constraints. The United States, then, should expect its allies and partners to join coalitions operating in the space domain at different times and in different ways. American policy makers and military leaders should not expect countries to march in lockstep with the United States. It is important, however, for allies to develop shared understandings of legal and constitutional issues in peacetime or between crises.

Furthermore, politics and national interests sometimes drive states' actions and their legal justifications. States and their domestic polities often (as the realist school of international relations predicts) assign more weight to their own interests and the relative stakes involved than to legal equities. In matters of war or peace, legal justifications will then follow along behind—the tail will not wag the dog.[66] In fact, absent consensus in this area and the unlikelihood of legally binding adjudication, determinations regarding force or armed attack will be essentially political.

Distorting the Law of Neutrality

The space strategist should expect that the law of neutrality, along with its distortion and misuse, will come into play. In its broadest sense, the law of neutrality defines the legal relationship between states engaged in an armed conflict (or belligerents) and states not taking part (or neutrals). The law of neutrality serves several purposes, such as to localize war, restrain its conduct on both land and sea, and lessen its impact on international commerce.[67]

Under customary international law, all nations have the option to refrain from an armed conflict by declaring or otherwise assuming a neutral status. Put succinctly: "The law of armed conflict reciprocally imposes duties and confers rights on neutral nations and on belligerents. The principal right of the neutral nation is that of inviolability; its principal duties are those of abstention and impartiality. Conversely, it is the duty of a belligerent to respect the former and its right to insist upon the latter."[68] A neutral state's right of inviolability is codified in Article I of Hague Convention V: "The territory of neutral Powers is inviolable." This is taken to mean that a belligerent may not occupy or conduct military operations from or within the territory of a neutral state.[69]

Another principal purpose of the law of neutrality is the regulation of belligerent activity with respect to neutral commerce. As considered here, *neutral commerce* comprises, first, all commerce between one neutral nation and another not involving materials of war or armaments destined for a belligerent nation; and second, all commerce between a neutral nation and a belligerent that does not involve contraband or otherwise contribute to a belligerent's war-fighting capability.[70] The law of neutrality does not prohibit neutral nations from engaging in commerce with belligerent nations; however, a neutral government cannot itself supply materials of war or armaments to a belligerent without violating its neutral duties of abstention and impartiality and risking the loss of its neutral status.[71]

While the law of neutrality is part of international law, its application and meaning in the context of wartime space operations are by no means clear. The primary treaties establishing neutral rights and obligations predate the launch of Sputnik I by half a century.[72] Warfare conducted in, from, or through outer space was not contemplated, much less addressed, in these early twentieth-century legal instruments. Even more than a century later, there is no state practice of applying these treaties or customary principles of neutrality to space warfare. In sum, the legal terrain in this area is unclear and therefore ripe for further development and, presumably, manipulation and misuse as well.

Space-law expert Robert Jarman observes that as space is increasingly considered a war-fighting domain, the applicability to it of the law of neutrality will be contested. As neutral states and commercial entities claim free access to outer space, belligerent states will capitalize on the dynamic nature of the law of neutrality to adapt and develop repressive measures.[73] In the context of satellite communications provided by a neutral party, Jarman asks whether a belligerent must simply acquiesce to the enemy's use of the neutral's satellites communication links for the duration of the conflict:[74] "One must question whether belligerents in the future conflicts will . . . idly stand by while enemy forces freely exploit neutral telecommunication satellites signals. A more likely scenario is that belligerents will act to deny this advantage to their enemies. They will not simply just act, however. They will also seek to justify their actions by promoting functional and reconceptualized interpretations of the law of neutrality based on a reappraisal of old precedents to meet new realities."[75] Indeed, historical experience suggests that states will seek to deny to neutrals the ability to operate space-enabled capabilities, especially if those capabilities provide a significant advantage to their opponents.

Specifically, then, in a future conflict that includes the space domain, both sides will take advantage of the space services of neutrals, whether states or companies. If these services may be vital for one belligerent's military success, the adversary may decide to deny it by degrading the neutrals' ability to provide it—that is, to render a neutral service not provided for its own use unavailable to anyone. Depending on the circumstances, this action could be considered lawfare and go against the law of neutrality and the customary international law on which it is putatively based. It is important for the United States and its allies to recognize that potential adversaries will likely seek to legitimize their actions with lawfare, distorting the law of neutrality for strategic advantage.

Establishing Excessive Safety Zones

The third example of lawfare in space concerns due regard and the establishment of safety zones. The issue is framed by the 1967 Outer Space Treaty, of which Article II states, "Outer space, including the moon and other celestial bodies, is not subject to national appropriation by claim of sovereignty, by means of use or occupation, or by any other means."[76] The beginning of Article IX lays down that "in the exploration and use of outer space, including the moon and other celestial bodies, States Parties to the Treaty shall be guided by the principle of co-operation and mutual assistance and shall conduct all their activities in outer space, including the moon and other celestial bodies, *with due regard to the corresponding interests* of all other States Parties to the Treaty."[77] Article IX further provides that if a state party to the treaty believes an activity would cause "harmful interference" with scientific exploration and the use of space, it may request consultation.[78]

In July 2021 the U.S. secretary of defense issued the memorandum "Tenets of Responsible Behavior in Space."[79] While not international treaty law, three of its five tenets are operating in, from, to, and through space with due regard to others and in a professional manner; avoiding the creation of harmful interference; and maintaining safe separation and safe trajectory.[80]

Under the Outer Space Treaty and the "Tenets of Responsible Behavior in Space," countries and commercial companies that operate on the Moon and other celestial bodies cannot own or claim territory exclusively, are to cooperate with due regard to corresponding interests, and avoid the creation of harmful interference. Yet, what does "exercising due regard in a professional manner" specifically mean in space? How close is too close? How are intentions and safety concerns to be communicated among countries and commercial companies?

That these questions are unanswered opens up room for distorting international treaty law by drawing a lunar analogy to the ongoing South China Sea situation. Presently, both the United States and China have expressed interest in scientific exploration and resource extraction on the Moon. The question is, what happens when the two countries have competing interests in a single lunar area? Will the two countries' robotic landers and autonomous vehicles—and those of their contractors— operate with due regard and maintain safe separation? Will the two countries' operations cause harmful interference to each other? What are the mechanisms for consultations between the two states, along with how will disputes be arbitrated and reconciled?

Finally, it would seem that "safe and professional responsible behaviors" could be promoted by establishing safety zones. But could they not be ultimately used as de facto "keep out" zones? This question is particularly relevant because countries and companies could reasonably promulgate safety zones around their lunar bases or robotic vehicles for reasons of safe separation and the exercise of due regard. In fact, the Artemis Accords—intended to provide a common vision through bilateral agreements to advance the U.S–led Artemis lunar program—note the need for them as well as for notification of space activities.[81] Yet safety zones could be taken to an extreme, declaring zones that are out of proportion to the ongoing lunar activity and any potential harm from nearby operations. Declaring safety zones might suggest itself as a method to circumvent the Outer Space Treaty prohibition of sovereignty claims or to establish what are effectively security zones around lunar bases and resource extraction sites.

States and commercial companies will interpret "due regard" and "safe and professional behavior" differently. Given that space is just another domain where competitive interests will play out, policy makers and space strategists should fully consider during peacetime the ramifications of different interpretations and of intentional efforts to distort the current rules-based international order.

Countering Lawfare

Every strategy has a viable counterstrategy: the same holds true for lawfare. It is important to recognize that while indirect approaches and cumulative strategy contribute to the success of lawfare, they can also be its undoing. A counterstrategy with any hope of success must recognize lawfare's strategic character and how it works. To account for its indirect-approach dimension, counter-lawfare should be in large part nonmilitary. To meet lawfare in its cumulative strategy dimension, counter-lawfare approaches should likewise use time for strategic effect.

Counter-lawfare strategies are of course not applicable to space-domain concerns alone, but in space, which is our concern here, the main ways to counter lawfare are integrating counter-lawfare approaches into overarching national strategies and military service education; relentlessly countering lawfare's narrative of misinformation; incorporating offensive-minded approaches; and coordinating with allies and trusted commercial partners.

Lastly, it is worth remembering that the purpose of space strategy is to ensure access to and use of space.[82] If one's counterstrategies against lawfare do not promote that end, they should be reevaluated to determine if they are indeed necessary. Because if a rival's distortion and misuse of the rule of law does no harm, then they are pointless, and no resources or efforts need be diverted to address them.

Integrating Counter-Lawfare into Strategies and Servicemember Education

Methods to counter lawfare and its long-term coercive effects must be integrated into national strategies and taught in military service education. The lesson for the United States is that rivals like China and Russia will continue to distort and misuse legal regimes and the rule of law, because it works. Even though effective counter-lawfare methods may seem difficult and outside of the traditional scope of military competition, the United States cannot wish the lawfare threat away. The United States must develop approaches that mitigate and directly frustrate it.[83] Policy makers and military planners should incorporate lawfare counterstrategies and countermeasures across the spectrum of conflict—during peace, quasi-war or gray-zone operations, and armed conflict. To accomplish this, policy makers and planners should address counter-lawfare in campaign plans and strategic communications, in synchronization with diplomats. A fully integrated counter-lawfare strategy must include a range of sustained non-military options that are synchronized across the government.

Additionally, American military servicemembers should be educated about lawfare as a tool of strategic competition and how the United States, its allies, and trusted commercial companies work together to thwart it. This military education promotes a more proactive, less reactive, maintenance of narratives based on the rule of law and recognized legal regimes beneficial to the United States and other liberal democracies. Specifically for the U.S. Space Force, a guardian's professional education and training should improve understanding of the key strategic, operational, and tactical-level issues arising from a competitor's use of lawfare. Ideally, this education and training would be incorporated throughout the service-member's military career. Moreover, the teaching and education should be honest as to how susceptible the United States has historically been to the indirect, protracted effects of lawfare.

Despite this frankness about susceptibility, American service personnel should be given reason for optimism about formulation of viable counterstrategies. Only through cold-eyed self-reflection about military predispositions and cultural biases can the United States move forward in addressing strategic competition.

Countering Lawfare Narratives

Lawfare looks for final success in the piling up of small ones and must be countered with equal relentlessness. As highlighted above, lawfare not only occurs below the threshold of force but may not provide a clear basis for resolute response. The United States, in particular, has historically found it challenging to maintain the political will and stamina to counter lawfare. In fact, rivals like China and Russia are counting on American lack of willpower, focus, and endurance. While some American policy makers and military leaders know of lawfare as a general concept for potential use, rivals seem already apt in its use for strategic competition.

Some counter-lawfare methods and approaches lend themselves to defensive strategies.[84] Defensive countermeasures to lawfare will be mostly reactive, not proactive, meant to thwart a competitor's actions as they occur. Steadfast and sustained defensive-minded efforts to frustrate a rival's misuse of the rules-based order or international treaties are effective and consequential. One example might involve direct legal and financial penalties designed to make the cost of lawfare greater than its perceived benefit. Some argue that defensive responses to lawfare are in fact passive and give competitors "first-mover advantage;" defensive counter-lawfare is a necessary, albeit not sufficient, solution.

Additionally, the United States must relentlessly counter lawfare's false narrative, to prevent the competitor's strategic gains being sought. Through a comprehensive approach to countering a competitor's lawfare and carrying the moral narrative of war, the United States can win in such competition.[85] A counternarrative should consistently and repeatedly uphold international treaty law, especially the Outer Space Treaty and Charter of the United Nations but also customary international law, international humanitarian law, and the law of neutrality. Lawfare counternarratives should clearly reflect America's interests and its desire to uphold the existing rules-based international order and democratic ideals. Certainly, the United States should convey the appeal of that order to rally support from other liberal democracies and strengthen its hand in the unfolding competition with China and Russia. Liberal democracies around the globe must diligently and continuously hold the line on responsible interpretation of law and acceptable international behavior.

Developing Offensive-Minded Approaches

In this context, *offensive* should not be construed as implying military force or hostile acts. In the general sense, strategies are "offensive" simply in that they seek to acquire something or wrestle something from the adversary.[86] Therefore, offensive approaches to address lawfare take away an opponent's freedom of action with respect to distortion and misuse of the law; their intent is to limit a competitor's present and future options. Offensive-minded measures to counter lawfare can achieve meaningful effects spanning all the levels of war—strategic, operational, and tactical. Counter-lawfare methods combining offensive approaches with defensive ones will be most effective, not only preventing the opponent's efforts to distort the law but creating additional opportunities to expand the rule of law.

The United States presently lacks such a combined strategy to counter lawfare, and as Orde Kittrie notes, problems have arisen as a result. Kittrie charges that the U.S. government's "failure over the last decade to adopt a broad and systematic lawfare strategy, with a robust offensive component, makes little sense."[87] Similarly, Jill Goldenziel, too, argues that "the United States must prepare to fight lawfare offensively and defensively, at the strategic, operational, and tactical levels."[88] The United States will be obliged to devote more resources to understanding lawfare's strategic implications and developing offensive and defensive strategies in response.

For the space domain specifically, several offensive-minded approaches are relevant. New international agreements and arrangements—whether multilateral or bilateral, binding, or nonbinding—can be pursued. Such instruments might codify future space norms of behavior, "norms" being standards defined in terms of rights and obligations.[89] Seeking and holding "new ground," not just thwarting individual attempts at lawfare, will mitigate rivals' prospects for future successes as well. An example is the set of Artemis Accords addressed above.[90] Another example is a draft United Nations resolution, circulated recently by the United Kingdom, that calls for creating new international norms and principles of responsible behavior for military activities in space.[91] Both look to make positive gains by defining appropriate and responsible behavior in space among the international community. Additional offensive-minded approaches would be new international legal and political instruments further implementing the Outer Space Treaty and promotion of interpretations of international law consistent with a free and open space domain.

It should be acknowledged, however, that in practice drawing a "bright line" between appropriate and inappropriate uses of law is not straightforward, especially given the lack of consensus on the meaning and scope of the UN Charter and the Outer Space Treaty. In the legal "gray zone" lie opportunities for states to promote interpretations of the law that may not be purposely distortive or abusive but are opportunistic and self-interested nonetheless. Certainly, judgment of such points is in the eye of the beholder.[92] In a competitive environment, the United States itself will not necessarily forego these opportunities and may consequently open itself up to charges of lawfare and hypocrisy. To avoid that trap the United States could proceed exclusively from the Artemis Accords principles of open access and transparency when developing or promulgating legal positions.[93]

Finally, security or legal experts occasionally suggest that the United States should use lawfare as China and Russia do.[94] This view holds that only by adopting the same unconventional and irregular methods as its rivals can the United States compete effectively with them. No, the United States should not use lawfare. If the United States were intentionally to misuse the rule of law and distort the legal basis of international treaties, it would undermine the foundation of trust and cooperation with its allies and partners—trust and cooperation that are essential to (if nothing else) success in protracted indirect competition. A comment from David Galula is apt here: "For him [the counterinsurgent] to adopt the insurgent's warfare would be the same as for a giant to try to fit into a dwarf's clothing."[95] Responding to lawfare with lawfare would be strategically simple—but also very wrong. Whatever a constraint refusal to fight like one's opponents may be, liberal democracies must not forget what they stand for and must not become what they are fighting against.

Coordinating with Allies and Commercial Partners

The last recommendation regarding methods to counter lawfare is to work with the global space community. The point has been made in previous chapters, but it is worth underscoring again here. Allies and partners are a U.S. advantage in strategic competition that should be capitalized on in response to such indirect approaches as lawfare. Allies who are signatories of treaties at issue are helpful for countering lawfare; collective and coordinated action by the international community is vital. The United States must proactively identify and promote actions that undermine competitors' attempts to employ lawfare in the space domain, and one of the best ways to do so is by working with allies and partners toward a common goal while upholding the rule of law. It is to be hoped that allies and partners will coordinate their efforts and remain vigilant for lawfare, especially in its early stages, and contribute to resolute counternarratives.

For its part, the United States must coordinate and synchronize with trusted commercial space entities. The commercial sector is critical to any broad strategy to counter lawfare, because most satellites in coming years will be commercial, not purely governmental, systems.[96] Hence, the United States should work with the commercial space sector to establish industry standards and day-to-day business practices that support the rules-based order and uphold—even, where appropriate, build on—the international legal regime. Commercial space enterprises will help shape future norms and perceptions of responsible behavior. In fact, the commercial space sector may become more influential in such ways than most countries' governments, much to the chagrin of their diplomats and some security experts.

Conclusion

Lawfare includes elements of "indirect approach" and a cumulative strategy, and policy makers and strategists may find developing suitable counterstrategies difficult and complex. Predictably, U.S. rivals use lawfare for precisely this reason. Countries like China and Russia may view lawfare in a variety of arenas as the best and cheapest way to oppose the United States and its extensive alliances and neutralize its technological advantages.

China has a documented history of lawfare, conspicuously so in the South China Sea. For this reason, the United States and its allies should expect to see China's use lawfare in the space domain. Indeed, China's political leaders appear to have no issue with misusing the law (if indeed they consider it "misuse") and upending the existing legal regimes.[97] If left unchecked, China's current use of lawfare will not only make its future access to and use of space easier but shape the international system to be supportive of its own long-term goals.[98] Lawfare in space, as in other domains, can enable China's political leadership, which is reinforcing its domestic control, to sustain an international order favorable to China's governance model, along with promoting its regional and global ambitions.

Because lawfare activities typically occur below the threshold of the use of force or hostile action, it can be difficult for American military planners to grapple with a suitable response. The nation's security experts and military leaders may even conclude that the lawfare "threat" does not warrant sustained and deliberate response. This thinking is dangerously wrong. If the target does nothing, a cumulative strategy works. The United States must develop and employ practical counterstrategies to lawfare before the damage cannot be undone. Because of lawfare's perceived effectiveness and the United States' difficulty in addressing it in a sustained way, lawfare and the practical ways to counter it are urgent subjects for consideration and debate now, and they will be for decades to come.

⟹ CHAPTER 6 ⟸

Commercial Companies, Privateers, and Space Pirates

Those who think the private military industry can be safely ignored, regulated, or categorically banned are too late.
—Sean McFate[1]

This chapter examines the role of commercial and quasi-commercial entities in competition and conflict in the space domain. This examination includes how the private space industry supports the ends of policy, potentially coercing a rival's calculations. Certainly, the commercial space sector will have the traditionally understood industry-centric objectives of increased market share, customer base, and profit margins. Also, government leaders may look to industry in a familiar manner: as enabling a technically educated workforce; increasing the gross domestic product; advancing technological innovation; and enhancing national prestige. However, commercial entities can also play a key role in irregular forms of competition and conflict in the space domain. Private entities and commercial companies providing paramilitary services are here to stay and will have roles in irregular space warfare.

As so often, there are few neat, tidy categories here, because commercial space activities can span the peace/conflict continuum, from benign presence, through coercive technology and capability demonstrations, to the use of force to compel acquiescence. Frequently, it is unclear whether or not these entities are acting in a traditional commercial sense, especially with respect to China's commercial sector and the American private military companies; how best to integrate commercial activities into the strategy of irregular space warfare is an open question.

Definitional issues regarding commercial space, proxies, private military companies, privateers, space pirates, and space militias are discussed in this chapter. It also examines the potential legal implications of blending governmental and commercial space capabilities and architectures in wartime, along with the long-term implications of whether or not space is defined as a global commons. These subjects are of ever-increasing importance as more and more states, organizations, and groups use commercial entities to advance political aims and even coerce others in the space domain.

The emerging commercial space ecosystem is opening new markets or expanding existing ones. In the last decade, commercial space activities have expanded significantly in both scale and diversity, resulting in new capabilities and services that take advantage of off-the-shelf technologies and lower barriers for market entry. These recent developments are contributing to a burgeoning space industry driven by entrepreneurial innovation and investment, advanced technology, and decreased costs. Governmental procurement professionals often seek to leverage these commercial developments as representing a faster, more responsive acquisition process than defense channels.

Furthermore, recent commercial advances raise questions as to which governmental missions and functions should be offloaded to space companies altogether. In the context of the U.S. military, national security space expert Doug Loverro observes that an understanding of recent commercial innovation "should inform not only which services can be commercialized, but can also be used to inform decisions on where the Space Force needs to focus its uniformed personnel versus relying on government civilian or contractor personnel."[2] Loverro believes that the U.S. Space Force must resolve clearly which space functions should be solely governmental and which functions can be shared or outsourced to commercial providers.

Many security professionals anticipate that entrepreneurial interest and investment in space companies will lead to significant changes in civil, military, and commercial use of and access to space. They consider commercial space innovation critical for developing novel ways of operating and of protecting national security interests that extend into space. For many, commercial space companies are a resource for achieving strategic and political objectives, and a relatively inexpensive one. Accordingly, commercial space companies will be instrumental in executing a strategy of irregular space warfare.

"Commercial": What Does That Mean?

Consensus on what is and is not a commercial space entity is currently elusive. That may surprise some security experts and analysts long familiar with that sector's pivotal role. But it is exactly this ambiguity that makes it especially valuable for irregular space warfare.

The U.S. and Western Perspective

Some consider a commercial activity one in which a private-sector entity risks its own capital and provides goods or services primarily to other private-sector entities or consumers instead of the government.[3] Examples of these entities would be providers of direct-to-home satellite television (e.g., DirecTV and DishTV), satellite radio (SiriusXM), and commercial satellites delivering Internet services (SpaceX's Starlink and OneWeb).[4]

From a U.S. policy perspective, determining what is and is not commercial typically has two dimensions. The first dimension is risk-taking—especially financial—by entities other than the government. Generally, at least some private capital must be at risk, or the company must sell to the private sector. The second dimension is the breadth of the customer base and the relationship between governmental and nongovernmental clients.[5] The 2020 U.S. National Space Policy defines *commercial* along these lines: "The term 'commercial,' for the purposes of this policy, refers to goods, services, or activities provided by private sector enterprises that bear a reasonable portion of the investment risk and responsibility for the activity, operate in accordance with typical market-based incentives for controlling cost and optimizing return on investment, and have the legal capacity to offer those goods or services to existing or potential nongovernmental customers."[6] This U.S. policy definition does include some ambiguous language, notably "reasonable portion of investment risk" and "typical market-based incentives." This lack of clarity likely resulted from an absence of any government-wide consensus that would support a more explicit statement. Also, it does not link commercial goods, services, and activities directly to space-based systems. The 2020 policy does establish, however, that *commercial* is best understood in the context of providing goods and services to nongovernmental customers.

Other, broader definitions of *commercial space* include entities that sell consumer equipment where the satellite constellation enabling the capability is government owned. An example of this arrangement is the Global Positioning System (GPS), a positioning, navigation, and timing satellite constellation owned and operated by the U.S. Space Force. Among its vast array of applications are automobile navigation, cell phones, and precision farming.[7] These devices are sold by commercial companies, but the satellite timing signal that makes them work is provided for free by the U.S. government.[8]

Another potential definition embraces capabilities and services provided by commercial entities primarily to governmental customers, such as the United Launch Alliance between Boeing and Lockheed Martin.[9] It is arguable, however, that these entities are not commercial, because they rely for most of their revenue on the government, which assumes the majority of the risk as the "anchor customer." Critics would call such entities *government contractors*.[10] The Space Foundation, a nonprofit space-industry advocacy group, makes a similar distinction in its definition of "commercial": "all space-related endeavors—including goods, services and activities—provided by private-sector enterprises with the legal capacity to offer their products to *nongovernmental customers*."[11] By the Space Foundation's definition, only companies that do not solely or primarily sell to or accrue revenue from governmental customers (such as the U.S. Department of Defense or the National Aeronautics and Space Administration) merit the label *commercial*.

Accordingly, the status of a given commercial actor may be unclear. Where doubt exists, especially in an American or Western context, the prefix *quasi-* is helpful. According to the Nasdaq stock exchange, a quasi-public corporation is operated privately and often traded publicly but is supported by the government.[12] The World Bank considers an arrangement whereby private-sector innovation and expertise delivers services needed by a government a "public-private-partnership" (PPP). These PPPs frequently leverage private finance and under the right circumstances can improve the provision of public services and facilitate economic growth.[13] For our purposes here, *quasi-commercial* denotes entities and activities that straddle the line between purely governmental and strictly nongovernmental actions, among them companies that operate in the private sector but also receive significant governmental backing.

The Chinese Perspective

Whatever "commercial space" might be in the West, a 2019 study by the Institute of Defense Analyses (IDA) explains that China's model, the state-owned enterprise (SOE), is different yet again. To date, nearly all of China's accomplishments in space have been achieved by the government, SOEs, or subsidiaries and suppliers. Historically, China's space industry has predominantly comprised SOEs controlled by central or provincial governments. Since 1999, two SOEs—the China Aerospace Science and Technology Corporation (CASC) and the China Aerospace Science and Industry Corporation (CASIC)—have had a near duopoly on launch and space technology in China, CASC being primary.[14]

In China, the IDA study suggests that what distinguishes a "commercial company" depends on whom one asks.[15] For example, many SOEs do business with the private sector, buying and selling goods and services from and to households and businesses. Of these, however, many prioritize state goals over making profit and do not face traditional market pressures—the government offsets any net losses.[16]

Ultimately, the study's authors define a Chinese commercial company as "an enterprise that is primarily operated in pursuit of profit, as opposed to an organization that prioritizes public policy goals over profits, even though it conducts commercial activities. Notably, this definition can include companies that are fully state-owned."[17] By this definition, China's space industry includes a variety of "players," from large SOEs and their subsidiaries to small, privately owned start-ups, all primarily motivated by the pursuit of profit. Some of these organizations—in particular, CASC, CASIC, and their subsidiaries—engage commercially, buying and selling goods and services, with the private sector.[18] At the time of the 2019 study, there were seventy-eight commercial space companies operating in China.[19] And more than half of them had been founded between

2014 and the 2019 study. The vast majority focus on satellite manufacturing and launch services. To a large extent, China seems to be following the American model, using government contracts and subsidies to give companies competitive advantages in the market.[20] China and the United States have in common strong linkages between their respective governments and commercial space sectors.

Chinese space companies may look private on paper, but they must acquiesce to government guidance and control and accept some degree of interference. It can be difficult for Chinese commercial entities to convince potential overseas and Western customers that they operate independently of governmental control and influence. The distinction between space companies that are truly private and those that are more or less state actors is still quite fuzzy, especially when the government is a frequent customer. "That could still lead to a lack of trust from other partners," explains China space scholar Namrata Goswami, and it does not help that the Chinese government is less than transparent about ownership and leadership within its national space programs.[21]

Throughout the remainder of this chapter, both commercial and quasi-commercial space entities will be mentioned to indicate the range of commercial entities' behavior and motivations, while acknowledging that different interpretations exist as to what constitutes "commercial." *Quasi-commercial* actors behave in some respect like commercial companies—such as seeking profit and increased market share—even though they may not operate in a purely commercial sense and may have noncommercial interests and relationships. Including both commercial and quasi-commercial space actors reflects the breadth of relevant capabilities and services available for irregular warfare and competition in space.

Commercial Space and Irregular Warfare Strategy

Commercial activities have significant places in irregular forms of competition and conflict in space. Strategy's function is balancing desired ends with available means, and commercial actors make means available. Both commercial and quasi-commercial actors support irregular warfare in primarily two ways: enabling indirect approaches by serving as proxies and creating asymmetric advantage with their novel capabilities.

Proxies and the Indirect Approach

As discussed in chapter 3, proxies are organizations, groups, and individuals that act on behalf of others. These third parties may intervene on behalf of a sponsor or benefactor to help influence events and achieve political aims. In the context of irregular forms of competition and conflict in space, commercial and quasi-commercial entities may act as surrogates for governments or other sponsoring organizations and groups. These sponsors may look to them for emerging technologies and capabilities useful for political objectives and strategic aims.

Furthermore, the use of commercial and quasi-commercial actors can relieve the sponsor from (possibly questionable) direct action. Commercial proxies allow sponsors to affect outcomes in competitions and conflicts in which they are engaged while being at arm's length and avoiding direct exposure to potential repercussions. Sponsors may use commercial proxies in irregular space warfare to make attribution of provocative or harmful actions more difficult, thereby ideally shielding themselves from responsibility and retribution.

The concept of commercial and quasi-commercial actors as alternates corresponds to the indirect approach as characterized by Liddell Hart—the idea of achieving positive results apart from direct, large force-on-force engagements.[22] As we have seen, through indirect approaches policy makers and military leaders can achieve greater operational success with fewer casualties.[23]

Liddell Hart never addresses the concept of commercial proxies per se, but the use of such surrogates is certainly in line with his thinking: a way for a government to help achieve political aims and military objectives without risking its own fighting forces. The commercial space sector's capabilities and services can help a sponsor throw an adversary off balance and achieve operational advantage, just as Liddell Hart recommends.[24] Examples would include paying commercial and quasi-commercial space services to shape public opinion about a competitor's actions, to conduct cyberattacks against a rival's space-enabled communications networks, or to run rendezvous and proximity operations (chapter 4) to coerce an adversary.

Buying Power and Creating Asymmetric Advantage

Fundamentally, by purchasing novel capabilities and services, sponsors of commercial proxies convert fiscal capital and economic power into other forms of power to achieve strategic effects. This is simply buying power.[25] A government, organization, or group not having its own capabilities to deter or compel (or the technological capacity to produce them) but possessing fiscal means can simply procure them.

By augmenting their access to and use of space by contracts or service agreements, sponsors avoid the costs of research and development: they pay only for specified commercial services. Contractual arrangements can give middle and emerging space powers access to greater capabilities than they might have had otherwise. Importantly, many commercial space capabilities and associated technologies are dual-use in nature, thereby causing useful ambiguity as to their implications. By procuring commercial technologies and services a state can lower its risks, gain dual-use capabilities, and achieve an operational advantage over a rival.[26] That advantage might also be asymmetric, one with potential to affect positively the strategic level of war or achieve strategic effect. A small amount of money can achieve big results. Commercial-enabled asymmetry uses fiscal means to create strength to exploit a rival's weakness and realize an advantage. Ultimately, the commercial-enabled asymmetric advantage exploits any imbalances in the competitive environment between rivals. To do so as part of a competitive strategy, sponsors of commercial proxies must first fully understand their own strengths and weaknesses relative to an opponent when seeking to create an asymmetric advantage. That is what competitive strategies do: they exploit one's own asymmetric advantages and the adversary's soft spots.

The use of commercial capabilities in competition and conflict is yet another manifestation of the irregular-warfare precept of "trying anything that might work" (chapter 2). There are several ways in which an entity might buy asymmetric advantage: entering into a service agreement for commercial satellite communications, with guaranteed availability throughout the peace/conflict continuum; purchasing commercial space-launch services, whether as the primary payload or a "rideshare"; procuring commercial on-orbit servicing and inspection capabilities; contracting for terrestrially based space situational-awareness services for detecting and tracking a competitor's spacecraft; contracting for active debris removal to respond to an uncooperative rival's defunct satellites; and acquiring commercial on-orbit, dual-use space capabilities to coerce a competitor.

Private Military Companies and Corporate Space Warriors

Commercial and quasi-commercial entities can directly support irregular space warfare, especially when coercion and force are being employed. This underlying concept is exemplified by today's routine use of private military companies, independent corporations offering training, logistical, security, and combat services to national governments, international organizations, and other actors.[27] Peter Singer, of the Washington, DC, think tank New America, calls these commercial entities "corporate warriors."[28] Terrestrially, the work of private military companies ranges from running small-scale training missions to fielding combat units of up to several hundred highly trained soldiers equipped with such heavy weapons as artillery and main battle tanks.[29]

The idea of private military forces is as old as warfare itself. Rulers of ancient Egypt and Rome used "armies for hire," or private forces, to supplement their imperial armies.[30] Even today, while a permanent, standing military may seem the norm, it is not. Armed forces of one's own can be ruinously expensive; renting them is much cheaper.[31]

As international security scholar Sean McFate explains, today's lexicon seeks to differentiate *private military companies* from the pejorative *mercenaries*: "There is no expert consensus on who exactly is a 'mercenary.' Those in the industry, their clients, and some outside experts spurn the 'M' word owing to the associated stigma, and give these private-sector fighters new labels: private military contractors, private security companies, private military companies, private security/military companies, private military firms, military service providers, operational contractors, and contingency contractors. Since the emergence of this new warrior class in the 1990s, volumes of academic ink have been spilt on differentiating them from mercenaries."[32] But, McFate notes, such expert labels are transitory: "There is no shining line between these categories, and it all depends on the individual warrior's will and market circumstances."[33] Frequently, academia overcomplicates already complex phenomena by imposing neat typologies, really helping no one.[34] It is exactly because private military companies are difficult to characterize—and because the recognition that private corporations routinely provide combat power is an uncomfortable one—that the topic is relevant for the strategy of irregular warfare in space.

Corporate space warriors should be expected to be conspicuous in irregular competition and conflict. However contentious a point that is for some policy makers and security experts, history documents it. Moreover, other governments and nonstate actors are imitating the private-military-company model, with the result that commoditized private force is turning into a global free-market sector.[35] States, organizations, and groups can outsource space capability, thereby buying plausible deniability by which to escape retaliation and international sanctions.[36] In general, corporate space warriors give sponsors the flexibility to adjust to complex and changing competitive environments, especially in irregular warfare.

More specifically, private military corporations can help support the strategy of irregular space warfare in primarily two ways. First, corporate space warriors may provide a coercive presence. Private space entities may serve the ends of policy through presence, proximity, and the perceived threat of force, especially because of the dual-use nature of much space technology. Private military companies' actions may be short of violence but significant for an irregular space warfare strategy. Corporate warriors providing dual-use, space-based capabilities may offer logistical services as well, such as active debris removal, refueling, and inspection. A current example of commercial space logistical support is Northrop Grumman's Mission Extension Vehicle, which docks with client satellites and uses its own thrusters and fuel supply to extend client satellites' operational lifetimes.[37] Second, whatever consternation and discomfort it may cause, private military companies may provide security and military services in, from, and through space. These services may involve the use of force: private military companies can be used to compel acquiescence. Furthermore, private military companies can play a part in complex strategies to exploit the gray zone between peace and war.

Privateers and Space Pirates

The purpose of using this catchy subhead is to underscore the fact that external third parties participate in irregular space warfare to confiscate property. Bleddyn Bowen warns, "Private property in space cannot be assumed [to be] immune to the effects of space warfare."[38] Maritime history offers valuable examples, and as has been argued throughout this book, shared strategic characteristics and considerations make it helpful for understanding irregular space warfare. Two aspects of naval irregular warfare are especially worthwhile here: privateers and pirates.

As briefly mentioned in chapter 3, privateers have been an enduring presence in naval warfare, including that of the American colonies and the early United States. The U.S. Constitution makes provision for privateers acting on behalf of the government: "The Congress shall have Power to . . . grant Letters of marque and reprisal."[39] Knowing that the early United States was not able to build and maintain a navy on a par with the sea powers of that day—like France, Great Britain, and Spain—the drafters wrote into the Constitution authority to commission the services of surrogates to achieve political and military objectives at sea.

In the Age of Sail, a "letter of marque and reprisal" from a government authorized a private person to operate as a privateer, attacking and capturing vessels of nations at war with the issuer. The privateer, that is, could legally pillage and take prizes (ships and their cargoes).[40] The privateer could take a prize before its own admiralty court, which would either take custody of the ship and cargo or transfer ownership to the privateer, who would probably sell it. A letter of marque and reprisal typically also included permission to cross an international border to conduct a reprisal, some action in response to an attack or injury.

Functionally related to privateers—but quite distinct from them—are pirates. The distinction, as Benjamin Armstrong explains, involved legal views on private property and neutral rights.[41] The American perspective was that a ship sailing under the flag of a neutral nation (such as the United States in those years) was inviolable, and likewise its cargo (see the law of neutrality discussion in chapter 5). Such countries as France, Great Britain, and Spain predictably held an opposing view: it was the ownership of the cargo and the cargo's destination that determined whether a ship was neutral or not. If the cargo was wartime contraband consigned to a foreign port, these European sea powers claimed for their own navies and privateers a legal right to seize it and the ship that carried it. From the American view it followed that privateers had no right to attack ships sailing under the U.S. flag, because such ships were neutral regardless of where their cargoes were bound. Any ship committing such an "outrage," the United States argued, should be considered a pirate instead of a privateer, even if it had a privateering commission.[42]

Pirates are more generally understood as persons at sea who, acting outside the law, robbed shipping for their own personal gain. The label of piracy can be applied to a wide-range of maritime misbehavior and unlawful action, including coastal raiding, robbery, kidnapping, and murder. Different names have been applied to pirates in various parts of the world, such as "corsairs" in the Mediterranean and "buccaneers" in the Caribbean.[43]

Given the lessons of historical experience, irregular space warfare should be expected to involve third parties, whether acting within the law or outside it. *Space privateers* pillage and take prizes legally, on the authority and on the behalf of a government, benefactor, or sponsor. The antiquated letter of marque and reprisal may not be useful in space in the future, but other, equally effective legal instruments are available. They include governmental licensing, contracting, and regulatory frameworks by which the services of third parties, whether companies or individuals, are employed or procured to raid, pillage, and take prizes on the licensor's behalf. In contrast, *space pirates* act outside of the law and rules-based order with no commission to commit nefarious, malicious, and unlawful acts against space capabilities, services, property, or architectures.

History suggests that rivals and belligerents will heatedly disagree as to the legalities, arguing from perspectives shaped by who is using privateers and who is being negatively affected by them. Nevertheless, space privateers and pirates and the spacecraft and space effects they use can help achieve political aims and military objectives through presence, coercion, force, and cyberattack.

Space Militias

Militias are relevant to irregular space warfare. While the concept of a militia—a body of civilians organized for military service—is similar in some respects to those of privateers and space pirates, militias and their use have a separate context, knowledge of which is helpful to understanding competition and conflict in space. Part of the effectiveness and appeal of militias is that they operate under the rubric of the indirect approach and can create asymmetric advantage by virtue of participation by a large number of citizens. If incorporated into a holistic strategy, militias may play a significant irregular role, which is part of a comprehensive approach to resisting a competitor's access to and use of space.

China's existing fishermen militia is an illustrative example of the concept. Countries in Southeast Asia have grown increasingly wary of China's coercive and aggressive actions in the South China Sea, particularly its maritime militia. For several years, the tension between China and Filipino fishermen in the Scarborough Shoal, as already mentioned, is contributing to instability in the South China Sea. China's maritime militia has acted in an unprofessional and escalatory manner to keep Filipino fishermen from reaching their fishing grounds and deter attempts to do so.[44] The maritime militia (detailed in chapter 5) acts as a proxy for the Chinese Communist Party, promoting its agenda in the South China Sea.

Space is not the sea. Therefore, it is best not to overstate any apparent parallels between China's maritime militia and a similar operation in the space domain. Certainly, there are not presently widespread private citizens working in space. While certain analogous aspects of maritime and space domains could be unscrupulously exaggerated, the fundamental idea and applicability of militias nonetheless applies in a strategic sense. Private citizens can work as proxies for their government to achieve political aims and military objectives; thus, private citizens can actively impact space and nonspace domains. In the near term, *space militias* are bodies of citizens organized for (but not formally enlisted into) military service, who, themselves predominantly not in space, negatively affect competitors' access to and use of space. Space militias may seek to deny a competitor's space-enabled communication and services through militia action on Earth denying a rival's access to its space architectures, networks, and ground segments. This idea of space militias is similar to the early 2022 actions of the Ukrainian "volunteer cyber army," civilians who defended their country by means of denial-of-service attacks against Russian networks.[45] When not acting in an aggressive manner, space militias may operate legally and peacefully, such as in coordinated and nonviolent demonstrations against a competitor's space-related activities. Space militias might obstruct the competitor's launches with large protests in launch safety areas—whether on land, at sea, or in the air. This tactic can diminish and hinder a competitor's command of space (if it had achieved that) and its overall effectiveness in the space domain.

Space militias should be part of a holistic strategy that allows for achieving military effects through private citizens' actions. If coordinated and synchronized as part of the overall plan for achieving political aims and military objectives, space militia capabilities and activities can improve the quality and performance of a government's overall military endeavors. Space militias hold the promise of providing exponentially more military effect than traditional fighting forces alone to promote a government's freedom of action and security.

Hybrid Space Architectures and Their Potential Downsides

The commercial space sector has advanced considerably, moving rapidly to provide robust and proliferated capabilities on-orbit, and some governments and defense agencies—like those in the United States—are blending governmental and commercial architectures. They see the commercial sector as a source of both cost savings and innovative capabilities. It would be foolish, so the thinking goes, not to take advantage of it, in part by incorporating commercial capabilities into government space architectures.

The U.S. Space Force's Space Capstone (that is, foundational) Doctrine describes a *space system architecture* as the space, terrestrial, and link segments that enable space capabilities and services.[46] First, the space segment consists of spacecraft in orbit beyond Earth's atmosphere, *spacecraft* being either remotely piloted, crewed, or autonomous. Second, the terrestrial segment encompasses all equipment on the ground required to operate spacecraft: control stations, antennas, tracking stations, launch sites, launch platforms, and user equipment. Third, the link segment comprises the electromagnetic spectrum and associated communication signals that connect the terrestrial and orbital segments. *Uplink* signals transmit data from Earth to spacecraft, *downlink* signals transmit data from a spacecraft to Earth, and *crosslink* signals transmit data from one spacecraft to another.[47]

Some space professionals view the interleaving of governmental and commercial architectures as dramatically improving deterrence and resilience.[48] In this view, deterrence is improved by distributing risk throughout proliferated and disaggregated capabilities across various orbital regimes.[49] Further, integration of governmental and commercial space architectures offers greater diversity of capabilities and services, reducing the inherent vulnerability of small numbers of exquisite governmental satellites.[50] Incorporating the commercial sector's rapid innovation cycle, novel technical capabilities, proliferated satellites, and diverse orbital regimes potentially means asymmetric advantage and at significant cost savings.[51]

Hybrid Space Architectures

As used here, *hybrid space architecture* is the intermingling of governmental and commercial capabilities and services across the space, terrestrial, and link segments. Hybrid space architectures frequently mix small constellations of large, exquisite, and expensive governmental satellites with large constellations of smaller, less costly commercial satellites, spanning various orbital regimes.[52] There are other definitions. In the view of NewSpace New Mexico, for example, "the Hybrid Space Architecture is the integration of emergent 'new space' smallsat capabilities with traditional US Government space systems."[53] Commercial space advocate Chuck Beames considers hybrid space architecture as the optimal way to operate old and new space technologies as an integrated whole to support military, civilian, and intelligence needs:[54] "There is not a lot of detail yet as to what precisely constitutes these hybrid space architectures or how they will work, but it is abundantly clear why they are necessary. With near parity in space competence and capability arising quickly worldwide, our government must no longer compete against, but instead harvest the innovations from the new commercial space sector. By integrating small, commercial space technologies, we can accomplish this and provide strength in numbers by mitigating vulnerabilities inherent in relying on a very small number of very expensive systems."[55]

In general, in a hybrid space architecture, governmental and commercial constellations work in an integrated fashion, forming a whole more effective and efficient than its individual parts. A substantial number of American national-security experts see overhauling the current space architecture into a hybrid design as offering the prospect of integrating the best of commercial and government capabilities and investments.[56]

For U.S. defense community leaders, moving toward a hybrid space architecture is vital. Gen. John Raymond, U.S. Space Force (USSF), commented when he was chief of space operations, "What we're looking at is to develop not a one size fits all, but a hybrid architecture, with large and small [spacecraft] so you don't have a vulnerability."[57] The Space Force wants to diversify its satellite architecture, like personal finances, "where you diversify your financial portfolio so you don't go broke if one stock takes a tumble."[58] Raymond sees other advantages as well: "If you go to a more proliferated architecture, rather than the handful of exquisite capabilities, you then open the opportunities for more commercial collaboration and you open opportunities for more collaboration with our allies and partners."[59] For example, a future architecture for space-based communications may include both exquisite and mass-produced satellites—that is, both high-end and low-end capabilities.[60] Hybrid architectures also hold promise for remote sensing. In comparison to high-demand, low-density government-owned satellites, commercial sensing satellites offer orders of magnitude more coverage and higher revisit rates (i.e., over the same point on Earth). They can augment and cue the capabilities of government-owned and -operated systems.

Potential Legal Implications

The intermingling of governmental and commercial space architecture for irregular competition and conflict, however, raises legal questions that must be fully considered and mitigated. The questions relate specifically to "targeting" and "distinction." Space policy analyst Robin Dickey warns that "in war, commercial actors can become strategic targets of combatants. This scenario applies to both commercial actors that are providing support to militaries, which could be valid military targets under the Law of Armed Conflict, and to those that are not."[61] The intermingling of military and civilian space activities can blur the line between civilian and military property and could lead some to construe commercial or civilian systems as legitimate military targets.[62]

One of the underpinnings of the law of armed conflict is the principle of *lawful targeting*, within which lies the principle of *distinction*. Lawful targeting requires that all "reasonable precautions" be taken to ensure that only military objectives are fired on, so that noncombatants, civilians, and civilian objects are spared as much as possible from the ravages of war.[63] Undergirding, in turn, this principle is the requirement that distinctions be made between combatants and noncombatants, so as, again, to spare the latter as much as possible. That is, lawful targeting is meant to minimize damage to civilian objects (collateral damage) or death and injury to civilians (incidental injury).[64] *Military objectives* are combatants and objects that, by their nature, location, purpose, or use effectively contribute to the enemy's war-fighting or war-sustaining capability. Obversely, civilians and civilian objects may not be made objects of attack. *Civilian objects* comprise all civilian property and activities not supporting or sustaining war-fighting capability.

The principles of targeting and distinction have implications for the use of commercial spacecraft in armed conflict. Legal scholar David Koplow argues that blurring the distinctions between civilian and military space systems and architectures poses serious issues for commercial customers and foreign nations.[65] Koplow explains, "This intermingling runs afoul of one of the most central requirements of the traditional law of armed conflict: the principle of distinction (or discrimination), which mandates that in combat, states may lawfully direct their attacks only against military objectives, not against civilians or their property."[66] Moreover, he points to an important corollary, "reverse distinction," which requires a state to separate its military assets from civilian objects to the extent feasible. This precaution aims, once again, to spare civilians and their property from the ravages of warfare by enabling an adversary to identify them and attack only military targets.[67] Reverse distinction is a somewhat "soft" obligation, as Koplow puts it; this duty is not absolute. For practical purposes parties are committed only to make the best efforts to separate military and civilian assets, and to the "maximum extent" feasible.[68]

An alternate viewpoint is that of legal scholar Charles Dunlap.[69] Dunlap explains that determining if something is "feasible" can properly take account cost and practicality. Conformance to the reverse-distinction corollary might be infeasible: "In theory, a government might be able to create a separate road system, electrical grid, petroleum refineries, internet, and so forth for its armed forces. However, doing so for such major infrastructure and systems that serve both civilian and military needs would be so enormously costly as to be impractical."[70]

The blending of commercial and governmental space capabilities is here to stay, and the concept of hybrid space architectures should be expected to become a normal part of how space capabilities and services are provided. Questions about how to reconcile space warfare with the law of armed conflict and the principles of targeting and distinction are important with respect to hybrid architectures. Policy makers and space strategists will need to consider how best to target military objects and discriminate between commercial and military systems and infrastructure. In cases involving hybrid space architectures, such consideration will need to include how to target specifically the adversary's military spacecraft and not negatively affect commercial capabilities. In cases when hybrid architectures include governmental *hosted payloads*—transponders, instruments, or other items occupying available space in commercial satellites—military planners and "targeteers" may need to attack a particular military subsystem or capability on a satellite that also includes nonmilitary components and functions.[71] Reversible, nonkinetic military effects may be the best choice. Distinctions need also to be made between military and nonmilitary users of the electromagnetic spectrum, such as when jamming and interfering with a rival's communication in a frequency spectrum that is used for both military and nonmilitary purposes.

To David Koplow's argument with respect to the potential obligations of defenders—or his "reverse distinction" corollary—states utilizing hybrid architectures should consider measures to minimize the likelihood or potential impact of an adversary targeting its dual-use capabilities. For example, states could limit the types of support provided by dual-use commercial capabilities in armed conflict, perhaps reserving commercial space services for baseline Earth observation and noncombat satellite communications, as opposed to direct, terrestrial targeting and fire control.[72] Such measures may be prudent, even if not strictly obligated as a matter of law. A lesson for American policy makers and military leaders (one taught all too often) is that they should consider these matters in peacetime and not in the chaos of combat.

Misinterpretation of Space as a Global Commons

This section describes some of the legal questions and implications resulting from the ill-advised advocacy of space as a global commons. While chapter 5 discussed lawfare—or the intentional distortion and misuse of legal regimes—here we address the unintentional self-inflicted harm done under the mistaken assumption that space is a global commons. The issue has implications regarding the fair and equitable use of space resources. In general, *global commons* refers to either physical or virtual areas where resources are shared at the international level. Examples are Antarctica, the high seas, and more recently cyberspace.[73] Because the preponderance of future space capabilities and services will be commercial in nature, the issue of space as a global commons is best examined here, along with commercial and quasi-commercial activity. The argument will be made that considering space to be global commons is wrong and such a determination would have a detrimental impact on the long-term success of commercial companies and on the U.S. competitive advantage.

Differing Interpretations

American policy on the topic has been inconsistent in recent years. For example, the 2010 National Security Strategy under the Obama administration declared that space is a global commons: "Safeguarding the Global Commons: Across the globe, we must work in concert with allies and partners to optimize the use of shared sea, air, and *space* domains. These shared areas, which exist outside exclusive national jurisdictions, are the connective tissue around our globe upon which all nations' security and prosperity depend."[74] According to advocates like L. A. Fisk of the non-governmental Committee on Space Research, "We thus need to recognize, encourage, and enable space as a global commons. A 'commons' in the English language is a piece of land owned by and used by all members of a community, as in a pasture used by all residents of a village. Many nations of the world view space as a global commons, a resource not owned by any one nation but crucial to the future of all humankind."[75]

During the Trump administration, the opposite view was taken. The White House issued Executive Order 13914 in April 2020 stating that "the United States does not view [space] as a global commons."[76] This statement agreed with language in a 2018 bill in Congress, "Notwithstanding any other provision of law, outer space shall not be considered a global commons."[77] Scott Pace, who spearheaded the development of space policy during the Trump administration, says emphatically, "Global commons as applied to space is bad law, bad diplomacy, bad economics, and bad politics."[78] Speaking in 2017 to a conference audience, he elaborated:

> Finally, many of you have heard me say this before, but it bears repeating: outer space is not a "global commons," not the "common heritage of mankind," not "*res communis*," nor is it a public good. These concepts are not part of the Outer Space Treaty, and the United States has consistently taken the position that these ideas do not describe the legal status of outer space. To quote again from a U.S. statement at the 2017 COPUOS [sixtieth session of the Committee on the Peaceful Uses of Outer Space] Legal Subcommittee, reference to these concepts is more distracting than it is helpful. To unlock the promise of space, to expand the economic sphere of human activity beyond the Earth, requires that we not constrain ourselves with legal constructs that do not apply in space.[79]

Sometimes American policy makers or security experts advocate "global commons" language in a conceptual rather than legal sense, but loose usage only increases the likelihood of confusion, especially in matters outside the American purview. The phrase should not be used to signal a general interest in deepening international cooperation with respect to certain domains; better choices for expressing such ideals, phrases without adverse connotations, would be "common interests" or "shared interests."[80]

Space is in actuality a domain without a government. Henry Hertzfeld, Brian Weeden, and Christopher Johnson took up this line of reasoning in a 2015 conference presentation examining possible legal bases for viewing space as a global commons. They recalled Article I of the 1967 Outer Space Treaty, which says, "The exploration and use of outer space, including the moon and other celestial bodies, shall be carried out for the benefit and in the interests of all countries, irrespective of their degree of economic and scientific development, and shall be the province of all mankind."[81] The three authors explain that the Outer Space Treaty's phrase "province of all mankind," in light of the rights and obligations enshrined elsewhere in Article I and across the treaty, lays down simply that the *activity* of exploring and using outer space is a right held by all and that no state can lawfully deny another state's freedom to do so.[82] That is, it is not the physical domain of outer space itself that is the province of all mankind but its exploration and use. The three authors observe pointedly, "All too often, commentators and pundits remark that outer space itself belongs to everyone. It is in fact just the opposite. Space itself belongs to no one and the right to access, explore, and use space is granted to everyone."[83] Because the Outer Space Treaty has been ratified or signed by all spacefaring nations, this provision is often regarded as customary international law. Under it, all countries around the world (and by inference, all peoples) enjoy the privilege of exploring and using outer space. Even if all states regarded outer space as a "commons," it would be a very different sort of commons from any that has been established in the past. It would be one with no real legal precedent, no true means of oversight or enforcement. That concept has been applied properly to territories or oceans of the Earth in many ways: it should not be applied to space.[84]

Negative Impact on the Commercial Space Sector

However attractive a metaphor, global commons in space is legally problematic in connections beyond the intentions of the Outer Space Treaty. It creates international misunderstandings and increases tension. For example, if space is a global commons, countries might infer that they get to tell other countries—like the United States and its commercially licensed companies—what to do or not do outside of written or customary international law. While space often may be viewed as a resource not owned by any nation, as explained above, "space as a global *commons*" means the opposite—that the domain belongs to everyone and that access to the area and its resources should be regulated only internationally.

Indeed, promulgating a view of space as a global commons will have significant downsides, including for the operations and profitability of commercial space companies. Advocates of space as a global commons could argue that any economic and monetary gains coming from resource extraction on the Moon or other celestial bodies belongs, like space, to everyone. Companies and countries operating in such a regime could realize little financial benefit and endure many constraints through the erosion of national sovereignty.[85] Failure to reach a common understanding of ownership rights versus enterprise rights with regard to commercial utilization and resource extraction could delay companies from advancing the technology for exploration and human space activity. Chronic debate and international disagreement could put commercial space in the false position of falling outside the law. The resulting negative effect on commercial space companies would redound against U.S. strategic advantage. Ultimately, the coexistence of different international understandings of the law in this matter can not only create uncertainty in relation to commercial space undertakings but more broadly impede the expansion of the economic sphere of human activity beyond the Earth.

Conclusion

Commercial and quasi-commercial entities can collectively play a key role in irregular forms of competition and conflict in the space domain, primarily in two ways: supporting an indirect approach and creating an asymmetric advantage. First, the commercial space sector is an alternative to military force for coercing others, which is a fundamental element of the indirect approach. Economically well-off sponsors and benefactors can purchase the services of commercial proxies to further policy aims and achieve military objectives. By acting as a proxy or third party, a commercial entity can, at a sponsor's bidding, coerce a competitor into not pursuing a certain course of action or to cease one. Second, the innovative capabilities that firms bring—which they routinely generate more quickly than many governments—can create an asymmetric advantage to be exploited in irregular space warfare. Because of these benefits, policy makers and military leaders will want to integrate and synchronize commercial space activities into their strategies and operational art of war.

Lastly, commercial entities can operate in a nontraditional manner, which makes some policy makers uncomfortable when they appear to be quasi-governmental in nature. This would be so in the case of private military companies providing security and military services on behalf of a government sponsor. Also, private citizens—whether acting as privateers or part of space militias—can directly support a government's political and military objectives. The blending of governmental and commercial roles and capabilities may raise legal questions regarding how best to discriminate between military and nonmilitary objects in conflict, and these questions must be debated and resolved well before the onset of hostilities.

≡ CHAPTER 7 ≡

Exploiting Space Technologies for Asymmetric Advantage

Technology is only as effective as the strategy it serves.
—Thomas Mahnken[1]

Warfare is both art and science. Much of this book has focused on the "art" aspect of space warfare, or the intangible features of conflict and competition. While creativity and human intuition are definitely important given the nature of war, warfare has strong scientific and technological dimensions, especially in the space domain. Consequently, this chapter examines the foundational reasons for and considerations of using technologies during irregular conflict and competition in the space domain.

In particular, this chapter details why space technologies might be used to achieve an asymmetric advantage—that is, to realize a benefit by using one's strengths against a rival's relative weakness. This examination also includes China's exploitation of innovative space technologies and the implications of dual-use space technologies. Furthermore, this chapter explains the potential unintended consequences of innovative space technologies in the context of international-relations theory, such as creating power imbalances among competitors and causing international instability generally. Lastly, this chapter highlights that a sound space strategy must guide the effective and efficient use of technology.

There is a danger here, given the rapidity of innovation and the fact that the future is unknowable in any meaningful and detailed way. It is vital to elucidate current and future competitive strategies beyond the latest "hot" space capabilities, neatly acronymic defense jargon, and fashionable buzzwords. While detailed analysis of today's popularized technologies—such as artificial intelligence, autonomy, hypersonic weapons, and proliferated low-Earth-orbit satellites—may be helpful in the short term, its utility diminishes rapidly as innovation marches ever onward.[2] As a result, this chapter will take a measured view of the technology, seeking to leave the space strategist with a sense of what it all means—that is, to answer the ever-present "So what?"

Indeed, there is a balance to be struck.[3] Thomas Mahnken, president and chief executive officer of the Center for Strategic and Budgetary Assessments, speaks to that balance: "If the enthusiasts are guilty of hyping technology, the skeptics have all too often discounted the role of technology in war. Although technology is not the only—or necessarily the most important—determinant of success, its effects should not be ignored."[4] Michael Handel offers a similar caution: that the point "is not . . . that technology is unimportant. It is simply . . . to remind us that technology, while of the greatest importance, is still only the *means*; as such, it is always secondary to the political and strategic non-material dimensions of war. Thus, technology and material victories are inseparable from the political and 'strategic' dimensions, but in the final analysis they are at best only a necessary but rarely sufficient condition for a final and complete victory."[5] A balanced understanding of technology's impact will lead to more complete space strategies and suggest better operational concepts for the space domain.

Novel Technologies

Novel advanced technologies can create asymmetric advantage between belligerents. Their employment has been an enduring part of both regular and irregular styles of warfare, but especially the latter, when one competitor is less capable than the other. A less-capable space power will seek any possible advantage, and the purpose of exploiting innovative technologies is just that, to nullify enemy advantages. Because the task of less-advantaged space strategists is to alter the military balance to their benefit, they are likely to turn to novel technologies and weapons of war. As we saw in earlier chapters, the lesser belligerent will likely eschew regular, conventional styles of warfare in favor of irregular modes where a technological edge can yield maximum benefit. For many space powers, the allure of finding a single, dominant technological war-fighting advantage will be just too great to resist.

Again, maritime history is illustrative of the relationships here. For example, torpedoes eventually became operationally effective, but only after early failures and then evolutionary improvement.[6] Employing weapons technology without fully understanding its utility can result in failure. The lesson is that new technology does not necessarily bring success, either tactically or operationally. Maritime experience also suggests that irregular warfare can be the impetus to test novel technologies. Benjamin Armstrong explains, "Early innovations with steam power and undersea warfare demonstrated how irregular operations offered an opportunity for early adoption of new and disruptive [i.e., transformative] naval technology."[7] Still, while innovation and disruptive technologies make important contributions during irregular warfare, sometimes change comes as evolution rather than transformation, and one should not expect too much too soon.[8]

It is helpful to think of technology's utility in terms of strategic effect. Technology and its applications are meaningless in a strategic sense apart from the effects achieved and outcomes realized at the strategic level of war. It is too often believed that superior technology is always the answer without understanding what the question is—How will the war's outcome be affected? Bigger, faster, and higher are seen as the ultimate criteria for technological success, but only in a world of unreality.[9] The strategic effect is determined by the target and not by the means of attack. Therefore, whether strategic effect is achieved or not is determined not by advanced technologies in themselves but by how they are used and how, if at all, the adversary's decision calculus is affected. Strategic effect—the common currency of military behavior and action—is ultimately generated by fortitude, blood, and treasure.[10]

An important side effect of successful advanced technology can be the dramatic improvement of the morale of fighting forces. Historian Jeremy Black explains, "Providing troops with better arms than their opponents not only enhances their effectiveness but also their morale, a point that is frequently ignored."[11] A strategy for irregular space warfare must embrace the centrality of human activity—warfare is primarily a human activity with a technological context, and not vice versa.[12] Advanced technologies can create a sense in a polity and its armed forces that the adversary can be beaten, encouraging them to envision victory and, in this context, carry out space operations that previously seemed unrealistic. Technological success in combat can beget further success and improve morale in the space domain as much as elsewhere. Many irregular wars have been won or lost in the minds of not only the militaries but the polities involved, and irregular space wars will probably be as well.[13] After all, victory or defeat in irregular space warfare will hinge on the beliefs, attitudes, and behavior of the public.

Creating New Operational Concepts

When innovations are first incorporated by armed forces, the primary benefit comes in the form of improved tactics, techniques, and procedures. Technological applications are most closely coupled with the tactical level of warfare. These improvements are significant and laudable, but much more is needed to produce a notable and positive effect on a war's outcome. One such need is new operational concepts.

Technological innovation is especially powerful if it leads to new operational concepts and organizational adaptations. In turn, those concepts and styles can lead to more efficient and effective employment of military forces to achieve political aims. As was true in Clausewitz's time, styles of warfare vary with the "spirit of the age," and warfare's character changes continually.[14] It is frequently the case that new operational concepts and styles of warfare are evolutionary rather than immediately transformative, meaning that trial and error—and certainly time—will be needed to understand how best to exploit them.

Although it is difficult to predict which future technologies will be incorporated into new operational concepts of irregular space warfare, it is safe to suggest some general areas. Liddell Hart writes emphatically, "Of all qualities of war it is speed which is dominant, speed of both mind and movement."[15] Accordingly, space-related technologies will be used to make decisions more quickly and to improve the lethality of space forces. Space forces will exploit technology-enabled asymmetric advantage to create and hold the initiative, along with improving intelligence collection and deception capabilities. Other examples are improved space domain awareness and space attribution (see chapter 8); faster decision-making processes, frameworks, and infrastructure; quicker responses to emergent threats; greater mobility and maneuverability of spacecraft; and improved range and precision of offensive space effects, whether kinetic or nonkinetic. Future irregular space warfare will mean incorporating technologies that improve information sharing with allies and trusted commercial partners and confidence in one's data and information. Less-capable space forces will use technology to weaken larger, stronger adversaries through attacks against exposed and vulnerable CLOCs, in the hopes of weakening the adversary and protracting the conflict.

Furthermore, operational concepts of irregular space warfare will often seek to offset an adversary's numerical preponderance in forces and systems with asymmetric advantages created through novel technologies. Stephen Biddle explains how the traditional military benefit of quantity is being diminished: "Increasing lethal technology has been progressively eroding the military utility of numerical preponderance, reducing superior actors' ability to bring their numbers to bear on the battlefield."[16] Smaller and less-capable space actors, out of scarcity of resources, will want to find creative ways to adopt technology to overcome, or at least offset, the advantages that a well-resourced opponent might have.

Any operational advantages from novel technologies may not be truly realized until organizational, bureaucratic, training, and educational changes are implemented. Former U.S. deputy secretary of defense Bob Work writes to the effect that technology alone is never the definitive answer—one has to incorporate it into new operational and organizational constructs.[17] New styles of space warfare will need to integrate innovative space technologies, military doctrine, education, and space operational concepts into a holistic strategy.

But even all that is not enough; meaningful change comes from abandoning outdated and ineffective concepts and styles, discontinuing obsolete behaviors and actions. Because personnel and fiscal resources—along with training and education opportunities—are limited, obsolete and ineffective operational concepts must be discarded as soon as possible to make room for new ones that address the changing character of space warfare. For whatever reasons—ones that impact space professionals and legacy acquisition programs—military services find it difficult to incorporate institutional and organizational changes that bring the abandonment of past ways. Space forces must be self-aware of this reluctance and seek out ways to fight institutional and bureaucratic resistance within their own structures to further helpful change.

Commercial Innovation for Competitive Advantage

Rapid technological developments in the commercial space sector are seen as a way to improve a country's competitiveness by creating an asymmetric advantage during competition and conflict. Indeed, innovation in the commercial space sector has expanded significantly in recent years, resulting in new capabilities and services that capitalize on commoditized, off-the-shelf technologies, and lower barriers for market entry.[18] The commercial space sector is leading the way in fielding innovative technologies and expanding potential markets. Current commercial space developments are being driven by entrepreneurs, venture capital, technological innovation, and decreased costs.[19]

Governmental decision makers are seeking to leverage these commercial developments, which present opportunities for gaining new capabilities more quickly. The U.S. Space Force planning guidance states that commercial technological innovation and competitive advantage "are also required of America's Space Force, and we will take industry's best practices, tools and benchmarks to create similar agility in military space development and operations."[20] Policy makers and military leaders seek to utilize novel commercial technologies when practical. In particular, commercial innovation in space technologies is acknowledged as being critical for national security interests extending into space.

A notable area of technological innovation is the commercial launch sector, which today is developing multiple new space launch vehicles across a range of payload classes—small to heavy lift. This development is international in scope, involves established and new launch providers, and is driven by both government and commercial demand to place larger constellations of satellites in orbit.[21] Many commercial launch providers are lowering launch costs and increasing competitiveness. Across the industry, the launch price per kilogram decreased 34 percent from 2011 to 2020.[22] Large and small launch vehicles are also enabling increased access to space for smaller satellites through expanded rideshare initiatives.

Additionally, advances in the commercial space sector are creating several markets, including on-orbit servicing and space domain awareness. Both established space companies and venture-backed start-ups are fielding capabilities for on-orbit servicing to extend the life of, repair, augment, and actively deorbit spacecraft. Several companies are seeking to advance in-space transportation through satellite delivery to custom and specific orbits.[23] Companies in the space domain awareness industry are developing ground- and space-based sensing capabilities for better tracking, cataloging, and prediction of activities in space. Such dramatic improvements are expected to continue bringing new space capabilities and services, technologies, and applications to market. Policy makers and military leaders will desire to take advantage of all this.

China's Space Industry and Technological Innovation

China's central government views both technological innovation and its application to be critical parts of its unified plan to advance the country's goals. In the expansion of its space industry, as with many of its policies and strategies, China adopts a holistic approach. The Chinese government seeks to mobilize and guide different sectors to take part and then coordinates their contributions under an overall plan. The space industry serves major Chinese strategic needs, and the central government pays special attention to the development and use of cutting-edge space technologies.

The intensity of that attention is evident in a January 2022 PRC white paper, *China's Space Program*.[24] The white paper discusses China's space achievements since 2016 and lays out its main objectives for the five years following 2021, in order "to help the international community better understand China's space industry."[25] *China's Space Program* declares that technology will play a greater role in promoting and guiding space science applications and that the quality and overall performance of China's space industry will be raised. The "space industry around the world has entered a new stage of rapid development and profound transformation that will have a major and far-reaching impact on human society. At this new historical start towards a modern socialist country, China will accelerate work on its space industry."[26]

Indeed, technological innovation undergirds China's space industry, and for this reason experimentation will be particularly important in the next five years. *China's Space Program* reports that innovation in space technology has helped traditional Chinese industries transform and upgrade themselves and has supported emerging industries in new energy, new materials, smart agriculture, autonomous driving, and environmental protection.[27] These space-related technological innovations are contributing to China's growing strengths generally in science and technology, manufacturing, cyberspace, and transportation.

During the next five years China plans in-orbit tests of and experimentation with new space materials, systems, and operational concepts: in particular, early warning services, self-management of spacecraft and autonomous collision avoidance, space mission–extension vehicles, propulsion, in-orbit servicing and maintenance, space-debris monitoring and clearing (i.e., active debris removal), and survivability of spacecraft.[28]

China is pursuing a holistic national plan for innovation as such, and the commercial space sector will have an important place in it. The relevance of space applications for governments, state-owned enterprises, and individuals is expanding. As the white paper puts it, "A group of competitive commercial space enterprises are emerging and realizing industrialized large-scale operation."[29] A variety of space-enabled products and services, such as satellite remote-sensing data, are improving transport, e-commerce, trade in agricultural products, assessment of losses and insurance claims after natural disasters, and the registration of real estate.

As always, the Chinese central government will establish and maintain strict guidelines on the commercializing of its space industry, tightly controlling what is and is not permitted. The central government will oversee and expand the procurement of space products and services, grant relevant state-owned enterprises access and sharing rights to major scientific research facilities and equipment, and support Chinese enterprises involved in the research and development of major engineering initiatives. Additionally, the central government will formally prohibit certain actions regarding market access to "ensure fair competition and the orderly entry and exit of participating enterprises."[30]

Dual-Use Technologies and Associated Risks

National security analysts have for some time perceived risks in technological innovation—that is, potential hazards, threats, challenges, and barriers that could be posed for space security. One perceived risk is the dual-use nature of many space technologies, in, for instance, satellite servicing and debris removal. In fact, some security analysts argue, there are difficulties in discriminating between purely military and commercial endeavors. Satellite-servicing systems capable of maneuver, rendezvous and proximity operations, and grappling have the potential, whatever their ostensible purposes, to inspect, disable, degrade, or destroy another satellite.[31] Technology historian Aaron Bateman explains that "the same techniques for benign proximity operations can be used to carry out observation of other countries' satellites or to attack them."[32] Finally, some security analysts warn of the risk to national security arising from the fact that antisatellite development, testing, and deployment could plausibly masquerade as peaceful and nonthreatening.[33]

The dual-use ambiguity inherent in these technologies could even lead to unintended escalations. Analysts theorize that decision makers would be unsure to whom systems belonged or were being leased.[34] Especially among China, Russia, and the United States, there is a particular risk of misperception in connection with contract satellite servicing or debris removal.[35] Problems can arise when commercial systems are not protected to the same extent as military systems. Yet government leaders often have no option but to integrate commercial capabilities and services into hybrid architectures (see chapter 6). Ultimately, governments must develop strategies to balance government-owned and -operated spacecraft versus reliance on commercial solutions.

The Benefits of Commercial Innovation Outweigh the Risks

The net benefit of integrating innovative commercial capabilities and services into governmental frameworks and architectures is far greater than the potential risk and cost. Notably, commercial systems help government customers do more, and more quickly, while spending less. Current federal procurement in the United States can take over a decade to field a complex space system.[36] Acquisitions of new space capabilities are cumbersome for many governments. Commercial services, by contrast, offer a way for states to circumvent lengthy traditional requirements, contracting, and development processes. Commercial systems, including off-the-shelf technologies and services, can rapidly increase the agility of space procurement.

Commercial systems may also enhance a state's deterrence posture through *deterrence by denial*—that is, according to the late Professor Glenn Snyder, "the capability to deny the other party any gains from the move which is to be deterred."[37] The growth in private-sector capabilities means that it will become more challenging for space powers to deny services in or degrade access to space. Particularly, architectures can be proliferated in ways that increase resilience, which in turn enhances deterrence by denial.[38] For instance, radio-frequency-spectrum diversity can complicate an adversary's attempts to jam communications.[39] Agile manufacturing processes become valuable in reconstitution efforts.[40] Therefore, simply placing commercial actors under contract can help convey the futility of hostile acts.[41] This futility may cause potential adversaries to avoid military confrontation in the first place. Also, commercial capabilities can provide support to space and terrestrial forces and enable "intrawar deterrence"— that is, mitigate the potential escalation of an ongoing war.

Technological Innovation and International-Relations Theory

A sound understanding of technological innovation, of its potential risks and benefits, is critical for developing practical and useful space strategies. Importantly, the commercial space sector will continue to drive trends and advances in technology while being further integrated into the governmental space ecosystem. Consequently, its role must be considered by policy makers and military leaders. Through a similar understanding national-security practitioners can better understand the impact of innovations on international stability. The following two sections detail, first, the international frameworks that are germane to space technological innovation and, second, some common misconceptions about technologies causing power imbalances and instability.

Technology, Power Imbalances, and Strategic Instability

In international relations, a state's power is often equated with material capabilities at its disposal. The late political scientist Kenneth Waltz explained that "the political clout of nations correlates closely with their economic power and their military might."[42] Commercially derived technological advances contribute directly to a state's power, through both the economic power of space-related commerce and the nonspace activities dependent on commercial space systems. Furthermore, innovation in commercial space bolsters military power by aiding war fighting and deterrence. Because the space industry is a contributor to national power, advances in new space technologies are significant to international relations. Policy makers must contemplate the future of strategic stability between competitors against the background of potential technology-driven power imbalances between states.

Among security professionals, a key concern is whether innovative commercial space technologies result in greater risk of escalation and propensity for conflict.[43] This concern pertains to a *security dilemma*, a term first used by international-relations scholar John Herz in 1950 to describe the creation—by one individual's or group's accumulation of power—of insecurity for neighboring individuals or groups.[44] Security dilemmas may arise as states seeking security for themselves make potential competitors less secure. In the security-dilemma context, the growing military reliance on relatively vulnerable space assets could make threats against them more attractive to adversaries. This can, in turn, prompt defensive countermeasures, and so on, causing a security dilemma and an arms race in space. Because many of the innovative commercial space advancements have appeared from commercial companies of the United States and its allies, it is thought that innovative space capabilities could cause instability of the international system on Earth, as the capabilities of China and Russia lag behind.

Brad Townsend agrees that a security dilemma for the space environment could result in arms races and grave unintended outcomes.[45] As a way of resolving it, Townsend proposes increased commercialization of traditionally military space functions.[46] In his view commercialization signals benign or at most defensive intentions, signals that, if reciprocated, would lead to a less threatening international environment. On the other hand, might not the military utility of those same space assets be lowered, resulting in a net loss of security to the commercializing country? Many space functions have dual-use applications, such as GPS signals used by both precision guided munitions and taxicabs. In the end, the existence of the dual-use capability and how it can be controlled is more important than who ultimately owns and operates it.

Some international-relations scholars contend that technological innovation, including commercially driven innovation, affects bilateral or multilateral relationships among states. For instance, states may experience a reordering of hierarchies and distributional changes in power.[47] Daniel Drezner asserts that technologies can radically shift the distribution of power among states, that "any technological change is also an exercise in redistribution. It can create new winners and losers."[48] The implication is space-technology innovation in the commercial sector will emerge as a key issue.

Shifts in power due to innovation could change the offense/defense balance in space, increasing the likelihood of conflict. Robert Jervis contends that the stability of the international system will be influenced by how clear it is that given technology is "offensive" or "defensive" and by perceptions of whether an offensive or defensive technology is more advantageous in strategic relationships.[49] Some scholars note that real or perceived shifts in the offense/defense balance increase the risk of conflict.[50] Brad Townsend argues that geography and technology are the typical determinants of such questions and that when adversaries share the space domain's "geography," technology could predominate.[51]

Today, military spacepower is perceived as largely offensive in character, in terms of conflict both on Earth and in space. First, the combination of satellite services with terrestrial military forces increases lethality and concentration of firepower.[52] Space capabilities and services can give terrestrial forces strategic effect. As a result, some security experts view spacepower as not only offensive but as creating a focused strategic effect. Second, satellites often follow predictable paths in orbit, with limited ability to hide or defend themselves. The economics of launch and constraints imposed by spacecraft size, weight, and electrical power create incentives to maximize mission payloads rather than defensive capabilities. Moreover, antisatellite weapons that destroy or disrupt satellites are usually significantly less expensive than their targets, especially exquisite governmental ones.[53]

In an offense-dominated domain, then, there is concern that innovations will create incentives for states to initiate offensive actions. Balance-of-power dynamics are susceptible to offensive actions taken to realize first-strike advantages.[54] A key variable here is the vulnerability of the technologies on which a country relies.

With regard to information technologies and first-strike advantages, Jacquelyn Schneider of the Hoover Institution asserts that certain technologies may generate significant benefits to the state that wields them but also dependence, challenges, and vulnerabilities. According to Schneider, the investments of the U.S. military on information-enabled forces, aside from their operational benefits, introduce digital-reliant and vulnerable architectures.[55] That is, the vulnerabilities of U.S. systems and architectures are heightened by dependence on information to support operations. In such situations, belligerents in a conflict are likely to see incentives to strike first.

In theory, the less capable state is driven to strike first against the more capable state's vulnerabilities and thereby cripple it at the onset of conflict. For its part, the more capable state may strike first out of fear of just such preemption against its vulnerabilities.[56] This argument is germane to innovative space technologies as well. Dependence on vulnerable space systems and technologies may give states reason to strike first in times of tension.

The final technological challenge is the rapid diffusion of innovative space technologies. For instance, the commercial sectors of launch, communications, remote sensing, space domain awareness, and on-orbit servicing are currently advancing rapidly. Moreover, this commercial innovation is concentrated largely in the United States, Western Europe, and Japan. International-relations scholars point to the potential influence of the diffusion of key technologies on the likelihood for war.[57] Political scientists Muhammet Bas and Andrew Coe suggest that a state may go to war to prevent a competitor from gaining a certain proliferating technology.[58] On this reasoning, the fact that commercial space innovations of the United States and its allies eventually diffuse to rivals such as China and Russia makes—in theory—the United States and its allies more likely to resort to preventive war.

Setting the Record Straight:
The Primacy of Politics and the Limitations of Technology

The previous section outlined many of the prevalent views of advanced technologies with respect to international relations, strategic stability, and the likelihood for conflict. Much international-relations scholarship posits that innovative technologies—such as those being developed by today's commercial space firms—can lead to inadvertent escalation and conflict if they manage to shift the offense/defense balance, create incentives for states to strike first, or advance the likelihood of preventive wars. International-relations theory paints a dismal picture of security risks, power imbalances, and conflict escalation. While these arguments merit engagement, many are misguided, reflecting a misunderstanding of the primacy of politics in strategy and international relations. As Todd Sechser, Neil Narang, and Caitlin Talmadge (political scientists themselves) note, "Very few technologies fundamentally reshape the dynamics of international conflict. Historically, most technological innovations have amounted to incremental advancements, and some have disappeared into irrelevance despite widespread hype about their promise."[59] Although innovation has destabilizing elements, advances in space technology will likely have less effect than will the primacy of politics, the limitations of technology, and the diffusion of innovation.

International-relations theory often emphasizes a specific technology's ability to shape the international environment. This view neglects the essential role of political and strategic choices, which are the primary drivers of escalation and instability in the international system.[60] Caitlin Talmadge finds that escalation and the risk of escalation in the Cold War was largely independent of technology.[61] In some cases technology enabled escalation, but escalation that would have occurred—or indeed did occur—even in the absence of the technology in question.[62] The emergence of particular technologies did not drive policy makers in the United States or the Soviet Union to adopt more escalatory strategies; instead, decision makers, having decided on military actions that would in themselves be escalatory, made use of advanced technologies in them.[63] Technology is merely a tool that polities leverage when they seek to escalate tensions or a conflict—actions that they would likely take regardless of the availability of a specific technology.[64]

The view that space is at an increased risk because spacecraft technologies and capabilities are offense-dominated fails, again, to account for the primacy of politics. The ubiquity of dual-use technologies shows that technology in itself should not be considered a threat. People decide how technologies are employed. Colin Gray explains that during the nineteenth and early twentieth centuries the state of technology largely favored the defense.[65] Nevertheless, wars—including the Crimean War, the American Civil War, and World War I—were still waged.[66] Whether peace or war is present in the international system at a given time is not determined by specific technologies or strategic preferences for defense or offense. War and peace always have technological dimensions, yet as Gray underscores, "Polities do not fight because they are armed, even potentially decisively well-armed; rather they do fight for political reasons."[67]

A common shortcoming in the international-relations scholarship on the role of technology is overstatement of its efficacy in practice. Scholarly discussions envision technological "silver bullets" bound to destabilize the international system. The actual strategic effect of technology, however, will be highly dependent on the context and character of the potential conflict, and in any case it may not live up to its promise.[68] Adoption of superior technologies does not guarantee success in strategy. Because war and strategy have so prominent a human element, the efficacy of specific technologies will depend on the skill of those who wield it and the military doctrine that they follow. However technologically well endowed a country may be, the adversary also has a vote. The efficacy of any technology is decided not unilaterally but through competition with an adversary that will seek to offset or mitigate it.

Moreover, scholarly international-relations theories often fail to consider fully the role of technology in strategy. Technology is one of several dimensions that must be considered in strategic planning and analysis. Gray explains the role of technology concisely: "Technology drives tactics, shapes operations, and enables strategy."[69] Some technologies are significant "game changers," altering how wars are waged. However, such powerful developments take place mostly at the tactical and operational levels of war. At the strategic level, policy ends driven by politics remain mostly unchanged by them.[70]

The final factor limiting the actual effect of technologies on strategic stability and propensity for conflict is the rapid diffusion and proliferation of technologies. Emily Goldman of U.S. Cyber Command and Richard Andres of the National War College note that neorealist logic predicts that "proven military methods, even if they are truly revolutionary, will have no lasting effect on the balance of international influence because diffusion occurs quickly among states that are within range of each other's war-making ability."[71] This diffusion and proliferation does not mean, however, that states will find themselves in escalatory or otherwise precarious arms races. States may acquire certain technologies simply as a matter of general military development, not specifically for their particular amassing capabilities.[72] In an example of technological diffusion, Barry Posen of the Massachusetts Institute of Technology writes that tank-related technologies, following their debut in World War I, proliferated even absent an arms race.[73] Any technological advantage of one state is likely to be fleeting.

Notwithstanding the warnings of inadvertent escalation and increased likelihood of conflict, the innovative space technologies being developed and fielded by governments and commercial companies will have marginal impacts on international relations and the achievement of political aims. Potential escalation in the strategic relationships between space powers will be driven predominantly by political considerations, not technological ones. The strategic effect of novel space technologies will be highly dependent on context. Future conflicts may take place in circumstances that make space technologies marginal or entirely moot. Finally, once again, any advantages that they do yield will be rapidly offset by their proliferation.

Conclusion

Technology is inevitably an important dimension of space warfare, irregular or regular. Historical experience in other domains suggests that space strategists and military leaders will seek to incorporate the latest advancements to mold new operational concepts and styles of space warfare. It is to be expected that space forces will exploit the latest technologies to make capabilities, resources, and space architectures more effective and efficient and also that advanced technologies will be used to address emerging space threats in original ways. Technological advancement is not a destination but an endless process. In irregular space warfare, technology's impact will be pronounced as belligerents seek asymmetric advantage, especially when a less-capable space power engages a more-capable enemy. For the less-capable space power, the pursuit of an all-powerful technological solution may become simply too tempting.

The space strategist must remember, however, that technology is only a tool.[74] Its application is not the end in itself but should serve the aims of policy to achieve strategic effect. As Thomas Mahnken puts it, "Technology is a poor substitute for strategic thinking."[75] Therefore, however technologies make for superior tactics, victory will likely be elusive if no sound strategy guides their use. Technology alone rarely confers insurmountable military or strategic advantage.

Lastly, policy makers and military leaders must fight the urge to specialize an already well-balanced military organization against one kind of foe in one domain. Irregular and regular strategies and associated operational concepts must be integrated across the peace/conflict continuum. To optimize space forces narrowly against any one segment of this range is to increase the likelihood that they will be ill prepared for the war they eventually fight. Policy makers and military leaders need to prepare for a range of possible futures, collecting a diversity of technologies as the tools.

≡ CHAPTER 8 ≡

How to Counter Irregular Space Warfare

For every complex problem there is a simple solution,
and it is always wrong.
—Colin Gray[1]

War is a duel on a grand scale, and competitive strategies must consider an adversary or competitor's own strategies and operational styles.[2] As illustrated in the previous chapters, irregular forms of warfare in the space domain are complex. Consequently, the space strategist should expect the development of suitable counterstrategies to irregular space warfare to be just as complex.

Often there is a desire in the security and defense communities for simple and easy solutions to complex problems, such as those posed by irregular warfare. As Colin Gray's remark above (notwithstanding its admitted hyperbole) warns, anyone looking for such a counter for irregular competition and conflict in space will be disappointed—or worse, misled by the purveyors of the next "big idea" wrapped in buzzwords and jargon.[3] Gray's observation agrees with the Clausewitzian "Everything in strategy is very simple, but that does not mean that everything is very easy."[4] The Prussian strategist gives hope, however, that "once it has been determined, from the political conditions, what a war is meant to achieve and what it can achieve, it is easy to chart the course."[5] Therefore, after careful study and consideration of the political objectives, strategic environment, and relevant strengths and weaknesses among rivals, the space strategist can develop useful wartime strategies, whatever the complexities.

The primary takeaway for space strategists is clear: difficult does not mean impossible. Furthermore, the strategists' role is not to "admire" the problem or lose themselves in contemplation of its nuances, because war fighters demand solutions. Space strategy and theoretical frameworks are useless if they do not lead to beneficial and practical approaches to competitive strategies. This chapter looks to discern and explain such approaches. The space strategist can rely on Gray's insight that "strategy, in its essence, works identically for regular and for irregular belligerents, and in regular and irregular warfare. The characteristics of different forms of war and styles in warfare will vary widely, but there is a common currency in strategic effect, no matter how that effect is generated."[6] Irregular space warfare can be understood in terms of the enduring nature of war, however different in character from regular forms of warfare in the other domains.

To begin with, two points should be underscored. First, the counterstrategies to be examined are relevant to both Clausewitzian "primordial violence" and competition short of armed conflict.[7] Although the most conspicuous feature of warfare is violence, space-warfare strategies and counterstrategies must also address general strategic competition, grayzone operations, and actions short of force.[8] Today's "strategic competition" involves from day to day much activity that, though coercive and competitive, is below the Western threshold of military conflict. Practical and useful space strategies must address it. Second, what follows is presented from an American perspective. The United States will likely face rivals using irregular forms of warfare to mitigate its advantages. Also, this nation still has a lot to learn—or more accurately, relearn—about countering irregular competition and conflict.

Pitfalls of the American Style of Warfare

Evocations of the styles of warfare to which the United States is inclined have been around for several decades. Whether accurate or not, popular perceptions of the existence, and specific content (i.e., that there is any and, if so, what it is), of an "American way of war" influence beliefs today, both inside the U.S. defense community and out. Many such generalizations are based on accurate readings of the historical record. For instance, the American and coalition involvement in Iraq and Afghanistan in the early 2000s has brought the U.S. military community frequent criticism for a style of warfare—a product of American historical, social, ideological, and material realities—not well suited to conflict with irregular enemies.[9] Of course, not all security scholars agree, and there are always exceptions.[10] Nevertheless, an understanding of broad, strategic preferences is helpful when forecasting the likely choices of competitors and belligerents.

The following section emphasizes the pitfalls of the American style of warfare and the military's insufficient self-awareness of its war-fighting propensities as well as how the U.S. military is perceived by others. Self-awareness is important because adversaries often develop counterstrategies to take advantage of one's perceived weaknesses or predictable operational tendencies, as Sun Tzu knew: "Know the enemy and know yourself; in a hundred battles you will never be in peril."[11] All strategies and operational styles have inherent flaws and weaknesses, and the American ones are not exceptions. Ultimately, better understanding and awareness are essential for building practical and relevant counterstrategies to irregular forms of competition and conflict in space. Space strategists must consider strategic preferences and conditions as they are, not how they would like them to be.

Optimization for Big, Traditional Wars

According to some security analysts of the past several decades, the United States has tailored its fighting forces for large-scale, traditional warfare. Even with the recent counterinsurgency and counterterrorism experience of Iraq and Afghanistan, the United States is primarily focused on organizing, training, and equipping for regular forms of warfare. An optimization of regular forces comes at the expense of the ability to combat irregular styles of warfare. Counterinsurgency scholar Seth Jones admonishes, "The United States is, to be blunt, *vulnerable* to irregular means," and it has demonstrated an inability to develop and implement effective counterstrategies for competition with China and Russia, two practitioners of irregular competition.[12]

The U.S. military routinely prepares logistically for regular forms of warfare in distant lands. Barry Posen explains how historically the United States has been master not only of the wide common of the high seas since Alfred Thayer Mahan's time but also of the new commons of the air, cyberspace, and (as Posen considers it), space.[13] Furthermore, an observation of

Samuel Huntington's has resonated with the national security community since he offered it in 1985: "The United States is a big country, and we should fight wars in a big way. One of our great advantages is our mass; we should not hesitate to use it. . . . Bigness, not brains, is our advantage, and we should exploit it. If we have to intervene, we should intervene with overwhelming force."[14] As a great power, the United States tends to excel at enterprises conducted on a scale that matches its total assets.[15] Indeed, the U.S. military and its amply endowed defense industrial base would seem to be most comfortable, when conditions necessitate, in mobilizing large, conventional forces to conquer distance and fight overseas. With its long-standing material superiority, it has had little reason to revisit its strategic preference and operational style. If necessity is the mother of invention, American fighting forces have seen none justifying substantial work-arounds to its primary mode of warfare.

Yet it has become a truism that future opponents of the United States will seek strategic advantage from the shortcomings of its style of warfare. In particular, emerging, and middle powers may be expected for that reason to use irregular forms of competition and conflict, as will those with less material wealth. As Colin Gray comments, "Poor societies are obliged to wage war frugally. They have no choice other than to attempt to fight smarter than their rich enemies. The United States has been blessed with wealth in all its forms. Inevitably, the armed forces, once mobilized and equipped, have fought a rich person's war."[16] An American strategic pref-erence for "bigness" and "large footprints" (i.e., presence at the scene, on the ground) and a war-fighting style that favors firepower, mobility, and aggressive hunting for the opponent's main body are apt to be ineffective against an elusive and irregular foe. Therefore, that America will continue to be required to fight irregular wars can be expected to challenge its estab-lished way of war severely—but not insurmountably.

Reliance on Technology

As Thomas Mahnken observes, "Reliance on advanced technology has been a central pillar of the American way of war, at least since World War II. No nation in recent history has placed greater emphasis upon the role of technology in planning and waging war than the United States."[17] Much of this proclivity stems from the breadth of the nation's high-tech industries and the size of its defense industrial base. The American defense community frequently looks to build new operational styles around the latest technological advances. This tendency is apparent in the 2019 *DoD Digital Modernization Strategy*, which states the Department of Defense will "increase technological capabilities across the Department and strengthen overall adoption of enterprise systems to expand the competitive space in the digital arena" so as to "enable increased lethality for the Joint warfighter."[18] Its already advanced technologies, capacity for defense and aerospace mass production, and wealth incline the United States to seek decisive advantage from novel technologies. This is true to some extent of many Western countries, but the United States has a well-established history of it.[19]

Yet there are downsides. All too often the American defense community has generated operational concepts for which technological applications are the centerpiece. This was the case in the late 1990s when the operational concept of "network-centric warfare" became popular. But in focusing on networked approaches to coordinate high-end military systems and weapons platforms against a future adversary, the United States was in effect setting up *itself* as that adversary. Historian Peter Mansoor perceived this consequence in 2012: "Concepts such as network-centric warfare, therefore, aimed at destroying mirror-image enemies. By the turn of the millennium, the U.S. military was well on its way to developing a system perfectly suited to fight itself."[20] That is, U.S. armed forces often envision and plan against future opponents as culturally attuned to favoring technological solutions as they are, only to face irregular enemies against whom technology typically offers few advantages. Certainly, future opponents of the United States will seek to negate any American technological advantage by employing irregular forms of warfare. The long-term risk of the current American approach is that time-consuming and costly programs may lead to the nations being ill-equipped to fight the commonplace irregular-warfare threat, doomed to perform poorly at the strategic level and fail to achieve the ends of policy.

The American tendency to be technologically reliant is evident in recent USSF publications. In 2020 its chief of space operations declared a need for harnessing "the best that technology has to offer and applying it in ways that can outpace the advances of our adversaries," by means of innovation in analytics, autonomy, and machine learning.[21] Additionally, in a 2021 publication the Space Force predicted that it, already the newest U.S. military service, will become the "world's first fully Digital Service."[22] The vision document goes on, "Given this operational reality, and the imperative we have to leverage data and information even more extensively to prevail in a highly contested and congested operating environment, the USSF will undergo a large-scale cultural and technical transformation by embracing modern technologies and methodologies to be a genuine Digital Service. The intent of this digital transformation is to enable us to recapture the initiative and maintain superiority in the domain our nation pioneered."[23] By implication the USSF's ultimate goal is to become an interconnected, innovative, and digitally dominant force.[24] But history cautions that the space strategist should be wary of becoming so reliant on technology in fighting wars that it has no response to an irregular opponent who finds a way to nullify a technological advantage.

Impatience and Eagerness for Quick, Decisive Victory

The U.S. military is culturally predisposed to attempt to win quickly and decisively, by means of mobility and firepower. Colin Gray once more: "The American way has the highly desirable characteristics of offensiveness, aggressiveness, seizing and keeping the initiative, and maintaining a high tempo of operations. The object is to defeat, indeed annihilate, the enemy in short order by a combination of maneuver and firepower. The idea that time is a weapon is somewhat alien—certainly, it is unwelcome. But in irregular warfare, an enemy who is greatly disadvantaged materially is obliged to use time against you. He expects to win by not losing because he believes that he can outlast you."[25] The American polity is typically uneasy about and avoids open-ended military conflicts in distant lands, and for good reason. It expects the U.S. military to be able to exploit its strategic and military advantage to get into the theater of operations, fight, win, and get out—quickly.

Of the many books and journal articles on American war-fighting preferences, an especially significant one, published in 1977 but frequently cited today, is Russell Weigley's *The American Way of War*. In it Weigley, a distinguished historian who died in 2004, examined how war and warfare have been understood and practiced by key American military and political figures. The book concludes that, except in the days of the nation's founding, the American way of war has centered on the desire to achieve a "crushing" military victory over an adversary, through either attrition or outright annihilation.[26] American political and military leaders often view the destruction of an adversary's war-fighting capability and the occupation of its capital as marking the end of war and the beginning of postwar negotiations.[27] However, because the American way of war seeks swift military victory independent of policy success, the desired political and military outcomes do not always align.[28] Weigley's book, while certainly not exhaustive, remains useful for understanding the U.S. desire to achieve a quick, decisive victory.

The way of war and the characteristic impatience of the United States form a contrast with irregular warfare and insurgencies. David Galula, writing for more-powerful counterinsurgency forces, advises, "The destruction of the guerrilla forces in the selected area is, obviously, highly desirable, and this is what the counterinsurgent must strive for. One thing should be clear, however: This operation is not an end in itself, for guerrillas, like the heads of the legendary hydra, have the special ability to grow again if not all destroyed at the same time. The real purpose of the first operation, then, is to prepare the stage for the further development of the counterinsurgent action."[29] A counterstrategy to irregular warfare will be a protracted affair, by virtue of how irregular warfare itself is fought. The United States should understand that when fighting an irregular opponent, the true purpose of any given military operation is to prepare the foundation for the next one.

The U.S. military should indeed employ any strategic advantages available in wartime. The purpose here is to argue not against that logic but for acknowledgment that any adversary capable of posing a threat will be a thinking, intelligent competitor, looking to maximize its probability of success and to offset perceived U.S. strengths. A rival in irregular warfare is not attempting to inflict a decisive defeat in a single battle but to harass, attack, fight another day, and hold out, hoping that time is in its favor.

Are Irregular Space Wars Winnable?

The "doom and gloom" of the discussion above may well leave the space strategist asking whether the United States can actually win in irregular warfare in space. Perhaps the most helpful answer to such a complex question—if not a very reassuring one—is "It depends," or "Perhaps."

History offers many examples of the failure of traditional, conventional fighting forces fighting irregular opponents. Whatever the inherent advantages of a large, traditional military, if asked to fight an irregular foe, it must perform in a way and for purposes for which it was almost certainly not designed. Not all wars can be won, and for a regular military not all tasks are doable however gallant and gifted its strategist. Even a sound, well-tested military doctrine of irregular warfare may stand no reasonable chance of succeeding in a given case. For space in particular, the strategist should not assume that all irregular wars are winnable, because of the innumerable unknown and unavoidable circumstances and forms of Clausewitzian friction that can undermine the best intentions and thwart the most desirable objectives.[30]

Still, there are examples in history of regular forces defeating irregular opponents. Indeed, such opponents as a group have a markedly uneven record of strategic and political success. To prevail against an irregular adversary, one's mindset must be holistic, alert to all aspects of a problem that is largely, though not entirely, political in nature.[31] This goes back to a fundamental observation by Clausewitz, that the supreme judgment "the statesman and commander have to make is to establish by that test [of fit with political aims] the kind of war on which they are embarking; neither mistaking it for, nor trying to turn it into, something that is alien to its nature."[32] While irregular conflict will, by necessity, have a military dimension, its outcome will not rely solely on military means but on political ones as well. Ultimately, those employing counterstrategies to defeat an irregular opponent can win given favorable strategic conditions and political latitude.

Profound cultural challenges to the U.S. military remain, despite two decades of nontraditional forms of combat and experience in Afghanistan and Iraq. Notwithstanding some meaningful changes, the services are still in large part organized, trained, and equipped to defeat regular adversaries. There can be no single military style of warfare that is equally well adapted to all forms of warfare. The strategic fit between the American regular style of fighting and that required for irregular warfare is far from perfect. Can, then, the nation's traditional way of war be effectively adapted for irregular enemies? Colin Gray replies, "Perhaps, but only with difficulty."[33] Yet difficult does not mean impossible, and the space strategist should be up for the challenge. Toward this end, the next section looks at the ways by which the United States can counter irregular forms of warfare and competition in the space domain.

Fortunately, One Need Only Be Good Enough

The strategy used to defeat an irregular foe in the space domain will be different from those of regular wars. Facing irregular opponents, the United States and many Western countries have tended toward "symmetrical" approaches—that is, attempting to beat the irregular force at its own game and in its chosen arena.[34] They frequently have concentrated on locating and destroying the irregular force.[35] That said, more recent American counterinsurgency theory recognizes the political nature of insurgencies and embraces the need for holistic rather than primarily military counter-strategies, to "win hearts and minds."[36] A holistic and integrated approach is needed to counter irregular forms of warfare in space, as well.

Presently there seems to be little literature on irregular warfare in the space domain generally or on counterstrategies specifically. That fact and repeated historical experience suggests, unfortunately, that irregular warfare in space will come as a surprise for American policy makers and military leaders—which by this time it should not. Perhaps the remainder of this chapter, with its outline of methods to counter irregular warfare, including in space, will minimize surprises. There are no definitive or authoritative lists; what follows arises from the author's sense of what is most necessary for fighting and winning irregular warfare in space and for prevailing in long-term strategic competition. They are relevant for any polity trying to counter irregular warfare or competition, though the discussion is tailored for the United States, its allies, and other liberal democracies. These ten counterstrategies may not be perfect, but warfare is a competition among imperfect polities and their militaries.

Invest in Integrated Irregular and Regular Warfare Education

The foremost requirement is to educate space war fighters. This point seems obvious but is mentioned first and explicitly because of the cyclical nature of American interest in irregular warfare. The United States has shown a regrettable "boom and bust" enthusiasm for study and education in irregular warfare, a great impediment to the long-term protection of its security interests and strategic advantages. Indeed, the need for foundational space education is a recurring lament; as far back as 2002 Michael Smith was arguing the importance of career education and specialization.[37] To avoid being caught unprepared yet again by irregular forms of competition and conflict, a dedicated and sustained military education program is needed that integrates them with regular modes of warfare. This is a task for the U.S. Space Force leadership, and it will help ensure the United States is prepared and proactive for its next round of irregular competition and conflict.

Such education should address how irregular and regular approaches can work together in a cohesive and unified strategic framework. The two strategies are mutually supportive, and space professionals need to master how they work together. Notwithstanding the different operational styles and tactical considerations, the same unifying strategy must rule and guide both. Combined irregular and regular warfare training and education will "educate the mind of the future commander" and guide his or her self-education, as Clausewitz foresaw.[38]

Not only space strategists but all military professionals need to be well informed of the strategies and operational styles of irregular warfare. Space professionals should be broadly educated in the styles and modes of irregular space warfare: active, reserve, and civilian personnel as well as both commissioned and enlisted guardians (as the USSF calls its personnel). Military service education and training on the subject should recur through the careers of servicemembers at all levels. Even for space professionals, irregular-warfare education should reflect a holistic, all-domain approach, spanning the entire spectrum of conflict. The education of military professionals on the subject of strategy—including that of both irregular and regular modes of warfare in space—should be an organized and structured affair, not left to happenstance. The space force it produces must be able to adapt and succeed in the ambiguous and rapidly changing environment of irregular space warfare.

Maintain Political Will and Domestic Support

Forces that adopt irregular forms of warfare and competition are likely seeking to erode their opponents' political resolve, and many irregular wars are won or lost in the minds of the polities involved.[39] Victory or defeat during irregular space warfare will involve the beliefs, attitudes, and behavior of the public and frequently of the international community. The military defeat of the irregular enemy is desirable but not essential. It is the foe's eventual political defeat and delegitimization that is crucial. Therefore, in the face of attempts to erode one's political support over time, one will need to maintain steadfastly the highly plausible political story that draws one's supporters. However tactically excellent and intellectually sophisticated one's counterstrategy or military doctrine is, if one's political support is hollow, victory may prove elusive.

Such steadfastness in irregular space warfare will be difficult and complex: policy makers and military leaders should not kid themselves. Inevitably, some in the American think-tank and defense communities will make extravagant promises that decision makers will embrace as simple, even dominant solutions.[40] History suggests that these promises will be unsound, misleading, and potentially dangerous.

Prepare for Protracted Competition and Have Patience

Successful counterstrategies to irregular space warfare need to envision protracted conflict and competition and the likelihood that their effects will mature only in the long term. An irregular opponent will use time as a weapon in ways that can be sources of endless frustration for those on the receiving end. Indeed, countering irregular space warfare will face tedium, setbacks, and likely a multitude of difficulties, predictable and not.

Broadly considered, irregular space warfare is not a problem to be solved but a condition to be endured. Success will be slow and gradual. Impatience is a military vice, but never more so than in irregular warfare. It is probably no overstatement to claim that a counterstrategy for irregular space warfare that is fueled by impatience will prove disastrous. An impatient belligerent will be seeking the impossible—a quick, decisive victory. Unless one side makes a truly irreversible error, swift and decisive victory is simply not attainable.[41]

Given a protracted strategy, there may be no practical or feasible way to hasten a favorable, decisive, and lasting outcome. The opponent will eschew large battles that might result in one. It is unlikely that an irregular space force can be brought to battle all at once, and an opponent fighting traditionally will not be able to solve the irregular problem at the tactical and operational levels. This is not to diminish the need for decisive military action but to frame that action in the larger context of strategic aims and political objectives.

To fight an irregular foe—much to a superior, regular opponent's dismay and potentially against its strategic culture—is to acknowledge the protracted character of the conflict and to tolerate the fact that the terms of the competition will be dictated by the adversary. This may prove awkward to explain to a doubting public and skeptical media. To undertake irregular warfare in space necessitates the measured, sustained application of all instruments of national power to achieve strategic aims and political objectives. Perseverance is required. History suggests that an ultimately victorious polity and its fighting force will have sustained its commitment and fortitude over a period of years or decades.

Have Credible Space Domain Awareness and Attribution Capabilities

The space domain, with its expansive CLOCs and distributed hubs of logistical activity, is well suited for exploitation by an irregular foe. An irregular opponent will certainly take advantage of its characteristics and employ dispersal, concentration, maneuverability, deception, and surprise. Furthermore, as national, organizational, and commercial interests expand outward from near-Earth into cislunar space and beyond, an irregular foe can find new celestial environments for exploitation, effect, and benefit.

To counter the exploitation of the space domain by an irregular adversary, robust space domain awareness (SDA) and space attribution capabilities are needed. They will help provide the needed intelligence, data, information, and overall understanding as to where an irregular force is operating, what kinds of activity is occurring, and who is conducting it.

Furthermore, SDA and space attribution will help frustrate an irregular foe's attempts at deception and surprise, help lift the "fog of war," and provide better and more-actionable intelligence.

The first requisite capability is SDA. The Space Force's 2020 *Space Capstone Publication* explains,

> Space Domain Awareness (SDA) encompasses the effective identification, characterization, and understanding of any factor associated with the space domain that could affect space operations and thereby impacting the security, safety, economy, or environment of our Nation. SDA leverages the unique subset of intelligence, surveillance, reconnaissance, environmental monitoring, and data sharing arrangements that provide operators and decision makers with a timely depiction of all factors and actors—including friendly, adversary, and third party—impacting domain operations. Furthermore, SDA must be predictive, synthesizing facts and evidence into an assessment of possible and probable future outcomes.[42]

The fact that SDA is defined as including prediction and forecasting is indeed noteworthy. This ability to predict and forecast will help focus space-relevant collection efforts and point to vulnerable space assets that should be moved or where they should be placed.

Yet SDA alone is not enough, as the 2020 U.S. Space Policy hints by stating the imperative to adapt policies, strategies, doctrine, and capabilities to deter hostilities, defeat aggression, and protect American interests through "robust space domain awareness of all activities in space with the ability to characterize *and attribute* potentially threatening behavior."[43] So in addition to SDA, *space attribution* is necessary—the ability to trace the origin, who or what, of an action against space architectures.[44] Without it, an appropriate response seems doubtful. Operational experiences in the other domains give caution that attribution will at times involve the reconciliation of conflicting data and information of varying confidence levels. The determination that results may be less than satisfying and definitive. For these reasons, attribution should be thought of *as a process*, not as a singular event or a piece of information or knowledge.

A beneficial framework for attribution combines SDA and space forensics, the intelligence community, allies, and commercial partners (see figure 8.1). First, while many of today's SDA ground- and space-based capabilities may be effective in collecting against kinetic actions, such as by direct-ascent and co-orbital antisatellites, more capabilities are needed against nonkinetic actions, such as jamming, lasing, and network cyber-attack. Among them is the discipline of *space forensics*—the science of analyzing and determining the source and pathway of an attack against space architectures after such an attack has occurred.[45] Space forensics gathers data and information from spacecraft, ground systems, and networks regarding actions that are nonkinetic, kinetic, reversible, or irreversible. Space forensics and SDA capabilities must work in synchronized fashion to support space attribution.

Second, the intelligence community must play a role. Executive Order 12333 directs the intelligence community to collect information for the president, the National Security Council, the secretaries of state and defense, and other executive branch officials and agencies; to produce and disseminate intelligence; and to collect information concerning hostile action against the United States.[46] It follows that the intelligence community should treat space attribution in the same way.[47] Toward this end, in June 2022 the U.S. Space Force activated the National Space Intelligence Center to deliver critical intelligence on threat systems, foreign intentions, and activity in the space domain.[48] Coordinated collection across

Figure 8.1. Space Attribution Framework (*author*)

the intelligence community will aid determinations as to how, where, and when harmful interference or an attack occurs, particularly during irregular space warfare.

Third, inasmuch as the space domain surrounds the Earth, the attribution network, if it is to be trusted and credible, must be global. Including allies and commercial partners can improve the sharing of SDA, intelligence, and forensics data. Involving commercial space companies is critical, because of the sheer number of commercial small satellites presently on-orbit and planned.[49]

Through the timely integration of all these, an irregular adversary in space can be countered. A credible and trusted attribution process may lead eventually to prosecution in civilian courts, or for more significant acts, an effective military response. While space attribution alone will not defeat an irregular foe in the space domain, it is critical to doing so.

Embrace Defensive Measures and Space Resilience

Defense is simply the stronger form of war. —Clausewitz[50]

The strategic culture of the U.S. military focuses on the offense to a fault. Offensiveness, aggressiveness, seizure of the initiative, and high-tempo operations are essential in regular warfare and are to be expected from a regular opponent. Not so for an irregular warfare—an intelligent opponent will not expose its limited forces to annihilation by a large, traditional military force. Irregulars understand that they would be greatly disadvantaged in traditional warfare and therefore maneuver, attack, and harass in a protracted and asymmetric manner. As a result, a regular force fighting an irregular enemy frequently will lack suitable targets.

Because an irregular belligerent intends to outlast its regular foe, the latter needs to incorporate in its counterstrategy defensive measures—which in fact should be key components of any wartime strategy, given the inherent strength of the defense. Sporadic and unexpected attacks by irregular belligerents cannot always be prevented; regular space forces must embrace defenses and resilience. The goal here is to render irregular attacks inconsequential, both to oneself and the achievement of the opponent's political and strategic aims—an endurable, strategically nugatory nuisance. Additionally, effective defensive and resilience efforts can expose the futility of the irregular opponent's operations to domestic audiences and the rest of the world.

In the space strategy lexicon, space defensive measures fall under the rubrics of *mission assurance* and *resilience*, which aim to prevent the natural or purposeful loss of space-reliant capabilities. A 2015 U.S. white paper defines *mission assurance* as "a process to protect or ensure the continued function and resilience of capabilities and assets—including personnel, equipment, facilities, networks, information and information systems, infrastructure, and supply chains—critical to the performance of DoD mission essential functions in any operating environment or condition."[51] Its elements, whatever the threat, are defensive operations, reconstitution, and resilience.[52] *Resilience*, for its part, connotes the probability that a space architecture can continue to support the mission and with minimal periods of reduced capability in the face of hostile action or adverse environmental and operational conditions, in a wide range of scenarios, conditions, and threat environments.[53] Improvement of resilience has six elements: disaggregation, distribution, diversification, protection, proliferation, and deception.[54]

Space is a domain where friend, foe, and neutral share the same environment and lines of communication. A space force in its zeal to dispatch an irregular threat by aggressive offensive action may unintentionally deny itself the very domain and lines of communication it needs. Also, indiscriminate kinetic and irreversible offensive actions can impact neutral parties and the global space industry. A Colin Gray warning about counterinsurgency rings true for irregular space warfare as well: "Aggressive offensive action against an enemy of uncertain location and identity is more likely to wreak political damage upon the [counterinsurgency] endeavor, a self-inflicted wound, than upon the enemy. Naturally, there is a time and place for offensive action. But, as the dominant characteristic of the official style of war, offensive action is likely to prove counterproductive against irregular enemies in many, perhaps most, circumstances."[55]

The takeaway is that offensive action in irregular space warfare is necessary but not sufficient and can be overdone. Strategy is about balancing ends and available means, while understanding the environment being contested. Any wartime strategy should have the right mix of offensive and defensive measures, and in irregular space warfare overly enthusiastic offensive action can be self-defeating.

Develop Gray-Zone and Intrawar Deterrence Strategies

Irregular space warfare lies in what is frequently termed the *gray zone* between peace and war. For some competing great powers, the gray zone may seem an enduring condition where rivals avoid large-scale, conventional conflict, but where they instead pursue competition, coercion, and compellence in a persistent manner to achieve political objectives. The methods employed during gray zone operations vary but include those areas covered in chapter 4, such as forward presence, power projection, coercion, proximity operations, and technological demonstrations.

For the United States and other liberal democracies, defense and response in the gray zone—aggression below the threshold of armed conflict (chapter 4)—are difficult. A targeted country cannot be certain ahead of time what acts of aggression and coercion it will face or, when it does know, what forms of defense and deterrence will be suitable or legal.[56] The latter is especially challenging because gray-zone actions often fall short of the UN Charter definition of armed force.[57] Democratic countries presumably consider observance of the law and the international legal regime vital, not least for ensuring the long-term legitimacy of their operations to counter gray-zone actions. Consequently, some governmental leaders may be reluctant to respond to gray-zone aggression for fear of being perceived as operating outside the law and international norms. As a result, rivals have been able in the past to achieve political and strategic objectives against Western countries in the gray zone. Therefore, space strategies must offer explicit options. Competitors with and adversaries of the United States have exploited and will continue to exploit perceived indecision or weakness in its responses.

Irregular space-warfare counterstrategies need also to provide for deterrence, in ways relevant to gray-zone competition and aggression. Yet deterrence—dissuasion from coercion and mitigation of unintended escalation—can be particularly difficult to achieve here. Elisabeth Braw explains, "Because gray-zone aggression can include any measures below the level of war, including illegal ones, it is impossible for the targeted countries to deter every act with the threat of punishment."[58] The space strategist should be fully aware that deterrence strategy in the gray zone must balance the risks of escalation, including diplomatic or economic, with the reality that some degree of risk tolerance is the price of effectiveness.

A suitable strategy will need to include a large measure of deterrence by denial—that is, of whatever the other party hopes to gain from aggressive or coercive behavior. *Deterrence by denial*, sometimes called *dissuasion*, can seek two different, but related, outcomes: discouraging military competition in the first place, and conveying the impossibility of achieving the desired objectives.[59] For the space strategist, the good news is that many of the key drivers in deterrence by denial are subsumed in defensive and resilience as described previously. Additionally, deterrence by denial can be made part of a hedging strategy against the possibility that gray-zone aggression escalates into armed conflict, by including robust space capabilities and defenses.

Gray-zone operations may occur in a condition of quasi-war or semi-conflict; therefore, an appropriate counterstrategy should include elements of *intrawar deterrence*, so that further escalation is dissuaded. By the nature of the space domain, the most comprehensive deterrence by denial utilizes all the instruments of national power—diplomatic, informational, economic, and military—and the active support of allies and trusted commercial partners.[60] Deterrence in the gray zone will need to be as multifaceted as the environment is complex.

Pursue Nonmilitary Solutions

As we have seen, most irregular space wars cannot be won solely through military means. Charles Callwell understood this over century ago: "It is the difficulty of bringing the foe to action which, as a rule, forms the most unpleasant characteristic of these [regulars against irregulars] wars."[61] Though military action is crucial, and an irregular war can be lost militarily, it generally cannot be won so.

In 1961 Roger Trinquier published *Modern Warfare,* on his counterinsurgency experience during the 1950s in Indochina and Algeria.[62] Trinquier described a new form of war, which he called "modern warfare," that includes guerrilla war, insurgency, terrorism, and political subversion.

One of his major points is that victory in modern war cannot come from the clash of armies on the battlefield but only from the support of the local population.[63] Trinquier advocates a comprehensive and interlocking system of political, economic, psychological, and military actions to undermine the insurgents' strategies, destroy their organization as a whole (not simply the military component), and gain the support of the people.[64] Despite its emphasis on counterinsurgency and local populaces, much of Trinquier's writing is relevant for irregular space warfare, particularly as to the limits to what can be achieved militarily. Military action is only one, albeit a vital one, dimension of strategy.

The nonmilitary dimensions of national power are needed to deal effectively with an irregular opponent. It is important to note that "nonmilitary" does not necessarily equate to a defensive mindset (i.e., focused on preventing the opponent from achieving something), but can also embrace offensive-mindedness and intent (to take or otherwise acquire something from the rival). A whole-of-government approach is less likely to be chronically reduced to reacting to a rival's actions. Nonmilitary but offensive-minded methods can diminish a rival's international power and diplomatic prestige; its standing among the global space community as portrayed in print, broadcast, or social media; and financial strength and access to markets.

Achieve Military Effects through Dispersal and Concentration

Space strategists may by now have concluded that offensive military activity is inconsequential. They would be wrong. Certainly, the military dimension is subordinate to the political in irregular-warfare strategy.[65] That is a powerful insight that must not be reduced to an article of faith, a dangerous error. Thus, to be clear, *the military use of force and offensive means are still a necessary component in countering irregular space warfare.* For indeed war is war, and war is an "act of force to compel our enemy to do our will."[66] Even defensive countermeasures often include military force in self-defense. Additionally, domestic support is critical for the long-term viability of any counterstrategy to irregular space warfare counterstrategy; it is essential that the public see its fighting forces succeed militarily against an irregular foe. A polity needs to believe that the irregular force is being, and will continue to be, defeated, and convincing it of that necessitates military force and offensive effects.

The strategic environment of space and its interconnectedness with cyberspace, however, necessitate offensive means of specific kinds. Its expansiveness, distances, and vast reaches involved do so as well. For the irregular space force, exposed lines of supply and communication and remote logistical bases are tempting targets. A strategy to counter the irregular space force will need to take into account these domain-specific elements.

The characteristics of irregular warfare in the space domain will necessitate the employment of offensive means through the flexible application of dispersal and concentration. Through dispersal and concentration of forces and offensive effects, a space force can counter an irregular foe by minimizing its own exposure as a consolidated, vulnerable target while being poised to concentrate force and military means to defeat irregulars prone to maneuverability and use of the "tyranny of distance." A pattern of dispersal and concentration in irregular space warfare should reflect the "continual conflict between cohesion and reach," as Julian Corbett explains regarding the concept's maritime application.[67]

The concept needs to be examined in two parts. First, resources are finite, so a counterstrategy to irregular space warfare must employ and distribute them to maximize the achievement of political ends and military objectives. Dispersing forces, assets, and effects to the widest practical extent provides for military presence across a wide region and increased freedom of action. Additionally, it may leave an irregular foe uncertain as to one's disposition and operational intent, to the benefit of defenses. The second is concentration, focusing firepower, assets, or other effects to defeat, defend against, or neutralize an irregular adversary. Swift concentration will minimize vulnerability as a target. After the concentrated force has successfully completed its task, it should disperse once again, so as to control expansive CLOCs and meet minor attacks in several regions at the same time. In the end, a fluid pattern of dispersal and concentration will help maintain the "elastic cohesion," to use Corbett's phrasing, needed in the space domain.[68]

Work with Allies and Commercial Providers

It is vital for any state or organization to work with allies and trusted commercial providers.[69] First, partnering will help solidify norms of safe and professional behaviors in space, which will help reduce ambiguity and miscalculation. Second, partnering, sharing information, and collective action can help to identify, characterize, and attribute anomalies or suspected malicious acts. Knowledge that information is shared helps deter potential aggressors, failing which it can lead to combined efforts and quicker and more judicious responses. Third, instances of partnership and collective action will advertise the existence of broad, shared, and credible capabilities for law-enforcement, economic, or military responses.

Much of this is relevant for the United States in today's strategic competition. The United States should lead international and multilateral efforts to help maintain peace and stability in the space domain, while ensuring unrestricted access and use to it. If collective responses to irregular actions in space are warranted, the United States should be prepared to take the lead, in accordance with international law and multilateral agreements. Also, the United States should work with allies and partners to enhance defensive measures and resilience to counter aggression and gray-zone actions and, as noted above, as a hedge.[70]

Further cooperation with the commercial space sector is needed. Its innovations and emerging capabilities are vital and must be integrated into the counterstrategies of irregular space warfare. The United States should do so when and where it makes sense. History makes clear, however, that the United States should also be prepared to "go it alone." All democratic governments have a duty and obligation to represent their polity's interests; multilateral approaches are ideal for irregular conflict and competition but are sometimes impossible to bring about.

Be Flexible and Adaptable

We cannot predict with certainty the pattern of the war for which we prepare ourselves. —J. C. Wylie[71]

Irregular warfare in any domain is highly variable and always complex.[72] A strategy to fight an irregular enemy in the space domain will need to be flexible and adaptable. Irregular space warfare on both sides must adapt to the specific circumstances. In his *Military Strategy*, Wylie warns, "The player who plans for only one strategy runs a great risk simply because his opponent soon detects the single strategy—and counters it. . . . [P]lanning for certitude is the greatest of all military mistakes, as military history demonstrates all too vividly."[73] We have seen that an irregular foe will eschew direct confrontation, seek asymmetric advantage in time or place, and act intelligently, attacking or harassing where the rival is weak and ill-prepared. Counterstrategies must be flexible and adaptive.

What would otherwise be a truism is worth special emphasis for irregular space warfare. An irregular foe will use maneuver, indirection, deception, and surprise; the opposing force will frequently be reduced to reacting to the irregular's actions as they occur. While less than ideal, that is the reality. Certainly, the need for flexibility and adaptability has been recognized at least as far back as Sun Tzu: "As water shapes its flow in accordance with the ground, so an army manages its victory in accordance with the situation of the enemy."[74] Those countering irregular warfare in the space domain must be like that water.

Policy goals and aims for warfare and peacemaking should be chosen in light of the actual conditions and probabilities of success, and then periodically revisited. Military services and defense establishments should continuously adapt their operational styles and preferences to future irregular wars. Colin Gray warns against the formulaic, "one size fits all strategy": "[The military service] cannot apply a simple template or rely on power-point wisdom that promises victory over irregulars in 'five easy steps.' Each historical case is different."[75] The irregular warfare threat does not present some single challenge to be met with a single doctrinal response.[76] War, again, is a duel between thinking, determined opponents.

The adversary aside, flexibility and adaptability are also required to deal with chance, uncertainty, and Clausewitzian friction. Even if a perfect counterstrategy for irregular space warfare could be developed and written, which seems doubtful, human error and miscalculation would upset it. Weather, luck, and the unimaginable have all proven worthy opponents of "the perfect plan." "No plan survives contact with the enemy"—true enough, but neither does it survive the multitude of things that always seem to go wrong.[77] A sound space strategy must account for and be tolerant of war's unpleasant surprises. Human error, chance, bad luck, and miscalculation cannot be entirely avoided, and the small errors often can be fixed eventually. What is ultimately important is to get the big things right enough.

Looking Up and Forward: Space Is Not Special

Don't Panic. —Douglas Adams, *Hitchhiker's Guide to the Galaxy*[78]

Irregular forms of competition and coercion have been part of the Space Age since it began. This is not all bad: one can look to the past to understand the function of strategy in the space domain and to derive solutions to complex problems. Because large-scale, regular warfare is less common than its irregular relative, the modes and actions of the latter will become very familiar in space. In any case, policy makers and military leaders can draw from an abundance of literature and historical experience that far predates the Space Age; contemplation of humankind's celestial future is no cause for panic.

Strategy and operational art in the space domain are supported by the irregular-warfare framework. We have seen that state and nonstate actors can expect to encounter irregular competition and conflict in space and that irregular space competitors will seek asymmetric advantage, use indirect approaches, and avoid decisive battle. They will act along distant, exterior CLOCs and against rearward logistical supply lines and bases. Any rival accustomed to fighting in traditional, regular ways should plan accordingly. *U.S. Space Force guardians, you have been warned.*

This is not to say that space is somehow "special," in a strategic sense. Primitive human nature reigns there too, as Michael Howard warns: "Nevertheless violence will continue to erupt in developed societies as well as undeveloped, creating situations of local armed conflict often indistinguishable from traditional war and requiring the continuing exercise of military skills."[79] Because future irregular space warfare can be understood in terms of humankind's strategic history, we know more about it than we do not know. Indeed, irregular space warfare notwithstanding, the future of warfare will look very much like its past.[80] The same foundational theory governs and guides both irregular and regular warfare, regardless of domain. Space strategists forecasting potential futures can be guided by the lore of war and its continuity. Irregular space warfare is still warfare, not something fundamentally different. Moreover, policy makers and military leaders must be wary of sharp distinctions between irregular and regular modes, because most wars have elements of both.

Many of today's most pressing security concerns are best considered using an irregular warfare and competition strategic lens. These current national security space concerns include: direct-ascent, antisatellite testing causing an inordinate amount of debris and threatening others in an indiscriminate manner; uncooperative rendezvous and proximity operations; purposeful lasing of space systems; and jamming of satellite communications and frequency spectra.[81] All these coercive and provocative actions fall short of the use of regular military force and armed conflict, and so by definition, these activities are irregular. Remarkably, these ongoing space activities are not widely recognized as being irregular in style or form. The value of using an irregular framework to contemplate existing space security concerns is that historical experience and strategic understanding can be used to consider solutions to known problems as well as to provide future insights into the solutions for problems as yet undiscovered.

Final Thoughts

Despite the shortcomings of the United States and other liberal democracies that this chapter has identified regarding irregular strategy and conflict, it is not all a "bad news story." The reason that rivals choose irregular modes against strong, liberal democracies is that they *are* strong. Rivals often see direct confrontation as out of the question: costs are unacceptable, and it will not achieve strategic advantage and success. Conversely, irregular competition with Western and other liberal democracies has been generally successful. Still, this is a positive situation, because it is the worldview of liberal societies, embracing rules-based order and free and open societies that defines the terms of the strategic competition in the first place. Irregular forms of coercion and aggression, "by definition," seek to degrade and subvert the rules-based order, upset the status quo, and change the competition paradigm.[82] Secretary of Defense Lloyd Austin has made this point: "The United States has an advantage that no autocracy can match: our combination of free enterprise, free minds, and free people."[83] The fact that individual liberties and freedoms are targeted by irregular methods only highlights their effectiveness and potency. Many liberal democracies in both the East and West are powerhouses of innovation and prosperity and can outcompete autocratic rivals by soft power, free speech, and economic strength.

The point is not to make oneself invulnerable—that is an unachievable absolute—but to make the effects of irregular action in space or against space architectures strategically inconsequential. In Julian Corbett's words, "To seek invulnerability is to fall into the strategical vice of trying to be superior everywhere, to forfeit the attainment of the essential for fear of risking the unessential, to base our plans on an assumption that war may be waged without loss, that it is, in short, something that it never has been and never can be."[84] Space strategy must not seek to be superior everywhere, control everything, and command all CLOCs. Doctrinal terminology like *space control* and *space superiority* are, in the end, unhelpful and misleading.[85] Losses to spacecraft and space architectures will happen: they cannot be avoided.

Finally, the United States and other space powers should be respectful of what history teaches and learn it well, so as not to be surprised by events for which historical understanding (and study of empirical evidence) could have prepared them. A well-read space force and historically informed space strategy can avoid much loss in both blood and treasure, a goal for anyone in the business of warfare.

In the end, there are no set answers, no schoolhouse solutions, no guarantees of success. Instead there are principles for space strategists to consider and rules for them to break in search of the genius of spacepower.

⇛ NOTES ⇚

Preface

1. Colin S. Gray, *Another Bloody Century: Future Warfare* (London: Weidenfeld and Nicolson, 2005), 214.
2. Carl von Clausewitz, *On War*, trans. and ed. Michael Howard and Peter Paret (Princeton, NJ: Princeton University Press, 1989), 87–89, 606.
3. Colin S. Gray, *Irregular Enemies and the Essence of Strategy: Can the American Way of War Adapt?* (Carlisle Barracks, PA: Strategic Studies Institute, March 2006), 50.

Chapter 1. The Enduring Nature of Irregular Warfare

1. Clausewitz, *On War*, 606 (emphasis original).
2. Clausewitz, 189.
3. Peter R. Mansoor, "Hybrid Warfare in History," in *Hybrid Warfare: Fighting Complex Opponents from the Ancient World to the Present*, ed. Williamson Murray and Peter R. Mansoor (Cambridge, U.K.: Cambridge University Press, 2012), 1.
4. Rosa Brooks, "Fighting Words: Has the Nature of 'War' Changed since the Days of Clausewitz?" *Foreign Policy* (February 4, 2014), https://foreignpolicy.com/2014/02/04/fighting-words/
5. Gray, *Another Bloody Century*, 291.
6. Clausewitz, *On War*, 89.
7. Department of Defense, *Summary of the Irregular Warfare Annex to the National Defense Strategy* (Washington, DC, 2020), 1, https://apps.dtic.mil/sti/pdfs/AD1112946.pdf.
8. Clausewitz, *On War*, 75 [emphasis original].
9. Colin S. Gray, "Irregular Warfare: One Nature, Many Characters," *Strategic Studies Quarterly* 1, no. 2 (Winter 2007): 37, https://www.jstor.org/stable/26267370.
10. Gray, *Another Bloody Century*, 248.
11. Clausewitz, *On War*, 81.
12. Peter Browning, *The Changing Nature of Warfare: The Development of Land Warfare from 1792 to 1945* (Cambridge, U.K.: Cambridge University Press, 2002), 2.

13. Clausewitz, *On War*, 75.

14. This does not discount that a war's conduct may include coercion through intimidation or threat of military force, a case that will also be discussed in this work.

15. See John J. Klein, *Space Warfare: Strategy, Principles and Policy* (Abingdon, U.K.: Routledge, 2006), 4.

16. Strategy and Force Planning Faculty, *Strategy and Force Planning*, 3rd ed. (Newport, RI: Naval War College, 2000), 20.

17. Gray, *Another Bloody Century*, 214.

18. Michael I. Handel, *Masters of War: Classical Strategic Thought*, 3rd ed. (Abingdon, U.K.: Routledge, 2001), xxii.

19. Gray, "Irregular Warfare," 43.

20. Department of the Army, *Insurgencies and Countering Insurgencies*, FM 3-24 / MCWP 3-33.5 (Washington, DC, with Change 1, June 2, 2014), 1-1.

21. Seth G. Jones, *Three Dangerous Men: Russia, China, Iran, and the Rise of Irregular Warfare* (New York: W. W. Norton, 2021), 11.

22. Jones, 11.

23. Department of Defense, *Summary of the Irregular Warfare Annex*, 2.

24. David Galula, *Counterinsurgency Warfare: Theory and Practice*, with forward by John A. Nagl (1964; reprint, Westport, CT: Praeger Security International, 2006), 3.

25. Galula, 36.

26. Galula, 4.

27. Galula, 7.

28. Galula, 8–9.

29. Stephen Biddle, *Nonstate Warfare: The Military Methods of Guerillas, Warlords, and Militias* (Princeton, NJ: Princeton University Press, 2021), 23.

30. Biddle, 23.

31. Biddle, xvi.

32. Gray, *Irregular Enemies and the Essence of Strategy*, vi.

33. Gray, vi.

34. Gray, vi.

35. Clausewitz, *On War*, 526; Julian S. Corbett, *Some Principles of Maritime Strategy* (London: Longmans, Green, 1911; reprint, Annapolis, MD: Naval Institute Press, 1988), 31–33, 310–11. Corbett viewed the offense as being the more "effective" form of warfare.

36. Clausewitz, *On War*, 357–58.

37. Clausewitz, 358 [emphasis original].

38. Tarik Solmaz, "'Hybrid Warfare': One Term, Many Meanings," *Small Wars Journal* (February 25, 2022), https://smallwarsjournal.com/jrnl/art/hybrid-warfare-one-term-many-meanings.

39. Colin S. Gray, *Fighting Talk: Forty Maxims on War, Peace, and Strategy* (Westport, CT: Greenwood, 2007), 12.

40. Brent Ziarnick, *Developing National Power in Space: A Theoretical Model* (Jefferson, NC: McFarland, 2015), 30.

41. Clausewitz, *On War*, 75.

42. This definition is a synthesis of Thomas Schelling, *Arms and Influence* (New Haven, CT: Yale University Press, 1966), 2–6.

43. Gen. John Hyten, "Space, Nuclear, and Missile Defense Modernization" (presentation, The Mitchell Institute for Aerospace Studies, Washington, DC, June 20, 2017), available at http://www.stratcom.mil/Media/Speeches/Article/1226883/mitchell-institute-breakfast-series/.

44. Defense Intelligence Agency, *Challenges to Security in Space: Space Reliance in an Era of Competition and Expansion* (2022), 4, https://www.dia.mil/Portals/110/Documents/News/Military_Power_Publications/Challenges_Security_Space_2022.pdf.

45. See John J. Klein, "Op-ed: To Deter Attacks on Satellites, U.S. Needs a Strategy to Identify Bad Actors," *SpaceNews*, June 5, 2020, https://spacenews.com/op-ed-to-deter-attacks-on-satellites-u-s-needs-a-strategy-to-identify-bad-actors/.

46. As cited in Jones, *Three Dangerous Men*, book epigraph, i.

47. Michael Howard, *The Lessons of History* (New Haven, CT: Yale University Press 1991), 9.

48. Howard, 188.

49. Gray, *Another Bloody Century*, 24.

50. Howard, *Lessons of History*, 188.

51. Howard, 189.

52. Howard, 11.

53. Howard, 9.

54. Williamson Murray, "The American Revolution," in Murray and Mansoor, *Hybrid Warfare*, 102–103; Murray citing Thucydides, *History of the Peloponnesian War*, trans. Rex Warner (London: Penguin Books, 1954), 48.

55. Williamson Murray, "Conclusion," in Murray and Mansoor, *Hybrid Warfare*, 290–91.

56. John B. Hattendorf, "The Uses of Maritime History in and for the Navy," *Naval War College Review* 56, no. 2 (2003): 27, https://digital-commons.usnwc.edu/nwc-review/vol56/iss2/4.

57. Brad Townsend, *Security and Stability in the New Space Age: The Orbital Security Dilemma* (Abingdon, U.K.: Routledge, 2020), 20.

58. Joshua P. Carlson, *Spacepower Ascendant: Space Development Theory and a New Space Strategy* (self-pub., 2020), 61.
59. Gray, *Fighting Talk*, 148.
60. Gray, 148.
61. See John J. Klein, "Corbett in Orbit: A Maritime Model for Strategic Space Theory," *Naval War College Review* 57, no. 1 7 (2004): 62; Hattendorf, "Uses of Maritime History," 19.
62. See Klein, *Space Warfare.*
63. Howard, *Lessons of History*, 2.
64. Everett C. Dolman, *Astropolitik: Classical Geopolitics in the Space Age* (Abingdon, U.K.: Frank Cass, 2002), 5.
65. Defense Intelligence Agency, *Challenges to Security in Space*, iv.
66. Brian Weeden and Victoria Samson, eds., *Global Counterspace Capabilities: An Open Source Assessment* (Washington, DC: Secure World Foundation, 2022), xii, https://swfound.org/media/207350/swf_global_counter space_capabilities_2022_rev2.pdf.
67. Weeden and Samson, xii.
68. Josh Rogin, "Opinion: A Shadow War in Space Is Heating Up Fast," *Washington Post,* November 30, 2021, https://www.washingtonpost.com/ opinions/2021/11/30/space-race-china-david-thompson/.
69. Rogin, "Shadow War in Space Is Heating Up Fast."
70. Seth G. Jones, "Commentary: The Future of Competition—U.S. Adversaries and the Growth of Irregular Warfare," *CSIS: Center for Strategic and International Studies*, February 4, 2021, https://www.csis.org/analysis/ future-competition-us-adversaries-and-growth-irregular-warfare.
71. Jones, "Future of Competition."
72. Jones.
73. See John J. Klein, *Understanding Space Strategy: The Art of War in Space* (Abingdon, U.K.: Routledge, 2019), 21.
74. Murray, "American Revolution," 103.
75. Mansoor, "Hybrid Warfare in History," 16–17.
76. Murray, "Conclusion," 307.
77. Jones, *Three Dangerous Men*, 4 [emphasis original].

Chapter 2. Characteristics of Irregular Space Warfare

1. Gray, "Irregular Warfare," 36.
2. Gray, *Another Bloody Century*, 291.
3. Gray, 312.
4. Clausewitz, *On War*, 605.
5. Clausewitz, 594.

6. Antulio J. Echevarria II, "War and Politics: The Revolution in Military Affairs and the Continued Relevance of Clausewitz," *Joint Force Quarterly* (Winter 1995–96): 78, https://ndupress.ndu.edu/portals/68/Documents/jfq/jfq-10.pdf.

7. Jones, *Three Dangerous Men*, 7–10.

8. Clausewitz, *On War*, 605.

9. Mao Tse-tung, *Selected Military Writings of Mao Tse-tung* (Seattle, WA: Praetorian-press.com, 2011), loc. 5017 of 10296, Kindle.

10. Gray, "Irregular Warfare," 44.

11. Colin S. Gray, *Airpower for Strategic Effect* (Maxwell Air Force Base, AL: Air University Press, 2012), 282–83.

12. Clausewitz, *On War*, 88–89.

13. Julian S. Corbett, "Green Pamphlet," in *Some Principles of Maritime Strategy* (London: Longmans, Green, 1911; reprint, Annapolis, MD: Naval Institute Press, 1988), 313.

14. Corbett, 313.

15. Andrew F. Krepinevich Jr., *The Army and Vietnam* (Baltimore, MD: Johns Hopkins University Press, 1986), 7 [emphasis original].

16. Handel, *Masters of War*, 293.

17. Corbett, *Some Principles of Maritime Strategy*, 67.

18. Corbett, 74.

19. Corbett, 59.

20. Corbett, 57.

21. Corbett, 58, 94.

22. See Klein, *Space Warfare*, 100–106.

23. Sun Tzu, *The Art of War*, trans. Samuel B. Griffith (Oxford, U.K.: Oxford University Press, 1963), 73.

24. Mao, *Selected Military Writings,* loc. 3250.

25. T. E. Lawrence, *Seven Pillars of Wisdom* (London, 1962), 202; as cited in Mansoor, "Hybrid Warfare in History," 7n15.

26. Gray, *Irregular Enemies and the Essence of Strategy*, 26.

27. Gray, 23.

28. John J. Mearsheimer, *Conventional Deterrence* (Ithaca, NY: Cornell University Press, 1983), 217n1.

29. B. H. Liddell Hart, *Strategy: The Indirect Approach*, 2nd ed. (London: Faber and Faber, 1967; reprint, BN Publishing, 2020), loc. 141 of 3881, Kindle.

30. Liddell Hart, loc. 152.

31. Liddell Hart, loc. 2417.

32. Liddell Hart, loc. 2314.

33. Liddell Hart, loc. 2442.

34. Mao, *Selected Military Writings*, loc. 3715.

35. Mao, loc. 5182.
36. J. C. Wylie, *Military Strategy: A General Theory of Power Control* (New Brunswick, NJ: Rutgers University Press, 1967; reprint, Annapolis, MD: Naval Institute Press, 1989), 26.
37. Wylie, 24.
38. Wylie, 24–25.
39. Wylie, 23.
40. Wylie, 23–24.
41. Wylie, 22–27.
42. Wylie, 22–27.
43. Wylie, 48–49.
44. Wylie, 48–49.
45. Wylie, 54.
46. Mao, *Selected Military Writings*, loc. 5145.
47. Gray, *Another Bloody Century*, 229.
48. Sun Tzu, *Art of War*, 69.
49. Qiao Liang and Wang Xiangsui, *Unrestricted Warfare: Assumptions on War and Tactics in the Age of Globalization*, trans. Foreign Broadcast Information Service (Beijing: People's Liberation Army Literature and Arts Publishing House, 1999), 211, https://www.c4i.org/unrestricted.pdf.
50. Qiao and Wang, 12, 206.
51. Qiao and Wang, 206.
52. Sandra Erwin, "STRATCOM Chief Hyten: 'I Will Not Support Buying Big Satellites That Make Juicy Targets,'" *SpaceNews*, November 19, 2017, https://spacenews.com/stratcom-chief-hyten-i-will-not-support-buying-big-satellites-that-make-juicy-targets/.
53. Sun Tzu, *Art of War*, 89.
54. Sun Tzu, 66, 69.
55. Sun Tzu, 98–99.
56. Office of the Assistant Secretary of Defense for Homeland Defense and Global Security [hereafter ASD-HDGS], *Space Domain Mission Assurance: A Resilience Taxonomy* (Washington, DC, September 2015), https://www.hsdl.org/?view&did=789773.
57. ASD-HDGS, 8.
58. ASD-HDGS, 8.
59. Sun Tzu, *Art of War*, 106.
60. Mao, *Selected Military Writings*, loc. 3728.
61. Alfred Thayer Mahan, *Sea Power in Its Relation to the War of 1812* (London: Sampson Low, Marston, 1905), 1:316.
62. Corbett, *Some Principles of Maritime Strategy*, 128.

63. Corbett, 152.
64. Mao, *Selected Military Writings*, loc. 3701.
65. Charles E. Callwell, *Small Wars: Their Principles and Practice*, 3rd ed. (London, 1906), 125–26.
66. See Klein, *Understanding Space Strategy*, 34–36.
67. Murray, "Conclusion," 307.
68. Mansoor, "Hybrid Warfare in History," 2.
69. Murray, "Conclusion," 307.
70. Murray, 290.
71. Mansoor, "Hybrid Warfare in History," 3.
72. Mansoor, 5.
73. Mansoor, 5–6.
74. William H. Natter, "Preface," in *Hybrid Warfare and Transnational Threats: Perspectives for an Era of Persistent Conflict*, eds. Paul Brister, William H. Natter, and Robert R. Tomes (New York: Council of Emerging National Security Affairs, 2011), 13.
75. Cited in Natter, 13.
76. Natter, 14.
77. Stephen Biddle, *Nonstate Warfare: The Military Methods of Guerillas, Warlords, and Militias* (Princeton, NJ: Princeton University Press, 2021), 89.
78. Theresa Hitchens, "For Space Force, It's Acquisition, Acquisition, Acquisition: 2022 Preview," *Breaking Defense*, December 29, 2021, https://breakingdefense.com/2021/12/for-space-force-its-acquisition-acquisition-acquisition-2022-preview/.
79. Patrick Howell O'Neill, "Russia Hacked an American Satellite Company One Hour before the Ukraine Invasion," *MIT Technology Review,* May 10, 2022, https://www.technologyreview.com/2022/05/10/1051973/russia-hack-viasat-satellite-ukraine-invasion/.
80. O'Neill.
81. O'Neill.
82. O'Neill.
83. Mao, *Selected Military Writings*, loc. 1931.

Chapter 3. Small Space Wars

1. U.S. Marine Corps, *Warfighting*, Marine Corps Doctrinal Publication 1 (MCDP-1) (Washington, DC, June 20, 1997), 80, https://www.marines.mil/Portals/1/Publications/MCDP%201%20Warfighting.pdf [emphasis original].
2. Biddle, *Nonstate Warfare*, xvi.
3. Clausewitz, *On War*, 75.
4. Callwell, *Small Wars*, 21 [emphasis added].
5. Callwell, 21.

6. Callwell, 25.

7. Callwell, 23.

8. U.S. Marine Corps, *Warfighting*, 27.

9. David Kilcullen, *Counterinsurgency* (Oxford, U.K.: Oxford University Press, 2010), ix–x.

10. Max Boot, *Savage Wars of Peace: Small Wars and the Rise of American Power* (New York: Basic Books, 2002), xvi.

11. U.S. Marine Corps, *Small Wars Manual*, FMFRP 12-15 (Washington, DC: 1940; reprint, 1990), 1, https://www.marines.mil/Portals/1/Publications /FMFRP%2012-15%20%20Small%20Wars%20Manual.pdf.

12. U.S. Marine Corps, *Small Wars Manual*, 1.

13. U.S. Marine Corps, 2.

14. Howard, *Lessons of History*, 19.

15. U.S. Space Force, *Space Capstone Publication: Spacepower, Doctrine for Space Forces* (Washington, DC: Headquarters U.S. Space Force, 2020), 16, https://apps.dtic.mil/sti/pdfs/AD1129735.pdf.

16. Howard, 172.

17. Gray, *Another Bloody Century*, 307.

18. See Klein, *Understanding Space Strategy*, 21.

19. Quoted in Klein, *Space Warfare*, 60; Klein, *Understanding Space Strategy*, 23–24.

20. Corbett, *Some Principles of Maritime Strategy*, 91.

21. Celestial lines of communication—or CLOCs—are those lines of communication in, through, and from space associated with trade, materiel, supplies, personnel, spacecraft, electromagnetic transmissions, and some military effects; and see Klein, *Space Warfare*, 51.

22. See Klein, *Understanding Space Strategy*, 24.

23. See Klein, 24–25.

24. This idea comports with "Where he is strong, avoid him." Sun Tzu, *Art of War*, 67.

25. Biddle, *Nonstate Warfare*, 36.

26. J. Boone Bartholomees Jr., "A Survey of the Theory of Strategy," in *U.S. Army War College Guide to National Security Issues*, 5th ed. (Carlisle Barracks, PA: June 2012), 1:31, https://publications.armywarcollege.edu/pubs/2182. pdf.

27. Biddle, *Nonstate Warfare*, 36

28. Biddle, 37.

29. Biddle, 36.

30. Bleddyn E. Bowen, *War in Space: Strategy, Spacepower, Geopolitics* (Edinburgh, U.K.: Edinburgh University Press, 2020), 113.

31. Joint Chiefs of Staff, *Joint Operations*, Joint Publication 3-0, JP 3-0 (Washington, DC, October 22, 2018, change 1), ix, https://www.jcs.mil/Portals/36/Documents/Doctrine/pubs/jp3_0ch1.pdf.

32. Joint Chiefs of Staff, xiv.

33. Jeff Becker and Todd Zwolensky, "Making Sense of Military Doctrine: Joint and Service Views on Maneuver," *War on the Rocks*, July 3, 2014, https://warontherocks.com/2014/07/making-sense-of-military-doctrine-joint-and-service-views-on-maneuver/.

34. Sun Tzu, *Art of War*, 106.

35. Mao, *Selected Military Writings*, loc. 1714 of 10296. This is somewhat similar in style to Sun Tzu's comment, "When the enemy is at ease, be able to weary him; when well fed, to starve him; when at rest, to make him move"; Sun Tzu, *Art of War*, 96.

36. Raoul Castex, *Strategic Theories,* trans. and ed. Eugenia C. Kiesling (Annapolis, MD: Naval Institute Press, 1994), 101–2, 110.

37. Castex, 102 [italics original].

38. Castex, 102, 105.

39. Castex, 113–14.

40. Galula, *Counterinsurgency Warfare*, 37 [emphasis original].

41. Galula, 37.

42. Joint Chiefs of Staff, *Space Operations*, Joint Publication 3-14, JP 3-14 (Washington, DC, October 26, change 1 2020), II-14, https://www.jcs.mil/Portals/36/Documents/Doctrine/pubs/jp3_14Ch1.pdf.

43. Joint Chiefs of Staff, *Space Operations*, II-14 through II-15.

44. Bowen, *War in Space*, 115.

45. Rodney Atwood, *The Hessians: Mercenaries from Hessen Kassel in the American Revolution* (Cambridge, U.K.: Cambridge University Press, 1980).

46. Biddle, *Nonstate Warfare*, xvi.

47. Andrew Mumford, *Proxy Warfare* (Cambridge, U.K.: Polity, 2013), 1; Andrew Mumford, "Proxy Warfare and the Future of Conflict," *RUSI Journal* 158, no. 2 (2013): 40, https://www.tandfonline.com/doi/pdf/10.1080/03071847.2013.787733.

48. Andrew Mumford, "The New Era of the Proliferated Proxy War," *Strategy Bridge*, November 16, 2017, https://thestrategybridge.org/the-bridge/2017/11/16/the-new-era-of-the-proliferated-proxy-war.

49. Mumford, "Proliferated Proxy War."

50. Mumford.

51. Mumford.

52. Mumford.

53. Sandra Erwin, "Space Force to Shore Up Cybersecurity as Threats Proliferate," *SpaceNews*, April 6, 2022, https://spacenews.com/space-force-to-shore-up-cybersecurity-as-threats-proliferate/.

54. Mike Gruss, "How Russia Telegraphed Invasion of Ukraine in Space and Online," *DefenseNews*, June 15, 2022, https://www.defensenews.com/digital-show-dailies/eurosatory/2022/06/15/how-russia-telegraphed-invasion-of-ukraine-in-space-and-online/.

55. Anthony J. Blinken, "Attribution of Russia's Malicious Cyber Activity against Ukraine," press statement, U.S. Department of State, May 10, 2022, https://www.state.gov/attribution-of-russias-malicious-cyber-activity-against-ukraine/.

56. Gruss, "How Russia Telegraphed Invasion."

57. Andrew F. Krepinevich, *Cyber Warfare: A 'Nuclear Option'?* (Washington, DC: Center for Strategic and Budgetary Assessments, 2012), 181–82, https://csbaonline.org/research/publications/cyber-warfare-a-nuclear-option.

58. See John J. Klein, "Some Principles of Cyber Strategy," *ETHzürich*, August 21, 2014, https://css.ethz.ch/content/specialinterest/gess/cis/center-for-securities-studies/en/services/digital-library/articles/article.html/182955.

59. See Klein.

60. See Klein.

61. Executive Office of the President, *National Security Strategy* (Washington, DC, 2017), 31–32, https://trumpwhitehouse.archives.gov/wp-content/uploads/2017/12/NSS-Final-12-18-2017-0905.pdf.

62. Department of Defense, *Summary: Department of Defense Cyber Strategy* (Washington, DC, 2018), 1, https://media.defense.gov/2018/Sep/18/2002041658/-1/-1/1/CYBER_STRATEGY_SUMMARY_FINAL.PDF

63. Executive Office of the President, *The National Space Policy of the United States of America* (Washington, DC, 2020), 29, https://history.nasa.gov/NationalSpacePolicy12-9-20.pdf.

64. Executive Office of the President, 10.

65. Executive Office of the President, 18.

66. Mumford, "Proxy Warfare and the Future of Conflict," 43.

67. Mumford, 43.

68. P. W. Singer and Allan Friedman, *Cybersecurity and Cyberwar: What Everyone Needs to Know* (Oxford, U.K.: Oxford University Press, 2014), 77.

69. Joint Chiefs of Staff, *Electromagnetic Spectrum Operations*, Joint Publication 3-85 (May 22, 2020), GL-6, https://www.jcs.mil/Portals/36/Documents/Doctrine/pubs/jp3_85.pdf.

70. Joint Chiefs of Staff, I-4.

71. Joint Chiefs of Staff, GL-6.

72. Stew Magnuson, "U.K.'s Upcoming Space Strategy to Focus on Collaboration," *National Defense*, September 13, 2021, https://www.nationaldefense magazine.org/articles/2021/9/14/uks-upcoming-space-strategy-to-focus-on-collaboration.

73. Magnuson.

74. Weeden and Samson, *Global Counterspace Capabilities*, 1-22 through 1-23, https://swfound.org/media/207350/swf_global_counterspace_capabilities_2022_rev2.pdf.

75. Aaron Bateman, "Mutually Assured Surveillance at Risk: Anti-satellite Weapons and Cold War Arms Control," *Journal of Strategic Studies* 45, no. 1 (January 2022): 6–8, https://doi.org/10.1080/01402390.2021.2019022.

76. Elon Musk, Twitter post, May 10, 2022, 8:56 p.m., https://twitter.com/elon musk/status/1524191785760788480?s=20&t=cnfRTIhC0Rl0q8wps3l5VA.

77. Sandra Erwin, "Space Force General: Commercial Satellite Internet in Ukraine Showing Power of Megaconstellations," *SpaceNews*, May 11, 2022, https://spacenews.com/space-force-general-commercial-satellite-internet-in-ukraine-showing-power-of-megaconstellations/.

78. Erwin.

79. Clausewitz, *On War*, 357–58.

80. Clausewitz, 526; Corbett, *Some Principles of Maritime Strategy*, 31–33.

81. Brian Weeden, email to author, March 15, 2022.

82. Antony J. Blinken, "Russia Conducts Destructive Anti-satellite Missile Test," press statement, U.S. Department of State, November 15, 2021, https://www.state.gov/russia-conducts-destructive-anti-satellite-missile-test/.

83. Jeff Foust, "Russian ASAT Debris Creating 'Squalls' of Close Approaches with Satellites," *SpaceNews*, February 18, 2022, https://spacenews.com/russian-asat-debris-creating-squalls-of-close-approaches-with-satellites/.

84. Blinken, "Russia Conducts Destructive Anti-satellite Missile Test."

85. Idrees Ali and Steve Gorman, "Russian Anti-Satellite Missile Test Endangers Space Station Crew—NASA," Reuters, November 16, 2021, https://www.reuters.com/world/us-military-reports-debris-generating-event-outerspace-2021-11-15/.

86. Foust, "Russian ASAT Debris."

87. Foust.

88. Foust.

89. Joint Chiefs of Staff, *Joint Operations*, VII-3.

90. Joint Chiefs of Staff, VII-3.

91. Joint Chiefs of Staff, VII-4.

92. Benjamin Armstrong, *Small Boats and Daring Men: Maritime Raiding, Irregular Warfare, and the Early American Navy* (Norman: University of Oklahoma Press), 191.

93. Armstrong, 191.

94. Armstrong, 191.

95. Armstrong, 192, 199.

96. James Cable, *Gunboat Diplomacy: Political Applications of Limited Naval Force* (New York: Praeger, for the Institute of Strategic Studies, 1971), 48.

97. James C. Bradford, "John Paul Jones and Guerre de Razzia," *Northern Mariner* 13, no. 4 (October 2003): 1–15, https://www.cnrs-scrn.org/northern_mariner/vol13/tnm_13_4_1–15.pdf.

98. Bradford, 2.

99. Armstrong, *Small Boats and Daring Men*, 199.

100. Clausewitz, *On War*, 480–81.

101. Gray, *Another Bloody Century*, 214.

102. Schelling, *Arms and Influence*, 17.

103. Bartholomees, "Survey of the Theory of Strategy," 32–33.

104. Bartholomees, 32–33.

105. Gray, *Irregular Enemies and the Essence of Strategy*, 19.

106. Bartholomees, "Survey of the Theory of Strategy," 33.

107. Howard, *Lessons of History*, 175.

108. See Klein, *Space Warfare*, 124–25.

109. Clausewitz, *On War*, 75 [emphasis original].

110. Gray, "Irregular Warfare," 40.

Chapter 4. Gray-Zone Operations and Gunboat Diplomacy:

1. Robert M. Gates, "A Balanced Strategy: Reprogramming the Pentagon for a New Age," *Foreign Affairs* 88, no. 1 (January/February 2009): 33, https://www.jstor.org/stable/20699432. Gates is paraphrasing Colin Gray.

2. Lyle J. Morris, Michael J. Mazarr, Jeffrey W. Hornung, Stephanie Pezard, Anika Binnendijk, and Marta Keep, *Gaining Competitive Advantage in the Gray Zone: Response Options for Coercive Aggression below the Threshold of Major War* (Santa Monica, CA: RAND, 2019), 8, https://www.rand.org/pubs/research_reports/RR2942.html.

3. Joint Chiefs of Staff, *Competition Continuum*, Joint Doctrine Note 1-19 (Washington, DC, June 3, 2019), https://www.jcs.mil/Portals/36/Documents/Doctrine/jdn_jg/jdn1_19.pdf. U.S. joint doctrine calls this concept the *competition continuum*.

4. Department of Defense Strategic Multi-Layer Assessment, "Gray Zone Effort Update," September 2016; as cited in Morris et al., *Gaining Competitive Advantage*, 8.

5. Morris et al., *Gaining Competitive Advantage*, 9.

6. Morris et al., 12.

7. U.S. Space Force, *Chief of Space Operations' Planning Guidance* (Washington, DC, November 9, 2020), 8, https://media.defense.gov/2020/Nov/09/2002531998/-1/-1/0/CSO%20PLANNING%20GUIDANCE.PDF.

8. Kathleen H. Hicks et al., *By Other Means Part I: Campaigning in the Gray Zone* (Washington, DC: Center for Strategic and International Studies [hereafter CSIS], July 2019), 7, https://csis-website-prod.s3.amazonaws.com/s3fs-public/publication/Hicks_GrayZone_interior_v4_FULL_WEB_0.pdf.

9. Melissa Dalton et al., *By Other Means Part II: Adapting to Compete in the Gray Zone* (Washington, DC: CSIS, August 2019), 19, https://csis-website-prod.s3.amazonaws.com/s3fs-public/publication/Hicks_GrayZone_II_interior_v8_PAGES.pdf.

10. Cable, *Gunboat Diplomacy*, 18.

11. Cable, 9.

12. Cable, 21.

13. Geoffrey Till, *Seapower: A Guide for the Twenty-First Century* (Abingdon, U.K.: Routledge, 2013), 34.

14. Till, 34.

15. Till, 34.

16. Chief of Navy, *Australian Maritime Doctrine: RAN Doctrine 1—2010*, 2nd ed. (Fyshwick, ACT, AU: Sea Power Centre, 2010), 109, https://www.navy.gov.au/sites/default/files/documents/Amd2010.pdf.

17. U.S. Marine Corps, *Small Wars Manual*, sect. 1-1.

18. Bateman, "Mutually Assured Surveillance at Risk," 10-13.

19. Joint Chiefs of Staff, *Joint Doctrine for Military Operations Other Than War*, JP 3-07 (Washington, DC, June 16, 1995), I-4, https://apps.dtic.mil/sti/pdfs/ADA323824.pdf. Though not the current version of U.S. joint doctrine, this publication remains comprehensive and useful on gray-zone operations.

20. Joint Chiefs of Staff, *Military Operations Other Than War*, I-4.

21. Cable, *Gunboat Diplomacy*, 63.

22. U.S. Navy, U.S. Marine Corps, and U.S. Coast Guard, *The Commander's Handbook on the Law of Naval Operations*, NWP 1-14M / MCTP 11-10B / COMDTPUB P5800.7A (Washington, DC, August 2017), 4-5, https://www.hsdl.org/?view&did=806860.

23. Joint Chiefs of Staff, *Military Operations Other Than War*, I-6.

24. Joint Chiefs of Staff, III-4.

25. Joint Chiefs of Staff, I-6.

26. Joint Chiefs of Staff, III-13.

27. Cable, *Gunboat Diplomacy*, 49.

28. Stansfield Turner, "Missions of the Navy," *Naval War College Review* 27, no. 2 (March–April 1974): 15, https://digital-commons.usnwc.edu/nwc-review/vol27/iss2/2. The article was reprinted in *Naval War College Review* 51, no. 1 (Winter 1998), https://digital-commons.usnwc.edu/cgi/viewcontent.cgi?article=2792&context=nwc-review.

29. Additionally, *power projection* is sometimes used interchangeably with *show of force*; Joint Chiefs of Staff, *Military Operations Other Than War*, III-15.

30. Joint Chiefs of Staff, III-15.

31. Till, *Seapower*, 184. Historically, the United States has viewed the projection of power in the context of both air power and seapower, but for brevity, the maritime domain alone is covered here.

32. Till, 185.

33. Till, 184.

34. U.S. Marine Corps, U.S. Navy, and U.S. Coast Guard, *Naval Operations Concept—2010: Implementing the Maritime Strategy* (Washington, DC, 2010), 60, https://www.mccdc.marines.mil/Portals/172/Docs/MCCDC/Documents/Concepts/NOC%202010.pdf.

35. U.S. Marine Corps, U.S. Navy, and U.S. Coast Guard, *Naval Warfare*, Naval Doctrine Publication 1 (Washington, DC: April 2020), 22, https://cimsec.org/wp-content/uploads/2020/08/NDP1_April2020.pdf.

36. U.S. Marine Corps et al., 22.

37. U.S. Space Force, *Space Capstone Publication*, 13.

38. U.S. Marine Corps et al., *Naval Operations Concept*, 54.

39. Joint Chiefs of Staff, *Military Operations Other Than War*, III-4.

40. Joint Chiefs of Staff, III-4.

41. U.S. Marine Corps et al., *Naval Operations Concept*, 52–54.

42. M. V. Smith, *Ten Propositions Regarding Spacepower* (Maxwell Air Force Base, AL: Air University Press, October 2002), 56, https://media.defense.gov/2017/May/05/2001742913/-1/-1/0/FP_0009_SMITH_PROPOSITIONS_REGARDING_SPACEPOWER.PDF.

43. Schelling, *Arms and Influence*, 69–72.

44. Schelling, 72.

45. Schelling, 69–72.

46. Daniel L. Byman, Matthew C. Waxman, and Eric Larson, "How to Think about Coercion," in *Air Power as a Coercive Instrument* (Santa Monica, CA: RAND, 1999), 10, https://www.jstor.org/stable/10.7249/mr1061af.9.

47. Schelling, *Arms and Influence*, 2, 31–34.

48. Cable, *Gunboat Diplomacy*, 23–65.

49. Cable, 29.

50. Cable, 39–40.
51. Cable, 39.
52. Cable, 32.
53. "SWF Releases New Compilation of Robotic Rendezvous and Proximity Operations in Space," *Secure World Foundation*, Tuesday, July 14, 2020, https://swfound.org/news/all-news/2020/07/swf-releases-new-compilation-of-robotic-rendezvous-and-proximity-operations-in-space/. [hereafter SWF, "Robotic Rendezvous and Proximity Operations."]
54. Rebecca Reesman and Andrew Rogers, *Getting in Your Space: Learning from Past Rendezvous and Proximity Operations* (Arlington, VA: Aerospace Center for Space Policy and Strategy, May 2018), 3, https://csps.aerospace.org/sites/default/files/2021-08/GettingInYourSpace.pdf.
55. Reesman and Rogers, 2.
56. SWF, "Robotic Rendezvous and Proximity Operations."
57. Todd Harrison, Kaitlyn Johnson, Makena Young, Nicholas Wood, and Alyssa Goessler, *Space Threat Assessment 2022* (Washington, DC: CSIS, 2022), 24, https://www.csis.org/analysis/space-threat-assessment-2022.
58. Gen. James H. Dickinson, "Presentation to the Senate Armed Services Committee," statement, Washington, DC, April 21, 2021, https://www.armed-services.senate.gov/imo/media/doc/Dickinson04.20.2021.pdf.
59. "China Launches Shijian-21 Satellite," XinhuaNet, October 24, 2021, http://www.news.cn/english/2021-10/24/c_1310265138.htm.
60. Harrison et al., *Space Threat Assessment 2022*, 24.
61. Harrison et al., 24.
62. Harrison et al., 24.
63. Corbett, *Some Principles of Maritime Strategy*, 211.
64. Corbett, 211.
65. Corbett, 211.
66. Corbett, 212–14.
67. Corbett, 224.
68. Kevin Rowlands, "Decided Preponderance at Sea: Naval Diplomacy in Strategic Thought," *Naval War College Review* 65, no. 4 (Autumn 2012): 92, https://digital-commons.usnwc.edu/nwc-review/vol65/iss4/9/.
69. Ministry of Defence, *UK Maritime Power*, Joint Doctrine Publication 0-10, 5th ed. (London, October 2017), 43, https://assets.publishing.service.gov.uk/government/uploads/system/uploads/attachment_data/file/662000/doctrine_uk_maritime_power_jdp_0_10.pdf.
70. Ministry of Defence, 43.
71. Corbett, *Some Principles of Maritime Strategy*, 212.
72. Dean Cheng, *Cyber Dragon: Inside China's Information Warfare and Cyber Operations* (Santa Barbara, CA: Praeger Security International, 2017), 166.

73. Cheng, *Cyber Dragon*, 186.
74. Dean Cheng, *Evolving Chinese Thinking about Deterrence: What the United States Must Understand about China and Space*, Backgrounder No. 3298 (Washington, DC: Heritage Foundation, March 29, 2018), 3, https://www.heritage.org/sites/default/files/2018-03/BG3298_0.pdf.
75. Cheng, *Evolving Chinese Thinking about Deterrence*, 3.
76. Cheng, 3.
77. Joint Chiefs of Staff, *Joint Operations*, VI-4 [emphasis added].
78. Joint Chiefs of Staff, xxii.
79. U.S. Space Force, *Chief of Space Operations' Planning Guidance*, i [emphasis added].
80. Joint Chiefs of Staff, *Space Operations*, I-10.
81. Joint Chiefs of Staff, *Department of Defense Dictionary of Military and Associated Terms,* Joint Publication 1-02 (Washington, DC, November 8, 2010, amended through February 15, 2016), 83.
82. Space Training and Readiness Command [hereafter STARCOM] Public Affairs, "STARCOM Uses High Fidelity Combat Simulation in SPACE FLAG," December 20, 2021, Peterson Space Force Base, CO, https://www.safia.hq.af.mil/IA-News/Article/2887362/starcom-uses-high-fidelity-combat-simulation-in-space-flag-22–1/.
83. Cheng, "Evolving Chinese Thinking about Deterrence," 3–4.
84. Colin S. Gray, *Modern Strategy* (Oxford, U.K.: Oxford University Press, 1999), 254.
85. Colin S. Gray, "The Influence of Space Power upon History," *Comparative Strategy* 15, no. 4 (October–December 1996): 303, https://doi.org/10.1080/01495939608403082.
86. Joint Chiefs of Staff, *Space Operations*, II-1 through II-8. "Timing is the ability to acquire and maintain accurate and precise time . . . anywhere in the world"; "Positioning, Navigation, and Timing (PNT)," August 7, 2017, https://www.jcs.mil/Portals/36/Documents/Doctrine/pubs/jp3_14Ch1.pdf.
87. Gray, *Modern Strategy,* 256. For further discussion of the space domain as geography, see Colin S. Gray, series editor's preface in Dolman, *Astropolitik*, xi–xii.
88. Gray, *Modern Strategy,* 264.
89. Corbett, *Some Principles of Maritime Strategy*, 60–63. Clausewitz does not use Corbett's phrasing but does discuss the concept.
90. Clausewitz, *On War*, 603.
91. Vanya Eftimova Bellinger, "When Resources Drive Strategy: Understanding Clausewitz/Corbett's War Limited by Contingent," *Military Strategy Magazine* 7, no. 1 (Spring 2020): 27–34, https://www.militarystrategymagazine.com

/article/when-resources-drive-strategy-understanding-clausewitz-corbetts -war-limited-by-contingent/.

92. Bellinger.

93. Michael I. Handel, "Corbett, Clausewitz, and Sun Tzu," *Naval War College Review* 53, no. 4 (Autumn 2000): 119, https://digital-commons.usnwc.edu/ cgi/viewcontent.cgi?article=2649&context=nwc-review.

94. Handel, 119.

95. Handel, 119. Handel is referring to Corbett, *Some Principles of Maritime Strategy*, 62–63.

96. Donald M. Schurman, *The Education of a Navy* (London: Cassell, 1965), 161n. Schurman is referring to Corbett's conclusions in *England in the Seven Years' War*, 2 vols. (London, 1907).

97. Corbett, *Some Principles of Maritime Strategy*, 67.

98. Corbett, 62 [emphasis original].

99. Corbett, 65.

100. Corbett, 66.

101. Corbett, 62.

Chapter 5. Lawfare and Space

1. Liddell Hart, *Strategy*, loc. 3705.

2. Charles J. Dunlap Jr., "Law and Military Interventions: Preserving Humanitarian Values in 21st Century Conflicts" (paper, Humanitarian Challenges in Military Intervention Conference, Washington, DC, November 29, 2001), https://people.duke.edu/~pfeaver/dunlap.pdf.

3. Charles J. Dunlap Jr., "Yes, There Is Consensus That 'Lawfare' Exists . . . but America Still Needs a Strategy for It," *Lawfare* (blog), September 23, 2021, https://sites.duke.edu/lawfire/2021/09/23/yes-there-is-consensus-that-law fare-exists-but-america-still-needs-a-strategy-for-it/.

4. Charles J. Dunlap Jr., "Lawfare amid Warfare," *Washington Times*, August 3, 2007, https://www.washingtontimes.com/news/2007/aug/03/lawfare-amid -warfare/.

5. Charles J. Dunlap Jr., "Lawfare Today: A Perspective," *Yale Journal of International Affairs* (Winter 2008): 146, https://scholarship.law.duke.edu/cgi/ viewcontent.cgi?article=5892&context=faculty_scholarship.

6. Dunlap, "Lawfare amid Warfare."

7. Benjamin Wittes, Robert Chesney, and Jack Goldsmith, "About Lawfare: A Brief History of the Term and the Site," *Lawfare* (blog), accessed January 5, 2023, https://www.lawfareblog.com/about-lawfare-brief-history-term-and -site (accessed March 2, 2023).

8. Joel P. Trachtman, "Integrating Lawfare and Warfare," *Boston College International and Comparative Law Review* 39, no. 2 (2016): 39, http://lawdigital commons.bc.edu/iclr/vol39/iss2/3.

9. Orde F Kittrie, *Lawfare: Law as a Weapon of War* (New York: Oxford University Press, 2016), 3.

10. Kittrie, 4–5.

11. Kittrie, 44–49.

12. Robert W. Jarman, video call with author, November 16, 2021.

13. Dean Cheng, *Winning without Fighting: Chinese Legal Warfare* (Washington, DC: Heritage Foundation, May 21, 2012), https://www.heritage.org/asia/report/winning-without-fighting-chinese-legal-warfare.

14. Cheng.

15. Jarman, video call.

16. PRC and Russia delegations to the United Nations, "Draft Treaty on the Prevention of the Placement of Weapons in Outer Space, the Threat or Use of Force against Outer Space Objects," (draft treaty, 2008), 1, https://www.reachingcriticalwill.org/images/documents/Disarmament-fora/cd/2008/documents/Draft%20PPWT.pdf.

17. PRC and Russia delegations, 1–2.

18. Todd Harrison, *International Perspectives on Space Weapons* (Washington, DC: CSIS, May 2020), 13, hhttps://aerospace.csis.org/wp-content/uploads/2020/05/Harrison_IntlPerspectivesSpaceWeapons-compressed.pdf.

19. Harrison, 15.

20. Robert A. Wood, "The Threats Posed by Russia and China to Security of the Outer Space Environment" (statement, Conference on Disarmament Plenary Meeting, Geneva, August 14, 2019), https://geneva.usmission.gov/2019/08/14/statement-by-ambassador-wood-the-threats-posed-by-russia-and-china-to-security-of-the-outer-space-environment/.

21. Wood.

22. Wood.

23. Cheng, *Winning without Fighting*.

24. Cheng.

25. Han Yanrong, "Legal Warfare: Military Legal Work's High Ground—An Interview with Chinese Politics and Law University Military Legal Research Center Special Researcher Xun Dandong," *Legal Daily* (PRC), February 12, 2006; cited in Cheng, "Winning without Fighting."

26. Cheng, *Winning without Fighting*.

27. Cheng.

28. Eric W. Orts, "The Rule of Law in China," *Vanderbilt Journal of Transnational Law* 34, no. 1 (January 2001): 43–116, https://scholarship.law.vanderbilt.edu/vjtl/vol34/iss1/2/.

29. "'Rule of Law' or 'Rule by Law'? In China, a Preposition Makes All the Difference," *Wall Street Journal*, October 20, 2014, https://www.wsj.com/articles/BL-CJB-24523.

30. Jones, *Three Dangerous Men*, 148n21.

31. Cheng, *Winning without Fighting*.

32. Cheng.

33. Jill Goldenziel, "The U.S. Is Losing the Legal War against China," *Forbes*, August 3, 2021, https://www.forbes.com/sites/jillgoldenziel/2021/08/03/the-us-is-losing-the-legal-war-against-china/.

34. Nguyen Thanh Trung and Le Ngoc Khanh Ngan, *Codifying Waters and Reshaping Orders: China's Strategy for Dominating the South China Sea* (Washington, DC: CSIS, September 27, 2021), https://amti.csis.org/codifying-waters-and-reshaping-orders-chinas-strategy-for-dominating-the-south-china-sea/.

35. Morris et al., *Gaining Competitive Advantage*, xii.

36. Emma Graham-Harrison, "South China Sea Islands Are Chinese Plan to Militarise Zone, Claims US," *Guardian* (U.S. edition), December 2, 2017, https://www.theguardian.com/world/2015/may/30/us-claims-south-china-sea-islands-are-beijing-plot.

37. Michael Green, Kathleen Hicks, Zack Cooper, John Schaus, and Jake Douglas, *Counter-Coercion Series: Scarborough Shoal Standoff* (Washington, DC: CSIS, May 22, 2017), https://amti.csis.org/counter-co-scarborough-standoff/

38. Goldenziel, "U.S. Is Losing the Legal War."

39. Goldenziel.

40. The Republic of the Philippines v. The People's Republic of China, PCA Case No. 2013–19, "The South China Sea Arbitration Award of 12 July 2016," Permanent Court of Arbitration, 12 July 2016, https://www.lawfareblog.com/south-china-sea-arbitration-award-five-years-later.

41. Sourabh Gupta, "The South China Sea Arbitration Award Five Years Later," *Lawfare* (blog), August 3, 2021, https://www.lawfareblog.com/.

42. Gupta.

43. Gupta.

44. Gupta.

45. Gupta.

46. "Kamala Harris Accuses Beijing of 'Coercion' and 'Intimidation' in South China Sea," *Guardian* (U.S. edition), August 24, 2021, https://www.theguardian.com/us-news/2021/aug/24/kamala-harris-accuses-beijing-of-coercion-and-intimidation-in-south-china-sea.

47. "Kamala Harris Accuses Beijing."

48. Cheng, *Winning without Fighting*.

49. Trachtman, "Integrating Lawfare and Warfare," 282.

50. Galula, *Counterinsurgency Warfare*, 9.

51. Galula, 9.

52. Liddell Hart, *Strategy*, loc. 2406.

53. Liddell Hart, loc. 2442 [emphasis original].

54. Trachtman, "Integrating Lawfare and Warfare," 267.

55. Trachtman, 280.

56. Wylie, *Military Strategy*, 77–78.

57. Wylie, 22–27.

58. Wylie, 24.

59. Mao, *Selected Military Writings*.

60. Joint Chiefs of Staff, *Military Deception*, Joint Publication 3-13.4 (Washington, DC, January 26, 2012),viii, ix, https://jfsc.ndu.edu/portals/72/documents/jc2ios/additional_reading/1c3-jp_3–13–4_mildec.pdf.

61. Sun Tzu, *Art of War*, 69.

62. Sun Tzu, 78.

63. Gen. John Hyten, "Space, Nuclear, and Missile Defense Modernization" (presentation, Mitchell Institute for Aerospace Studies, Washington, D.C., June 20, 2017), http://www.stratcom.mil/Media/Speeches/Article/1226883/mitchell-institute-breakfast-series/.

64. United Nations, *Charter of the United Nations and Statute of the International Court of Justice* (San Francisco, June 26, 1945) [hereafter UN Charter], Article 2(4), https://legal.un.org/repertory/art2/english/rep_supp7_vol1_art2_4.pdf [emphasis added].

65. UN Charter, Chapter 7, Article 51, https://legal.un.org/repertory/art51.shtml [emphasis added].

66. Robert W. Jarman, email to author, January 31, 2022.

67. A. R. Thomas and James C. Duncan, *International Law Studies, Volume 73: Annotated Supplement to the Commander's Handbook on the Law of Naval Operations* (Newport, RI: Naval War College, 1999), 365n1, https://ia801601.us.archive.org/11/items/annotatedsupplem73thom/annotatedsupplem73thom.pdf

68. Thomas and Duncan, 367n12.

69. International Peace Conference of 1907, *Convention (V) respecting the Rights and Duties of Neutral Powers and Persons in Case of War on Land* (The Hague, October 18, 1907), Article 1, https://ihl-databases.icrc.org/ihl/intro/200.

70. Thomas and Duncan, *Annotated Supplement to Handbook*, 381n88.

71. Thomas and Duncan, 381n91. While beyond the scope of this chapter, it is worth noting that the application of the law of neutrality may be impacted

by the UN Charter and decisions of the UN Security Council in certain circumstances. For example, see UN Charter, Chapter VII.

72. Hague Convention V. *Convention (XIII) concerning the Rights and Duties of Neutral Powers in Naval War* (The Hague, October 18, 1907), https://ihl-databases.icrc.org/applic/ihl/ihl.nsf/INTRO/240.

73. Robert W. Jarman, "The Law of Neutrality in Outer Space" (thesis, Institute of Air and Space Law, McGill University, 2008), 66, https://escholarship.mcgill.ca/concern/theses/vx021j773.

74. Jarman, 90.

75. Jarman, 91.

76. United Nations General Assembly, Resolution 2222 (XXI), *Treaty on Principles Governing the Activities of States in the Exploration and Use of Outer Space, including the Moon and Other Celestial Bodies*, or *The Outer Space Treaty* (1967), Article II, http://www.unoosa.org/oosa/en/ourwork/spacelaw/treaties/outerspacetreaty.html.

77. United Nations General Assembly, Article IX [emphasis added].

78. United Nations General Assembly, Article IX.

79. Secretary of Defense, "Tenets of Responsible Behavior in Space" (memorandum, Washington, DC, July 7, 2021), https://media.defense.gov/2021/Jul/23/2002809598/-1/-1/0/tenets-of-responsible-behavior-in-space.pdf.

80. Secretary of Defense.

81. *The Artemis Accords: Principles for Cooperation in the Civil Exploration and Use of the Moon, Mars, Comets, and Asteroids for Peaceful Purposes* (October 13, 2020), 2, 5–6, https://www.nasa.gov/specials/artemis-accords/img/Artemis-Accords-signed-13Oct2020.pdf.

82. See Klein, *Understanding Space Strategy*, 21.

83. Cheng, *Winning without Fighting*.

84. Clausewitz, *On War*, 357–58.

85. Kittrie, *Lawfare*, 32–33.

86. Clausewitz, *On War*, 526.

87. Kittrie, *Lawfare*, 31.

88. Goldenziel, "U.S. Is Losing the Legal War."

89. Dolman, *Astropolitik*, 87.

90. *Artemis Accords*, 5.

91. Theresa Hitchens, "Exclusive: UK Pushes New UN Accord on Military Space Norms," *Breaking Defense*, September 13, 2021, https://breakingdefense.com/2021/09/exclusive-uk-pushes-new-un-accord-on-military-space-norms/.

92. Jarman, email.

93. Jarman, email.

94. Goldenziel, "U.S. Is Losing the Legal War."

95. Galula, *Counterinsurgency Warfare*, 51.

96. Carissa Christensen, "Commercial Space in 2033" (presentation, Schriever Wargame 2023 Commercial and Civil Workshop, Les Mureaux, France, May 17, 2022).

97. See Peter Dutton, ed., *Military Activities in the EEZ: A U.S.-China Dialogue on Security and International Law in the Maritime Commons*, China Maritime Studies Institute Red Book 7 (Newport, RI: Naval War College Press, 2010).

98. Carlson, *Spacepower Ascendant*, 79.

Chapter 6. Commercial Companies, Privateers, and Space Pirates

1. Sean McFate, *Mercenaries and War: Understanding Private Armies Today* (Washington, DC: National Defense University Press, 2019), 43, https://ndupress.ndu.edu/Portals/68/Documents/strat-monograph/mercenaries-and-war.pdf.

2. Doug Loverro, "If Commercial Space Is Ready to Set Sail, Why Are We Still Missing the Boat?" *Breaking Defense*, August 25, 2021, https://breakingdefense.com/2021/08/if-commercial-space-is-ready-to-set-sail-why-are-we-still-missing-the-boat/.

3. "Commercial Space Activities," SpacePolicyOnline.com, updated January 26, 2021, https://spacepolicyonline.com/topics/commercial-space-activities/.

4. "Commercial Space Activities."

5. Irina Liu, Evan Linck, Bhavya Lal, Keith W. Crane, Xueying Han, Thomas J. Colvin, *Evaluation of China's Commercial Space Sector*, D-10873 (Washington, DC: Institute of Defense Analyses, September 2019), 3, https://www.ida.org/-/media/feature/publications/e/ev/evaluation-of-chinas-commercial-space-sector/d-10873.ashx.

6. Executive Office of the President, *National Space Policy*, 20.

7. "Basics of GPS," *Schriever Space Force Base* (Archived), October 2020, https://www.schriever.spaceforce.mil/GPS/.

8. "Commercial Space Activities."

9. "United Launch Alliance," *Boeing*, https://www.boeing.com/space/united-launch-alliance/ (accessed January 5, 2023).

10. "Commercial Space Activities."

11. Space Foundation Editorial Team, *Space Briefing Book* (Colorado Springs, CO: Space Foundation), https://www.spacefoundation.org/space_brief/space-sectors/

12. "Quasi-Public Corporation," *Nasdaq*, https://www.nasdaq.com/glossary/q/quasi-public-corporation (accessed January 5, 2023).

13. "Public-Private Partnerships (PPP): How Can PPPs Help Deliver Better Services?" *World Bank Group*, https://ppp.worldbank.org/public-private-

partnership/about-us/about-public-private-partnerships# (accessed January 5, 2023).

14. Liu et al., *China's Commercial Space Sector*, 1.
15. Liu et al., 2–3.
16. Liu et al., 3.
17. Liu et al., 27.
18. Liu et al., 2–3, 27.
19. Liu et al., 6.
20. Neel V. Patel, "China's Surging Private Space Industry Is Out to Challenge the US," *MIT Technology Review*, January 21, 2021, https://www.technology review.com/2021/01/21/1016513/china-private-commercial-space-industry -dominance/.
21. Patel.
22. Liddell Hart, *Strategy*, loc. 152.
23. Liddell Hart, loc. 2442.
24. Liddell Hart, loc. 2417.
25. See Klein, *Understanding Space Strategy*, 131–32.
26. Dani Haloutz, "Air and Space Strategy for Small Powers: Needs and Opportunities," in *Towards a Fusion of Air and Space: Surveying Developments and Assessing Choices for Small and Middle Powers*, ed. Dana J. Johnson and Ariel E. Levite (Santa Monica, CA: RAND, 2003), 148.
27. Rodrick H. McHaty and Joe Moye, "The US Military Must Plan for Encounters with Private Military Companies," *Brookings*, March 30, 2021, https:// www.brookings.edu/blog/order-from-chaos/2021/03/30/the-us-military- must-plan-for-encounters-with-private-military-companies/.
28. P. W. Singer, *Corporate Warriors: The Rise of the Privatized Military Industry* (Ithaca, NY: Cornell University Press, 2003), 2–3.
29. McFate, *Mercenaries and War*, 1.
30. Alexander Casendino, "Soldiers of Fortune: The Rise of Private Military Companies and Their Consequences on America's Wars," *Berkeley Political Review*, October 25, 2017, https://bpr.berkeley.edu/2017/10/25/soldiers-of- fortune-the-rise-of-private-military-companies-and-their-consequences- on-americas-wars/.
31. McFate, *Mercenaries and War*, 10.
32. McFate, 6.
33. McFate, 6
34. McFate, 6.
35. McFate, 26.
36. McHaty and Moye, "US Military Must Plan for Encounters."

37. "SpaceLogistics," *Northrop Grumman*, https://www.northropgrumman.com/space/space-logistics-services/. (accessed January 5, 2023).
38. Bowen, *War in Space*, 125.
39. U.S. Const., art. I, § 8, cl. 11.
40. "Pirate or Privateer, the Law of the Sea," *Escales: Ponant Magazine*, https://escales.ponant.com/en/differences-pirate-privateer/ (accessed January 5, 2023).
41. Armstrong, *Small Boats and Daring Men*, 126–27.
42. Armstrong, 126–27.
43. "Pirates, Privateers, Corsairs, Buccaneers: What's the Difference?" *Encyclopedia Britannica*, https://www.britannica.com/story/pirates-privateers-corsairs-buccaneers-whats-the-difference. (accessed January 5, 2023).
44. Morris et al., *Gaining Competitive Advantage*, xii.
45. "Ukraine's Volunteer 'IT Army' Is Hacking in Uncharted Territory," *Wired*, February 27, 2022, https://www.wired.com/story/ukraine-it-army-russia-war-cyberattacks-ddos/.
46. U.S. Space Force, *Space Capstone Publication*, 5, 37.
47. U.S. Space Force, 5, 37.
48. "Hybrid Space Architecture: Statement of Principles," *NewSpace New Mexico*, https://www.newspacenm.org/wp-content/uploads/2021/01/Nixon-Hybrid-Architecture-Statement-of-Principles-v21.pdf. (accessed April 30, 2022).
49. ASD-HDGS, *Space Domain Mission Assurance*.
50. "Hybrid Space Architecture."
51. Chuck Beames, "Why Hybrid Systems Will Enable the United States' Space Future," *Forbes*, November 29, 2019, https://www.forbes.com/sites/charlesbeames/2019/11/29/why-hybrid-systems-will-enable-the-united-states-space-future/.
52. Hitchens, "For Space Force, It's Acquisition."
53. "Hybrid Space Architecture." "Smallsats," small satellites, constitute the largest of several categories of satellites purposefully miniaturized for economy or efficiency.
54. Beames, "Hybrid Systems."
55. Beames.
56. John Paul (JP) Parker, "Op-ed: Why a 'Hybrid' Space Architecture Makes Sense for Economic and National Security," *SpaceNews*, August 14, 2022, https://spacenews.com/op-ed-why-a-hybrid-space-architecture-makes-sense-for-economic-and-national-security/.
57. John Raymond, as quoted in Sandra Erwin, "Raymond: U.S. Space Command Needs Satellites to Be Built Fast, to Be Survivable," *SpaceNews*, Sep-

tember 17, 2019, https://spacenews.com/raymond-u-s-space-command-needs-satellites-to-be-built-fast-to-be-survivable/.

58. John Raymond, as quoted in Theresa Hitchens, "Space Force Targets 2027 for Resilient On-Orbit Posture Initial Capability," *Breaking Defense*, May 17, 2022, https://breakingdefense.com/2022/05/space-force-targets-2027-for-resilient-on-orbit-posture-initial-capability/.

59. John Raymond, as quoted in Sandra Erwin, "Military Space Chiefs from 15 Countries Gather amid Growing Security Concerns," *SpaceNews*, April 4, 2022, https://spacenews.com/military-space-chiefs-from-15-countries-gather-amid-growing-security-concerns/.

60. Erwin, "Military Space Chiefs . . . Gather."

61. Robin Dickey, *Commercial Normentum: Space Security Challenges, Commercial Actors, and Norms of Behavior* (Arlington, VA: Center for Space Policy and Strategy, August 2022), 11, https://csps.aerospace.org/papers/commercial-normentum-space-security-challenges-commercial-actors-and-norms-behavior.

62. David A. Koplow, "Reverse Distinction: A U.S. Violation of the Law of Armed Conflict in Space," *Harvard National Security Journal* 13, no. 1 (2022): 25–26, https://harvardnsj.org/2022/01/07/reverse-distinction-a-u-s-violation-of-the-law-of-armed-conflict-in-space/.

63. U.S. Navy et al., *Commander's Handbook on the Law of Naval Operations*, 8-1.

64. U.S. Navy et al., 8-3.

65. Koplow, "Reverse Distinction," 25–26.

66. Koplow, 25–26.

67. Koplow, 25–26.

68. Koplow, 34.

69. Charles Dunlap, as cited in Amanda Miller, "Resilient Architecture vs. Civilian Risk," *Air Force Magazine*, February 16, 2022, https://www.airforcemag.com/article/resilient-architecture-vs-civilian-risk/.

70. Miller.

71. "Category: Hosted Payloads," *Office of Space Commerce*, https://www.space.commerce.gov/category/government-business/hosted-payloads/ (accessed January 5, 2023).

72. Robert W. Jarman, email message to author, May 20, 2022.

73. Iris Kyriazi, "Outer Space as Global Commons," *Katoikos*, May 25, 2020, https://katoikos.world/analysis/outer-space-as-global-commons.html.

74. Executive Office of the President, *National Security Strategy* (Washington, DC, May 2010), 49–50, https://obamawhitehouse.archives.gov/sites/default/files/rss_viewer/national_security_strategy.pdf [emphasis added].

75. L. A. Fisk, "Space as a Global Commons" (presentation, United Nations Office for Outer Space Affairs, Dubai, n.d.), 3, https://www.unoosa.org/documents/pdf/hlf/1st_hlf_Dubai/Presentations/26.pdf (accessed January 5, 2023).

76. Executive Office of the President, Executive Order 13914, April 6, 2020, 1, https://www.govinfo.gov/content/pkg/FR-2020-04-10/pdf/2020-07800.pdf.

77. American Space Commerce Free Enterprise Act of 2018, 51 U.S.C. § 80308, Global Commons, https://www.congress.gov/bill/115th-congress/house-bill/2809/text#toc-H031D6DABEAC04942A835BDD8E49A903B. This bill was passed by the House but has not become law.

78. Scott Pace, email message to author, April 15, 2022.

79. Scott Pace, "Space Development, Law, and Values" (keynote address, IISL Galloway Space Law Symposium, Washington, D.C., December 13, 2017), 4, https://spacepolicyonline.com/wp-content/uploads/2017/12/Scott-Pace-to-Galloway-Symp-Dec-13-2017.pdf.

80. Pace, email message.

81. United Nations General Assembly, Resolution 2222 (XXI), Article I, http://www.unoosa.org/oosa/en/ourwork/spacelaw/treaties/outerspacetreaty.html.

82. Henry R. Hertzfeld, Brian Weeden, and Christopher D. Johnson, "How Simple Terms Mislead Us: The Pitfalls of Thinking about Outer Space as a Commons" (presentation, 2015 International Astronautical Conference, IAC-15—E7.5.2 x 29369) 7, https://swfound.org/media/205390/how-simple-terms-mislead-us-hertzfeld-johnson-weeden-iac-2015.pdf.

83. Hertzfeld et al., 4.

84. Hertzfeld et al., 11.

85. Pace, email message.

Chapter 7. Exploiting Space Technologies for Asymmetric Advantage

1. Thomas G. Mahnken, *Technology and the American War of War since 1945* (New York: Columbia University Press, 2008), 227.

2. For space-related technologies, see Sandra Erwin, "On National Security: Moving Data through Space a Linchpin of DoD's Strategy for Winning Wars," *SpaceNews*, June 30, 2021, https://spacenews.com/on-national-security-moving-data-through-space-a-linchpin-of-dods-strategy-for-winning-wars/.

3. David J. Lonsdale, *The Nature of War in the Information Age: Clausewitzian Future* (London: Frank Cass, 2004), 53.

4. Mahnken, *Technology and the American War of War*, 220.

5. Handel, *Masters of War*, xxi [emphasis original].

6. Armstrong, *Small Boats and Daring Men*, 194.
7. Armstrong, 193.
8. Howard, *Lessons of History*, 4.
9. Jeremy Black, *Rethinking Military History* (Abingdon, U.K.: Routledge, 2004), 110.
10. Gray, *Fighting Talk*, 55.
11. Black, *Rethinking Military History*, 111.
12. Colin S. Gray, *The Strategy Bridge: Theory for Practice* (Oxford, U.K.: Oxford University Press, 2010), 72.
13. Gray, *Irregular Enemies and the Essence of Strategy*, 25.
14. Clausewitz, *On War*, 594.
15. B. H. Liddell Hart, "The Development of the 'New Model' Army: Suggestions on a Progressive, but Gradual Mechanicalization," *Army Quarterly* 9, no. 1 (1924): 49.
16. Biddle, *Nonstate Warfare*, 55.
17. Bob Work, "Remarks by Deputy Secretary Work on Third Offset Strategy" (speech as delivered, Brussels, Belgium, April 28, 2016), https://www.defense.gov/News/Speeches/Speech-View/Article/753482/remarks-by-d%20eputy-secretary-work-on-third-offset-strategy/.
18. See John J. Klein and Nickolas J. Boensch, "NewSpace and New Risks in Space Security," in *Oxford Handbook of Space Security*, ed. Saadia M. Pekkanen and P. J. Blount (Oxford, U.K.: Oxford University Press, forthcoming).
19. See Klein and Boensch.
20. U.S. Space Force, *Chief of Space Operations' Planning Guidance*, 10.
21. See Klein and Boensch, "NewSpace and New Risks."
22. Satellite Industry Association, *State of the Satellite Industry Report* (2021), https://sia.org/news-resources/state-of-the-satellite-industry-report/.
23. See Klein and Boensch, "NewSpace and New Risks."
24. State Council Information Office of the People's Republic of China, *China's Space Program: A 2021 Perspective*, white paper (January 2022), http://www.cnsa.gov.cn/english/n6465652/n6465653/c6813088/content.html.
25. State Council Information Office.
26. State Council Information Office.
27. State Council Information Office.
28. State Council Information Office.
29. State Council Information Office.
30. State Council Information Office.

31. Brad Townsend, "Strategic Choice and the Orbital Security Dilemma," *Strategic Studies Quarterly* (Spring 2020): 74, https://www.airuniversity.af.edu/Portals/10/SSQ/documents/Volume-14_Issue-1/Townsend.pdf.

32. Aaron Bateman, "Restraint, Not Superiority, in Space," *War on the Rocks,* March 4, 2021, https://warontherocks.com/2021/03/restraint-not-superiority-in-space/.

33. James Vedda and Peter Hays, *Major Policy Issues in Evolving Global Space Operations* (Arlington, VA: Mitchell Institute for Aerospace Studies, 2018), 44, https://aerospace.org/sites/default/files/2018-05/Space_Policy_FINAL_interactive_0.pdf.

34. Mariel John Borowitz, Lawrence Rubin, and Brian Stewart, "National Security Implications of Emerging Satellite Technologies," *Orbis* 64, no. 4 (Fall 2020): 524, https://doi.org/10.1016/j.orbis.2020.08.002.

35. Bateman, "Restraint, Not Superiority."

36. David Hebert, Karen Jones, and Russell Rumbaugh, *Outpacing the Threat with an Agile Defense Space Enterprise* (Arlington, VA: Aerospace Center for Space Policy and Strategy, September 24, 2019), 2, https://csps.aerospace.org/papers/outpacing-threat-agile-defense-space-enterprise.

37. Glenn H. Snyder, "Deterrence and Power," *Journal of Conflict Resolution* 4, no. 2 (June 1960): 163, https://doi.org/10.1177/002200276000400201.

38. See John J. Klein, *The Influence of Commercial Space Capabilities on Deterrence* (Washington, DC: Center for a New American Security, March 25, 2019), https://www.cnas.org/publications/reports/the-influence-of-commercial-space-capabilities-on-deterrence.

39. Jamie Morin and Robert Wilson, *Leveraging Commercial Space for National Security* (Arlington, VA: Aerospace Center for Space Policy and Strategy, November 16, 2020), 7, https://csps.aerospace.org/sites/default/files/2021-08/Morin-Wilson_Leveraging_20201113.pdf.

40. Matthew A. Hallex and Travis S. Cottom, "Proliferated Commercial Satellite Constellations: Implications for National Security," *Joint Force Quarterly* 97 (2nd Quarter 2020): 25, https://ndupress.ndu.edu/Portals/68/Documents/jfq/jfq-97/jfq-97_20-29_Hallex-Cottom.pdf?ver=2020-03-31-130614-940.

41. See Klein, *Influence of Commercial Space Capabilities.*

42. Kenneth Waltz, *Theory of International Politics* (Reading, MA: Addison-Wesley, 1979), 153.

43. Borowitz et al., "National Security Implications of Emerging Satellite Technologies."

44. John H. Herz, "Idealist Internationalism and the Security Dilemma," *World Politics* 2, no. 2 (1950): 157, https://doi.org/10.2307/2009187.

45. Townsend, "Strategic Choice," 64.

46. Townsend, 74–75.
47. Charles Weiss, "Science, Technology, and International Relations," *Technology in Society* 27, no. 3 (2005): 303, https://doi.org/10.1016/j.techsoc.2005.04.004.
48. Daniel W. Drezner, "Technological Change and International Relations," *International Relations* 33, no. 2 (2019): 286–87, https://doi.org/10.1177/0047117819834629.
49. Robert Jervis, "Cooperation under the Security Dilemma," *World Politics* 30, no. 2 (1978): 186–87, https://doi.org/10.2307/2009958.
50. Stephen Van Evera, *Causes of War* (Ithaca, NY: Cornell University Press, 1999), 13–14.
51. Townsend, "Strategic Choice," 73.
52. M. V. Smith, "Spacepower and the Strategist," in *Strategy: Context and Adaptation from Archidamus to Airpower,* ed. Richard Bailey, James Forsyth, and Mark Yeisley (Annapolis, MD: Naval Institute Press, 2016), 171.
53. John B. Sheldon, *Reasoning by Strategic Analogy: Classical Strategic Thought and the Foundations of a Theory of a Space Power* (Ph.D. thesis, University of Reading, 2007), 199.
54. Jacquelyn Schneider, "The Capability/Vulnerability Paradox and Military Revolutions: Implications for Computing, Cyber, and the Onset of War," *Journal of Strategic Studies* 42, no. 6 (2019): 847, https://doi.org/10.1080/01402390.2019.1627209.
55. Schneider, 842.
56. Schneider, 848.
57. Muhammet Bas and Andrew Cole, "Arms Diffusion and War," *Journal of Conflict Resolution* 56, no. 4 (2012): 651–74.
58. Bas and Cole, 652.
59. Todd S. Sechser, Neil Narang, and Caitlin Talmadge, "Emerging Technologies and Strategic Stability in Peacetime, Crisis, and War," *Journal of Strategic Studies* 42 no. 6 (2019): 728, https://doi.org/10.1080/01402390.2019.1626725.
60. Caitlin Talmadge, "Emerging Technology and Intra-War Escalation Risks: Evidence from the Cold War, Implications for Today," *Journal of Strategic Studies* 42 no. 6 (2019): 865, https://doi.org/10.1080/01402390.2019.1631811.
61. Talmadge, 866.
62. Talmadge, 879.
63. Talmadge, 866.
64. Talmadge, 883.
65. Colin Gray, *Perspectives on Strategy* (Oxford, U.K.: Oxford University Press, 2013), 179.

66. Gray, *Perspectives on Strategy*, 179.
67. Gray, *Perspectives on Strategy*, 180.
68. Sechser et al., "Emerging Technologies and Strategic Stability," 728.
69. Gray, *Perspectives on Strategy*, 170.
70. Gray, *Perspectives on Strategy*, 184.
71. Emily Goldman and Richard Andres, "Systemic Effects of Military Innovation and Diffusion," *Security Studies* 8, no. 4 (1999): 83, https://doi.org/10.1080/09636419908429387.
72. Samuel Huntington, "Arms Races: Prerequisites and Results," *Public Policy* 8 (1958): 42.
73. Barry Posen, *The Sources of Military Doctrine: France, Britain, and Germany between the World Wars* (Ithaca, NY: Cornell University Press, 1984).
74. Michael Howard, "IISS: The First Thirty Years—A General Overview," in *A Historical Sensibility: Sir Michael Howard and the International Institute for Strategic Studies, 1958–2019*, International Institute for Strategic Studies (Abingdon, U.K.: Routledge, 2020), 294.
75. Mahnken, *Technology and the American War of War*, 6.

Chapter 8. How to Counter Irregular Space Warfare

1. Gray, "Irregular Warfare," 51.
2. Clausewitz, *On War*, 75.
3. Gray, "Irregular Warfare," 51.
4. Clausewitz, *On War*, 178.
5. Clausewitz, 178.
6. Gray, *Irregular Enemies*, 51.
7. Clausewitz, *On War*, 89.
8. From the Charter of the United Nations: "All Members shall refrain in their international relations from the threat or use of force against the territorial integrity or political independence of any State, or in any other manner inconsistent with the Purposes of the United Nations." UN Charter, Chapter I, Article 2(4).
9. Gray, *Irregular Enemies*, 7.
10. For an argument against popular perceptions of an American way of war, see Antulio J. Echevarria II, *Reconsidering the American Way of War: US Military Practice from the Revolution to Afghanistan* (Washington, DC: Georgetown University Press, 2014).
11. Sun Tzu, *Art of War*, 84.
12. Jones, *Three Dangerous Men*, 19–20 [emphasis original].
13. Barry R. Posen, "Command of the Commons: The Military Foundation of U.S. Hegemony," *International Security* 28, no. 1 (Summer 2003): 5–46, https://www.jstor.org/stable/4137574.

14. Samuel P. Huntington, *American Military Strategy*, Policy Papers in International Affairs, no. 28 (Berkeley, CA: Institute of International Studies, University of California, 1986), 16.
15. Gray, *Irregular Enemies*, 38.
16. Gray, 38.
17. Mahnken, *Technology and the American War of War*, 5.
18. Department of Defense, *DoD Digital Modernization Strategy* (Washington, DC, June 5, 2019), 3, https://media.defense.gov/2019/Jul/12/2002156622/-1/-1/1/DOD-DIGITAL-MODERNIZATION-STRATEGY-2019.PDF.
19. Geoffrey Parker, ed., *The Cambridge History of Warfare* (New York: Cambridge University Press, 2005), 8.
20. Mansoor, "Hybrid Warfare in History," 13.
21. U.S. Space Force, *Chief of Space Operations' Planning Guidance*, 10.
22. U.S. Space Force, *Vision for a Digital Service* (Washington, DC, May 2021), 2, https://media.defense.gov/2021/May/06/2002635623/-1/-1/1/USSF%20VISION%20FOR%20A%20DIGITAL%20SERVICE%202021%20(2).PDF.
23. U.S. Space Force, 3.
24. U.S. Space Force, 4.
25. Gray, "Irregular Warfare," 44–45.
26. Russell F. Weigley, *The American Way of War: A History of United States Military Strategy and Policy* (Bloomington: Indiana University Press, 1977).
27. Antulio J. Echevarria II, *An American Way of War or Way of Battle?* (Carlisle Barracks, PA: U.S. Army War College, 2004), https://press.armywarcollege.edu/monographs/774/.
28. Rose Lopez Keravuori, "Lost in Translation: The American Way of War," *Small Wars Journal*, November 17, 2011, https://smallwarsjournal.com/jrnl/art/lost-in-translation-the-american-way-of-war.
29. Galula, *Counterinsurgency Warfare*, 75.
30. Clausewitz, *On War*, 119.
31. Gray, "Irregular Warfare," 47.
32. Clausewitz, *On War*, 88.
33. Gray, *Irregular Enemies*, 55.
34. Bartholomees, "Survey of the Theory of Strategy," 33.
35. Bartholomees, 33.
36. Carl E. Mundy III, "Spare the Rod, Save the Nation," *New York Times*, December 30, 2003, https://www.nytimes.com/2003/12/30/opinion/spare-the-rod-save-the-nation.html.
37. Smith, *Ten Propositions Regarding Spacepower*, 74.
38. Clausewitz, *On War*, 141.
39. Gray, *Irregular Enemies*, 25.
40. Gray, "Irregular Warfare," 39.

41. Gray, *Irregular Enemies*, 44–45.

42. U.S. Space Force, *Space Capstone Publication*, 38.

43. Executive Office of the President, *National Space Policy*, 27 [emphasis added].

44. See Klein, "To Deter Attacks on Satellites."

45. See Klein.

46. Executive Office of the President, Executive Order 12333, "United States Intelligence Activities," December 4, 1981, https://www.archives.gov/federal-register/codification/executive-order/12333.html.

47. Eric Rosenbach and Aki J. Peritz, *Confrontation or Collaboration? Congress and the Intelligence Community* (Cambridge, MA: Belfer Center for Science and International Affairs, July 2009), https://www.belfercenter.org/publication/confrontation-or-collaboration-congress-and-intelligence-community.

48. Annika Moody, "DNI Haines Speaks at the Activation of the National Space Intelligence Center," Director of National Intelligence Office of Strategic Communications, June 27, 2022, https://www.dni.gov/index.php/newsroom/news-articles/news-articles-2022/item/2304-dni-haines-speaks-at-the-activation-of-the-national-space-intelligence-center.

49. Carissa Christensen, "Commercial Space in 2033" (presentation, Schriever Wargame 2023 Commercial and Civil Workshop, Les Mureaux, France, May 17, 2022).

50. Clausewitz, *On War*, 380 [emphasis original].

51. ASD-HDGS, *Space Domain Mission Assurance*, 2.

52. Joint Chiefs of Staff, *Space Operations*, viii.

53. ASD-HDGS, 3.

54. ASD-HDGS, *Space Domain Mission Assurance*, 6.

55. Gray, *Irregular Enemies*, 42.

56. Elisabeth Braw, *Building a Wall of Denial against Gray-Zone Aggression* (Washington, DC: American Enterprise Institute, April 2021), 2, https://www.aei.org/research-products/report/building-a-wall-of-denial-against-gray-zone-aggression/.

57. UN Charter, Chapter I, Article 2(4).

58. Braw, *Building a Wall of Denial*, 1.

59. Andrew F. Krepinevich and Robert C. Martinage, *Dissuasion Strategy* (Washington, DC: Center for Strategic and Budgetary Assessments, 2008), vii–viii, https://csbaonline.org/research/publications/dissuasion-strategy/publication/1.

60. See Dean Cheng and John J. Klein, "A Comprehensive Approach to Space Deterrence," *Strategy Bridge*, March 31, 2021, https://thestrategybridge.org/the-bridge/2021/03/31/a-comprehensive-approach-to-space-deterrence.

61. Callwell, *Small Wars*, 38.
62. Roger Trinquier, *Modern Warfare: A French View of Counterinsurgency*, trans. Daniel Lee (London: Pall Mall, 1964; reprint, Fort Leavenworth, KS: Combat Studies Institute, 1985), https://www.armyupress.army.mil/Portals /7/combat-studies-institute/csi-books/Modern-Warfare.pdf.
63. Trinquier, 6–8.
64. Bartholomees, "Survey of the Theory of Strategy," 34.
65. Gray, "Irregular Warfare," 54.
66. Clausewitz, *On War*, 75.
67. Clausewitz, 97, 358; Corbett, *Some Principles of Maritime Strategy*, 132.
68. Corbett, 132.
69. Hertzfeld et al., "How Simple Terms Mislead Us," 4.
70. Morris et al., *Gaining Competitive Advantage*, xvi.
71. Wylie, *Military Strategy*, 70 [emphasis original].
72. Gray, "Irregular Warfare," 54.
73. Wylie, *Military Strategy*, 71–72.
74. Sun Tzu, *Art of War*, 101.
75. Gray, *Irregular Enemies*, 10.
76. Gray, 9.
77. A paraphrase of an adage attributed to Helmuth von Moltke in 1871. Ralph Keyes, "The Quote Verifier," *Antioch Review* 64, no. 2 (2006): 256–66, https://doi.org/10.2307/4614974.
78. Douglas Adams, *The Hitchhiker's Guide to the Galaxy* (New York: Pocket Books, 1979), 27.
79. Howard, *Lessons of History*, 176.
80. Gray, *Another Bloody Century*, 14.
81. Weeden and Samson, *Global Counterspace Capabilities*, xii–xxii.
82. Sean Monaghan, "Bad Idea: Winning the Gray Zone," *Defense360: Center for Strategic and International Studies*, December 17, 2021, https://defense 360.csis.org/bad-idea-winning-the-gray-zone/.
83. Lloyd J. Austin III, "Remarks at the Reagan National Defense Forum" (speech as delivered, December 4, 2021), https://www.defense.gov/News/ Speeches/Speech/Article/2861931/remarks-by-secretary-of-defense-lloyd- j-austin-iii-at-the-reagan-national-defen/.
84. Corbett, *Some Principles of Maritime Strategy*, 279.
85. Joint Chiefs of Staff, *Space Operations*, I-4, II-2.

≋ SELECTED ≋
BIBLIOGRAPHY

Published Government Documents

Defense Intelligence Agency. *Challenges to Security in Space.* Washington, DC, 2022.

Department of the Army. *Insurgencies and Countering Insurgencies*, FM 3-24 / MCWP 3-33.5. Change 1. Washington, DC, June 2, 2014.

Department of Defense. *Summary: Department of Defense Cyber Strategy.* Washington, DC, 2018.

———. *DoD Digital Modernization Strategy.* Washington, DC, June 5, 2019.

———. *National Defense Strategy of the United States of America: Sharpening the American Military's Competitive Edge.* Washington, DC, 2018.

———. *Summary of the Irregular Warfare Annex to the National Defense Strategy.* Washington, DC, 2020.

Executive Office of the President. *The National Space Policy of the United States of America.* Washington, DC, 2020.

Joint Chiefs of Staff. *Joint Doctrine for Military Operations Other than War*, JP 3-07. Washington, DC, June 16, 1995.

———. *Military Deception*, Joint Publication 3-13.4. Washington, DC, January 26, 2012.

———. *Space Operations*, Joint Publication 3-14. Change 1. Washington, DC, October 26, 2020.

Office of the Assistant Secretary of Defense for Homeland Defense and Global Security. *Space Domain Mission Assurance: A Resilience Taxonomy.* Washington, DC, September 2015.

State Council Information Office of the People's Republic of China. *China's Space Program: A 2021 Perspective.* White paper. January 2022.

U.S. Marine Corps. *Small Wars Manual*, FMFRP 12-15. 1940. Reprint, Washington, DC, 1990.

———. *Warfighting.* Marine Corps Doctrinal Publication 1, MCDP-1. Washington, DC, June 20, 1997.

U.S. Marine Corps, U.S. Navy, and U.S. Coast Guard. *Naval Operations Concept—2010: Implementing the Maritime Strategy.* Washington, DC, 2010.

———. *Naval Warfare.* Naval Doctrine Publication 1. Washington, DC, April 2020.

U.S. Navy, U.S. Marine Corps, and U.S. Coast Guard. *The Commander's Handbook on the Law of Naval Operations.* NWP 1-14M / MCTP 11-10B / COM-DTPUB P5800.7A. Washington, DC, August 2017.

U. S. Space Force. *Chief of Space Operations' Planning Guidance.* Washington, DC: Headquarters U.S. Space Force, November 9, 2020.

———. *Space Capstone Publication: Spacepower, Doctrine for Space Forces.* Washington, DC: Headquarters U.S. Space Force, June 2020.

———. *Vision for a Digital Service.* Washington, DC: Headquarters U.S. Space Force, May 2021.

Journals and Magazines

Air Force Magazine

Antioch Review

Berkeley Political Review

Boston College International and Comparative Law Review

Breaking Defense

Forbes

Foreign Affairs

Harvard National Security Journal

Joint Force Quarterly

Journal of Conflict Resolution

Journal of Strategic Studies

MIT Technology Review

National Defense

Naval War College Review

Northern Mariner

Ponant Magazine

RUSI Journal

Small Wars Journal

SpaceNews

SpacePolicyOnline.com

Strategic Studies Quarterly

Strategy Bridge

Vanderbilt Journal of Transnational Law

War on the Rocks

Yale Journal of International Affairs

Books and Monographs

Armstrong, Benjamin. *Small Boats and Daring Men: Maritime Raiding, Irregular Warfare, and the Early American Navy.* Norman: University of Oklahoma Press. 2019.

Biddle, Stephen. *Nonstate Warfare: The Military Methods of Guerillas, Warlords, and Militias.* Princeton, NJ: Princeton University Press, 2021.

Black, Jeremy. *Rethinking Military History.* Abingdon, U.K.: Routledge, 2004.

Bowen, Bleddyn E. *War in Space: Strategy, Spacepower, Geopolitics.* Edinburgh, U.K.: Edinburgh University Press, 2020.

Braw, Elisabeth. *Building a Wall of Denial against Gray-Zone Aggression.* Washington, DC: American Enterprise Institute, April 2021.

Cable, James. *Gunboat Diplomacy: Political Applications of Limited Naval Force.* New York: Praeger, for the Institute of Strategic Studies, 1971.

Callwell, Charles E. *Military Operations and Maritime Preponderance: Their Relations and Interdependence.* Introduction by Colin S. Gray. London: William Blackwood and Sons, 1905; reprint, Annapolis, MD: Naval Institute Press, 1996.

———. *Small Wars: Their Principles and Practice.* 3rd ed. London: Harrison and Sons, for His Majesty's Stationery Office, 1906.

Carlson, Joshua P. *Spacepower Ascendant: Space Development Theory and a New Space Strategy.* Self-published, 2020.

Castex, Raoul. *Strategic Theories.* Translated and edited by Eugenia C. Kiesling. Annapolis, MD: Naval Institute Press, 1994.

Cheng, Dean. *Cyber Dragon: Inside China's Information Warfare and Cyber Operations.* Santa Barbara, CA: Praeger Security International, 2017.

Clausewitz, Carl von. *On War.* Translated and edited by Michael Howard and Peter Paret. Princeton, NJ: Princeton University Press, 1989.

Corbett, Julian S. *Some Principles of Maritime Strategy.* London: Longmans, Green, 1911; reprint, Annapolis, MD: Naval Institute Press, 1988.

Dolman, Everett C. *Astropolitik: Classical Geopolitics in the Space Age.* Abingdon, U.K.: Frank Cass, 2002.

Echevarria II, Antulio J. *Reconsidering the American Way of War: US Military Practice from the Revolution to Afghanistan.* Washington, DC: Georgetown University Press, 2014.

Gray, Colin S. *Another Bloody Century: Future Warfare.* London: Weidenfeld and Nicolson, 2005.

———. *Fighting Talk: Forty Maxims on War, Peace, and Strategy.* Westport, CT: Greenwood, 2007.

———. *Irregular Enemies and the Essence of Strategy: Can the American Way of War Adapt?* Carlisle Barracks, PA: Strategic Studies Institute. March 2006.

————. *Weapons Don't Make War: Policy, Strategy, and Military Technology.* Lawrence: University Press of Kansas, 1993.

Galula, David. *Counterinsurgency Warfare: Theory and Practice.* Foreword by John A. Nagl. 1964; reprint, Westport, CT: Praeger Security International, 2006.

Handel, Michael I. *Masters of War: Classical Strategic Thought.* 3rd ed. Abingdon, U.K.: Routledge, 2001.

Harrison, Todd, Kaitlyn Johnson, Makena Young, Nicholas Wood, and Alyssa Goessler. *Space Threat Assessment 2022.* Washington, DC: Center for Strategic and International Studies, 2022.

Howard, Michael. *The Lessons of History.* New Haven, CT: Yale University Press, 1991.

Jones, Seth G. *Three Dangerous Men: Russia, China, Iran, and the Rise of Irregular Warfare.* New York: W. W. Norton, 2021.

Kittrie, Orde F. *Lawfare: Law as a Weapon of War.* New York: Oxford University Press, 2016.

Klein, John J. *Space Warfare: Strategy, Principles and Policy.* Abingdon, U.K.: Routledge, 2006.

————. *Understanding Space Strategy: The Art of War in Space.* Abingdon, U.K.: Routledge, 2019.

Liddell Hart, B. H. *Strategy: The Indirect Approach.* 2nd ed. London: Faber and Faber, 1967; reprint, BN Publishing, 2020. Kindle.

Lonsdale, David J. *The Nature of War in the Information Age: Clausewitzian Future.* London: Frank Cass, 2004.

Lutes, Charles, and Peter L. Hays eds., with Vincent A. Mazo, Lisa M. Yambrick, and M. Elaine Bunn. *Toward a Theory of Spacepower: Selected Essays.* Washington, D.C.: National Defense University Press, 2011.

Mahnken, Thomas G. *Technology and the American War of War since 1945.* New York: Columbia University Press, 2008.

Mao Tse-tung. *Selected Military Writings of Mao Tse-tung.* Beijing: Foreign Language Press, 1963; reprint, Seattle, WA: Praetorian-press.com, 2011. Kindle.

McFate, Sean. *Mercenaries and War: Understanding Private Armies Today.* Washington, DC: National Defense University Press, 2019.

Morris, Lyle J., Michael J. Mazarr, Jeffrey W. Hornung, Stephanie Pezard, Anika Binnendijk, and Marta Keep. *Gaining Competitive Advantage in the Gray Zone: Response Options for Coercive Aggression below the Threshold of Major War.* Santa Monica, CA: RAND, 2019.

Mumford, Andrew. *Proxy Warfare.* Cambridge, U.K.: Polity, 2013.

Murray, Williamson, and Peter R. Mansoor, eds. *Hybrid Warfare: Fighting Complex Opponents from the Ancient World to the Present.* Cambridge, MA: Cambridge University Press, 2012.

Pace, Scott. *Merchants and Guardians: Balancing U.S. Interests in Space Commerce*. Santa Monica, CA: RAND, 1999.

Posen, Barry. *The Sources of Military Doctrine: France, Britain, and Germany between the World Wars*. Ithaca, NY: Cornell University Press, 1984.

Qiao Liang and Wang Xiangsui. *Unrestricted Warfare: Assumptions on War and Tactics in the Age of Globalization*. Translated by Foreign Broadcast Information Service. Beijing: People's Liberation Army Literature and Arts Publishing House, 1999.

Schelling, Thomas C. *Arms and Influence*. New Haven, CT: Yale University Press, 1966.

Singer, P. W. *Corporate Warriors: The Rise of the Privatized Military Industry*. Ithaca, NY: Cornell University Press, 2003.

Smith, M. V. *Ten Propositions Regarding Spacepower*. Maxwell Air Force Base, AL: Air University Press, 2002.

Sun Tzu. *The Art of War*. Translated and with an introduction by Samuel B. Griffith. Oxford, U.K.: Oxford University Press, 1963.

Till, Geoffrey. *Seapower: A Guide for the Twenty-First Century*. 3rd ed. Abingdon, U.K.: Routledge, 2013.

Townsend, Brad. *Security and Stability in the New Space Age: The Orbital Security Dilemma*. Abingdon, U.K.: Routledge, 2020.

Trinquier, Roger. *Modern Warfare: A French View of Counterinsurgency*. Translated by Daniel Lee. London: Pall Mall, 1964; reprint, Fort Leavenworth, KS: Combat Studies Institute, 1985.

Weeden, Brian, and Victoria Samson, eds. *Global Counterspace Capabilities: An Open Source Assessment*. Washington, DC: Secure World Foundation, 2022.

Weigley, Russell F. *The American Way of War: A History of United States Military Strategy and Policy*. Bloomington: Indiana University Press, 1977.

Wylie, J. C. *Military Strategy: A General Theory of Power Control*. With introduction by John B. Hattendorf. New Brunswick, NJ: Rutgers University Press, 1967; reprint, Annapolis, MD: Naval Institute Press, 1989.

Ziarnick, Brent. *Developing National Power in Space: A Theoretical Model*. Jefferson, NC: McFarland, 2015.

≋ INDEX ≋

ABOUT THE AUTHOR

Dr. John J. Klein is a Senior Fellow and Strategist with Falcon Research, Inc., and also instructs space policy and strategy courses in the Washington, D.C., area at the undergraduate, graduate, and doctorate levels. He routinely writes on space policy, strategy, and deterrence. He is a retired commander in the U.S. Navy.